MIDDLE SISTERS

MIDDLE SISTERS

MARGUERITE DUVIVIER
Cover art by: A.C. Piessens

PALMETTO
PUBLISHING
Charleston, SC
www.PalmettoPublishing.com

© 2024 M. M. Stilmant
Cover art by A.C. Piessens
All rights reserved.
No portion of this book may be reproduced,
stored in a retrieval system, or transmitted in
any form by any means–electronic, mechanical,
photocopy, recording, or other–except for
brief quotations in printed reviews,
without prior permission of the author.

Hardcover ISBN: 9798822970052
Paperback ISBN: 9798822970069
eBook ISBN: 9798822970076

Excerpt(s) from WOULDN'T TAKE NOTHING FOR MY JOURNEY NOW *by Maya Angelou, copyright © 1993 by Caged Bird Legacy, LLC. Used by permission of Random House, an imprint and division of Penguin Random House LLC. All rights reserved.*

Author can be reached at middlesisterbook@gmail.com

"The woman who survives intact and happy must be at once tender and tough. She must have convinced herself, or be in the unending process of convincing herself, that she, her values and her choices are important. In a time and world where males hold sway and control, the pressure upon women to yield their rights of way is tremendous. And it is under those circumstances that the woman's toughness must be in evidence."

— Maya Angelou, *Wouldn't Take Nothing for My Journey Now*

FOREWORD

My youngest daughter has long been fascinated with photography, her hobby and passion. She has been exhibiting her art for many years, won prizes and has photos in private collections.

A couple of years ago, she asked me if I had interesting family photos she could use for a project, and we spent time looking at old photos together. She asked, "Who was this person? What is the story of our family?"

Born in Belgium in 1942, I emigrated to the United States in 1970, with my husband and two young daughters, and divorced four years later.

A single mother building a career in medicine, I did not have the time to talk about my family in Belgium, nor did I know much of my parents' and grandparents' history.

After my mother died, her journals were discovered. My own sisters did not want the journals; I did not want to read them, assuming they would be full of anger and sadness, but I wanted to preserve them, brought them back from Europe, and my daughter expressed the desire to read them. Later, "Grandmother's journals are handwritten in French, and I cannot read her handwriting," she complained, "I am curious, would you read them, tell me what they say?"

At her urging, I finally began to read what my mother had written over decades of her life. The many journals were disorganized, repetitive, some torn apart, and, as I had suspected, often heartbreaking, raw, full of anger, despair and resentment. I paused many times, emotionally torn, and was advised by family and friends to stop reading, but I persisted.

I discovered a trove of information about my mother's early life in poverty, her upbringing, parents and siblings, her difficult life as a young bride in an arranged marriage. The journals contained a rich, detailed portrait of a family and an era, they were informative and factual. Mother could be lyrical, writing surprisingly good poetry, or nakedly documenting her own feelings, longings and sorrows. There were some good times, she had a sharp sense of humor. She wrote of her love for her granddaughters. At the end of her life, her writings became a desperate cry for help.

My own life has also seen turmoil, and I slowly developed the idea of writing a book about the women in my family.

Both my mother and I were the middle child, the middle sister, in our respective families.

In the book, my mother speaks with her own voice. My father was a secretive person, and, at times, I had to surmise his thoughts and feelings from his actions, my mother's writings, confidences he made late in life, and details provided by my older sister.

This book covers the lives of six generations of women of the same family. It takes place over some hundred and twenty years and two world wars, and is factual, with rare assumptions when information was lacking, for the sake of a coherent story.

Marguerite Duvivier is a pen name, most of the names of the characters in the book have been changed. Aimeries is not the real name of a community in Belgium, but we lived somewhere like it. The institutions are real.

This book is in memory of my mother, who wrote in secret, and is dedicated to my two daughters.

CHAPTER I

At the beginning of the twentieth century, in Belgium's Wallonia, Lydie, a fifteen-year-old seamstress apprentice, falls in love with Clement, a hardworking and resourceful nineteen-year-old coal miner.

Lydie, the oldest of a family with six children, becomes pregnant at the age of sixteen and is thrown out of her parents' home. She finds refuge with her mentor, the seamstress; she and Clement marry as soon as he turns twenty-one. In September 1908, when Lydie is seven months pregnant, there is an accident in the coal mine where Clement is toiling. She rushes to the mine in her wooden shoes and falls, triggering an early delivery. Clement escapes injury in the mine accident, and, at barely three pounds, the baby who has deformed feet and legs is miraculously breathing on her own though not expected to live. She is placed behind the stove in a cardboard box. A couple of hours later, the baby makes small sounds. "God wants us to raise this child," says the deeply religious Clement. The child grows up to be physically and mentally impaired.

Within five years, three more girls are born into the desperately poor family: the second in 1911; the third, Clementine, in 1913;

and, thirteen months later, at the very beginning of World War I, Zilda is born in August 1914 by a difficult breach birth, as if reluctant to be born. The twenty-two-year-old young mother, overwhelmed, cries at the birth of the fourth child.

She despairs and wonders how she and Clement will be able to feed and raise their four daughters.

It is wartime. Unable to continue working in the coal mines because of asthma, Clement enlists as an apprentice in a metal workshop. To make ends meet, Lydie opens a small food store at the front of their tiny house. She sells dry goods and some fresh fruit. Their house has no running water; rainwater is collected in a cistern. Lighting is from petrol lamps, and the house is heated with coal that must be carried by foot or in a horse cart.

Laure, Lydie's mother, a laundress who has already lost four of her six children to accident and infectious diseases, helps with the growing family's laundry. Fond of her grandchildren and wanting to be around them, she is the one providing the affection that the young mother has no time to give. Zilda, the youngest, frail and timid, is her favorite and she takes her along whenever she can; the child rides on top of dirty laundry in a wheelbarrow, she walks alongside when washed and ironed laundry is returned.

During the war, the four young girls all sleep in the same bed. The family eats black bread and the fruits too bruised to sell in the small shop. Lydie sews all the children's clothes and the little girls hear their mother at her sewing machine as she pedals late in the night.

After his long hours at the workshop, Clement breaks wartime curfews and sneaks into local farms at night to obtain animal fat, which he combines with lye to make soap to sell on the black market. When he can obtain flour, he makes bread. He sleeps only a few hours a night and is becoming very thin. He rarely sees his children.

For a period, the family is forced to flee from their house; the Germans are bombarding the area. They take temporary lodging in an abandoned brewery, sharing space with English and Scottish Allied soldiers.

There are lighter moments in their grim life; the soldiers share food rations and like to play with the children, putting them in their blankets, and holding onto the corners, they send the children high into the air which makes them laugh. Clement has a sense of humor: he and one of his brothers exchange clothing with the Scottish soldiers and a photo is taken.

Lydie, destitute, depressed, is at the nadir of her life, and would be astonished to know that she is destined to become the powerful matriarch of a wealthy family.

CHAPTER 2

Lydie and Clement are exhausted. Lydie, running the store while taking care of four young daughters, one severely handicapped, can barely cope with the pressure.

Clementine, the third born, an audacious, restless, vigorous child leads her sisters into mischief, she is the ringleader.

Zilda is often sick, she is very pale. The doctor advises that she should be outdoors more often. "I do what I can, doctor," says Lydie, "I make her sit outside under the tree."

Clementine is difficult to handle; she plays in the street with young neighbor boys and comes home with dirty torn clothes. She starts school at the age of six and walks to school alone, crossing a bridge over a canal. Twice, she throws her schoolbag into the canal when a barge passes under the bridge and yells at the boatman to retrieve the bag with his long pole. Goods are delivered to the store by horse-drawn carriages; while a delivery man is in her mother's store, she climbs into the carriage and urges the horse to run, falling with the barrels and breaking two teeth. She is irrepressible and too much to handle along with the sister who requires constant care.

The young parents decide to place Clementine, six and a half, and little Zilda, who just turned five, in a boarding school run by nuns that is a day's train ride from home.

It is a bare-bones, strict Catholic boarding school.

On the day that Lydie brings the two little girls to the school, Clementine rushes into the central courtyard to join a game in progress, while Zilda clings to her mother's skirt and cries. The sisters sleep in the same narrow bed in the unheated attic dormitory: the tuition is cheaper if the children share the same bed.

The Catholic school where the children are sent is a forbidding, large, square brick building with a single entrance and no outside windows; a central court serves as a recreation area where the children run, play ball games.

The nuns teach writing, reading, rudimentary mathematics, history, and geography. Bible study is mandatory. The children are expected to learn segments of the Bible by heart. Zilda is upset by the story of Joseph being sold by his brothers, and in a rare incidence of rebellion, she refuses to memorize it and is punished. They are also taught to sew, embroider, and knit. The children have no toys or books except for school textbooks and the Bible.

Parents are allowed to visit for an afternoon three times a year. Clementine and Zilda's parents do not make the visit every time. The children anxiously await: Zilda is crushed if her parents fail to come. On those visits, Clement, in a constant state of exhaustion, usually falls asleep.

Clementine, strong-headed and healthy, adapts well to her life at the school. She quickly learns to write and read. She plays pranks on other pupils. She takes advantage of her younger sister whenever she can: she steals her candy and raids her meager piggybank.

Clementine is often told by the nuns to lower her devil's eyes, but she is irrepressible. Clementine excels at schoolwork and gets very poor marks for behavior.

Zilda gets top marks for behavior but fails schoolwork—she flounders. She is the youngest and smallest of the pupils, and though a sister takes her under her wing, the attention is limited to small acts of kindness. The nuns are not allowed to hug or single out children for attention. The five-year-old is often sick, spends much time in the infirmary. She develops eczema, faints in class and in church, and is unable to stay on her knees for long prayers. She has repeated ear infections, intestinal worms, and every childhood disease. When the children are vaccinated against smallpox, Zilda develops a large abscess at the site of vaccination and stays for days in the infirmary.

Zilda misses classes and is not interested in learning. She does not start to read until she is nine years old. At her First Communion, she is told not to bite into the holy wafer, that she would have Christ's blood in her mouth if she did. She grows up with fears, misconceptions, and apprehension, lacking love, guidance, and affection. She does not develop the ability to form or express her own opinions. She is very docile and obedient. She is a dreamer.

CHAPTER 3

For the first four of years at boarding school, the children hardly see their parents. During summer vacation, they are sent to relatives, farmers, each child with a different family. It is heaven for Zilda. She plays outside, learns to do farm chores, how to cook. She receives attention and affection.

Christmas vacation is spent at home. Lydie gives each child some coins but asks to have the coins back the next day, for safekeeping she says. She does this every year until the children wise up, rebel, and ask to keep the money. There is no money for gifts and toys.

On one of the rare visits the parents make to the boarding school, Lydie gives five cents to Clementine to buy some candy on the way home from church but gives only one cent to Zilda. Bewildered, the child asks why and Lydie tells her that she is younger and does not need the five cents. Unnoticed by Lydie, Clement slips Zilda a five-cent coin and she realizes for the first time that her mother treats her differently. She is baffled and hurt. She is jealous of her sister and starts to develop a deep, lifelong adoration for her father.

Clement and Lydie's fortune improves. They have acquired a house with a small attached workshop; Clement is now fabricating wagon wheels and has two employees. Soon, they enlarge the workshop that becomes a small factory. Their parents move Clementine and Zilda to a closer, less strict and more comfortable boarding school. Still, the children do not see their parents often.

Like the previous one, the school has strict rules, and prayers still occupy a great part of the day. There is a large garden, and the children are now able to spend more time outdoors. They are tasked with picking berries growing at the back of the garden but have to recite prayers loudly while harvesting the fruit, as the sisters do not want them to eat any of the berries.

The parents begin taking the children home during vacation and make short trips to the North Sea in the summer. The young girls have never seen the sea before and are enchanted. It is during one of these brief vacations at the North Shore with her parents that Zilda meets a year younger boy, Victor, the only son of prosperous merchants. The children play on the beach and a lifelong bond develops.

The new house where Clement and Lydie have moved their family is adjacent to a four-acre property surrounded by a brick wall; it is possible to peek over the wall by climbing the rabbit hutch at the back of the garden. Zilda's godfather tells her that the property belongs to Sleeping Beauty. It is a vast wooded park bordering two streets with a large mansion at the back. The property contains majestic old trees, a pond, stables at the far end, a small pavilion with columns, and a large glass greenhouse. Zilda is mesmerized. She dreams of living there, one day.

Clement and Lydie have saved sufficient funds to acquire a piece of machinery in Germany. Clement makes the trip to Germany by train, acquires the machinery just before he has an accident; a large iron piece falls on his leg, causing a worrisome gaping wound. The wound gets infected and there is talk of amputation. While confined to bed for several weeks, he reads about a new German machine—an electric compressor. Clever, he thinks about modifying the compressor and attaching a pick. From his years working in the coal mines, he is keenly aware of the hard and dangerous work of the miners; maybe he can devise a safer, more effective mechanical tool than handpicks.

Recovered, he acquires a compressor, then designs and builds a prototype of pneumatic hammer that could be used in the coal mines. Tested in a local mine, it is enthusiastically received. Clement patents the invention and is authorized to build a factory in an adjacent town. The sale of the first one hundred pneumatic hammers is celebrated. The family's fortunes have changed.

The family has become rich, but the older children are not told of the extent of the family's successes. Clementine and Zilda remain in boarding school, unaware of their parents' turn in fortune. Zilda, at seven, asks to leave the school and come live with her family, but Lydie refuses and tells her that she will have a nice surprise soon.

Lydie, almost eight years after having her fourth child, is pregnant again. A little sister is born in 1921. Zilda does not see the new baby until she is almost seven months old. Sheltered at the school, ignorant of the facts of life, she still has no knowledge of how children are created and born. She tells a classmate that her parents have found another child in a bed of roses. The classmate is astonished, incredulous that Zilda is still ignorant and does not know that children come from their mother's belly. Zilda talks to Clementine who knows that yes, children come from the mother's belly, but she does not know how they get there or how they come out.

Later, a son, Jean, is born in 1925, and finally a last girl, in 1927. Lydie is thirty-five years old and has seven children. Zilda is the middle child.

Zilda has her first menstruation at the age of sixteen, at the boarding school. She has belly pain and discovers that she is bleeding. Having soiled the bedsheets, she thinks that she is dying and does not get up. Her mother has never explained to her children the workings of the body, and the Catholic school's teachings do not include those subjects.

Unbeknownst to Clementine and Zilda, their parents buy a large tract of farmland in the small community of Aimeries, on Alliance Road, opposite a row of narrow brick houses and an elementary school. They build a huge, luxurious house with a glass veranda, two living rooms, two dining rooms, a large kitchen and servants' quarters, multiple bedrooms and bathrooms, a large garden, and a front wrought-iron gate.

Taken by their father to the newly built house with marble and wood floors, stained-glass windows, paintings, oriental rugs and new furniture, Clementine and Zilda enter through a back veranda and are told to explore. They are astonished to find their mother reclining on a daybed in a well-appointed bedroom, and they are told to choose a bedroom.

Zilda is allowed to come home more frequently and when there, she spends all her time with her baby brother, whom she adores.

He is the toy that she did not have at school and she lavishes love and attention on him. She bathes him and sees a penis for the first time. Leaving her baby brother to return to school is always a heartbreak, but she is to remain at the boarding school for most of the year.

The four older children were born and raised in poverty. They have had a strict upbringing and except for the physically and mentally handicapped firstborn, they were raised away from home and deprived of their parents' attention and affection.

The three much younger children are brought up at home and in luxury. The family has maids, gardeners, a cook, and the mother can devote time to the younger ones; she is enamored of her fifth daughter, and she spoils the very pretty child. She can finally be a mother and she lavishes all of her time on the newborn.

Born four years later, Jean is rambunctious; the only son, he is favored and indulged. He is lazy and does poorly in school, loves pranks and jokes, gossip. The difference in upbringing is stark—the last three children have a sense of entitlement.

Lydie luxuriates in her new life; she accompanies her husband on business trips and buys designer clothes in Paris. The family acquires a large apartment building fronting the boardwalk and the beach at the North Shore, and they occupy the first floor on vacation.

While Clementine survived and even thrived in boarding school, Zilda, younger and in poor health, has not fared well. Deprived of her parents' attention and affection, she suffers emotional consequences. She is deeply religious, insecure, and obedient. Her mother reigns over and makes decisions for her children. She has little patience for the fragile Zilda, who is always feeling slighted, inferior, and that others have more luck. Lydie initially favored Clementine, who like herself is a survivor. Later, she lavishes time on the baby girl born eight years after Zilda, and her only son, Jean.

CHAPTER 4

Zilda, seventeen, has finally come home from boarding school. She has a room of her own for the very first time. She washed with cold water at the boarding school, now she luxuriates in warm baths. She is a pretty young woman, slender, with long, light brown, wavy hair and hazel eyes. She is bought nice clothes and enjoys her family life.

Clement, Lydie, and their two teenage daughters are invited to a ball. Zilda and Clementine are hurriedly given dancing lessons and taken to Brussels to buy ball gowns and dancing shoes. Zilda receives her first grown-up dress, a frilly confection of white muslin with a cape of white velvet, which enchants her. She gets her hair cut short in a fetching style.

She is very sweet, and several young men line up to ask her to dance. A twenty-seven-year-old hovers and takes her to the dance floor several times, holding her close. Other young men also pay her a lot of attention; one of them, too timid to come close, follows her with his eyes the entire evening.

Clementine, with her close-set eyes, long nose and forceful personality, is not asked to dance. She is jealous of her prettier sister.

The youngsters are allowed to socialize over the next several weeks, gathering in homes, dancing, going to the movies chaperoned by parents. Victor, a frequent visitor to Zilda's parents' home, often joins the others; his friendship with Zilda deepens and he starts to view her differently, with feelings of love.

The father of the twenty-seven-year-old young man visits Clement and asks for Zilda's hand in marriage to his son. It is a good respectable family of prosperous merchants.

Zilda is bewildered. She just made her debut a few weeks ago—it is too soon, and she is not in love. She just started enjoying a social life and is having fun, but the young man is a serious potential husband. She is hesitant, asks for a little more time.

A well-meaning person visits Clement and tells him that the suitor has a mistress. Lydie argues that a twenty-seven-year-old man has physical needs; the young man will break up with the mistress when he marries Zilda. But Clement is furious. Zilda is troubled; her beloved father is angry; she would like more time to decide her future. Victor, visiting at the same time, takes Zilda aside. He is only sixteen years old but loves Zilda. He tells her that if she is willing to wait for him to finish his education, he would like to marry her. Zilda too realizes that she loves Victor more than as a friend, and they talk to Zilda's parents of their hope for the future.

Realizing that young Zilda, attractive, sweet, and the daughter of a rich man, will continue to attract eligible men, Clement asks her if she would spend another year in a pension in Brussels. Zilda agrees; the new school is close to where Victor goes to university, they will be able to visit each other regularly. At eighteen, finally out of boarding school for good, Zilda and Victor, seventeen, become officially engaged. They plan to wait to marry for a few years until Victor finishes at the university and is established in his career.

Then follows a period of peace, joy, and deepening affection for the two young people, who see each other often and are compatible and happy.

Meanwhile, the Belgian factory is at maximum capacity, and Clement decides to build a second factory just over the border in France. To have company on the drive to the building site, and to distract her, he takes Clementine with him on a couple of visits. Ferdinand, a young electrical engineer, is working on wiring the factory. He is tall and good looking, and he follows Clementine with his eyes, which the father notices. Told of Ferdinand's interest, Clementine starts to pay attention to the young man. She does not have any suitors, and whether Ferdinand is calculating and realizes that the rich industrialist daughter is available, or whether he is truly smitten, the two young people start dating.

Some time later, Zelda and Victor are at a dance when Victor complains of feeling ill; he faints and is taken to the hospital. He is diagnosed with leukemia with no hope of survival. Zilda's dreams and hopes are shattered. Shortly before her fiancé's passing, Zilda is allowed to visit him. He is skeletal, jaundiced; his eyes are bulging, his lips retracted. The two young people embrace and tell each other of their love. Both very religious, they believe they will eventually be reunited. Zilda is nineteen years old; she is immensely sad and depressed. Her love has died; she is listless.

To occupy and distract his daughter, Clement brings her to his factory where she learns to do accounting and filing. She finds the work enjoyable. She is surprisingly good with numbers, though she laments her lack of grasp of orthograph.

One day, Zilda is diagnosed with appendicitis. She undergoes an operation, but she develops a large abdominal abscess. She is gravely ill. The abscess is drained, and she lingers, weak and listless for several weeks in the hospital. Lydie visits her only once with her four-year-old youngest daughter in tow.

Clementine and Ferdinand have a short courtship and get married. The wedding at the family home is lavish. Zilda has recovered, and her timid suitor at her first ball is her partner at the wedding.

The newlyweds honeymoon in Italy and settle in a large house that Clement built for them next to the factory in northern France. They are happy; Ferdinand, whether he calculated well or is truly in love, is now the director of the French factory and receives a large salary. He is attentive to and defers to his young wife, who is making most of the decisions. She is in her element and flourishing with a suitable husband.

Clementine confides in Zilda that married life is lovely, that there is nothing to fear. Marital activities are delightful and great fun. She does not give details. Zilda, who wants to have children, has a renewed interest in life. She resumes meeting other young people; she refuses a young doctor who vies for her hand. Her partner at Clementine's wedding approaches Zilda and asks if she would like to date. Zilda refuses, saying, "I like you as a friend, and I am still mourning the loss of Victor."

Days later, Lydie's only surviving sibling visits her. They chat and the sister remarks that a young doctor has just opened an office down the street in the house of a teacher. "Interesting," says Lydie. "I was not aware that he had a son."

CHAPTER 5

The young doctor, a newly minted physician trained in pediatrics, is named Maximilien. Born in 1908, he is an only child. After his birth, his mother Victoire refused to have sexual relations with her husband. Maximilien's delivery was a long and painful ordeal, she does not want to give birth to more children.

Victoire, the daughter of farmers, takes the tramway to her parents' farm with her young son every weekend and vacation, exposing him to many experiences that shape his life.

Short and sturdy like his mother, the boy enjoys farm life, the outdoors, and physical exercise. The family, with access to the farm's production of food, does not suffer deprivations during the First World War, and Maximilien grows to be healthy and muscular.

At his grandparents' farm, he witnesses the churning of butter, the baking of bread and fresh pies. He takes part in the raising and butchering of chickens, ducks, pigeons, and sheep. He learns how to milk the cows. A stream crosses his grandparents' farm, where he catches crayfish.

A bright child, he is urged by his father to become a physician, and he trains in pediatrics. He would have preferred to study agronomy or be a farmer, but he does not cross his father.

He has one cousin who becomes a pharmacist. The two young men practice close by in the same small community, remaining friendly throughout their lives. Thus, Maximilien as a young adult has few family ties, one cousin and his parents.

Aime, Maximilien's father, a handsome man, is determined, ambitious. From modest beginnings as an elementary school teacher, he becomes a school principal, then a regional. and later, a district administrator with abundant responsibilities. He is often away on inspections of schools in his district. A liberal, he actively participates in local politics. Very popular, he gets easily elected to committees.

Aime has a mistress, an educator like himself, who teaches mathematics in secondary school. It is a poorly kept secret that the mathematician's only son is Maximilien's half-brother. The families vacation together and there are photographs of Aime at the beach with his wife on one side and his mistress on the other, holding Aime's hand.

Maximilien, exposed early to this way of life, accepts it as normal. He is friendly with his father's mistress and her son. His parents have a peaceful life, each going about their days in their chosen ways, both cherishing their only son.

The family is not rich but lives comfortably in a narrow brick house on Alliance Road in Aimeries, near the elementary school where Aime started his teaching career. Their house has four rooms on the first floor, two on each side, separated by a long corridor leading to a brick-walled garden. His parents cede two of their narrow house's first-floor rooms to serve as Maximilien's medical suite. Some farmlands from Victoire's family is sold to equip the young doctor's office; patients are few and although Maximilien trained in pediatrics, much of his practice consists of adult patients.

Maximilien has his father's gray eyes and an attractive face with a generous mouth. He has short arms and slightly bowed legs with thick knees, and he is happiest outdoors.

He is an atheist, believing that religion and the belief in God have no rational justification and are for weak people; he does not have a sense of humor, and he is quick to anger, impatient. He is dedicated to his profession and hardworking.

As an only child, he is self-centered, selfish, and unused to sharing; he remains devoted to his parents, whom he visits almost every day for his entire life. His father has great influence, dictating most of his life's choices.

Unsentimental, he has a healthy sexual appetite. He has a lover, a widow a few years older than he is, who does not desire to have children, a source of concern for and disapproval from his parents who dream of having grandchildren.

CHAPTER 6

Hitler comes to power in 1933.

Clement is keenly aware of, and concerned about, political events, but Lydie's preoccupation is to get Zilda married and away from the family home. The first born, handicapped daughter is cared for by living-in aides and a governess, the second born has joined the convent at the age of fifteen. Clementine has married. Lydie wants her middle daughter out of her new house. She has a different life now, with three much younger children.

She hatches a plan to have her daughter and the young doctor meet, and she enlists the help of a matchmaker.

At first, there are chance meetings between the two young neighbors. At the local fair there is a new entertainment, electric bumper cars, that Zilda wants to try. Two young men are nearby in another car. One of them has bet his companion that he can jump into Zilda's car when the ride begins. He jumps into Zilda's bumper car, and she is greatly annoyed. She learns that the two young men are cousins, and that one of them is her neighbor, the young doctor.

Zilda runs into the young man again at the local swimming pool. Her father has decided that she needs strengthening and should learn how to swim. Attached to a harness and suspended in the water, Zilda dutifully follows instructions and learns to swim. She notices her neighbor in the water swimming with his lips pursed, puffing, and she thinks to herself that he looks like the backend of a chicken. He is waiting, leaning on his car outside the swimming pool when she gets out.

"We are neighbors. My name is Maximilien," he says. "I would be glad to take you home."

She says, "I prefer to walk."

Now, Lydie has plotted with the matchmaker, and Aime and Victoire are party to the scheme.

Zilda is invited to tea at acquaintances and is annoyed to find out that Maximilien and his parents are there. She is invited by a friend of the family to see a movie, only to find Maximilien and his parents again are in attendance. The seats are reserved, and she has no choice but to sit next to the young man during the movie. He eats gummies and masticates during the entire movie, greatly irritating Zilda.

A few days later, Maximilien rings the bell at the front gate and asks if Zilda will walk with him. They go for a walk in the nearby fields, the reluctant Zilda looks down, barely answers the young man's many questions.

"I do not like him," she tells her mother. "He has a cold stare, he does not smile, he is short and has thick lips and I am not attracted to him. Victor was much taller. His mother is slovenly; she has been seen on the sidewalk with her hair undone and her stockings down to her ankles."

"The young man is a serious prospect," responds Lydie. "You will get used to him."

Lydie argues that Zilda needs to marry, that she is in fragile health and that the young doctor would be able to take care of her and their children. She secretly wants the delicate Zilda to leave the family home; she has no patience for the daughter who lacks Clementine's sturdiness and independence. She is really tired of Zilda.

In reality, Maximilien, almost seven years older than Zilda, is a reluctant suitor. His parents, especially Aime, want grandchildren. Aime is fully aware that Clement is a very rich man. Though delicate looking, Zilda is a beautiful young woman. Aime and Victoire have asked around and have sensed that she is vulnerable, probably docile and malleable. They are determined to have the rich Zilda as a daughter-in-law, a womb for their grandchildren.

Maximilien, who loves another woman, unsuitable in his parents' eyes, is unable to resist the pressure. He again invites the reluctant Zilda on walks in the fields, to the movies, and asks many questions of the young woman who is as demure and evasive as she can be. He is always eating candy. When she returns from the outings, Lydie presses Zilda with questions.

"Has he kissed you?"

"No," says Zilda.

"Has he taken your hand?"

"No, no, nothing happened, he just talks and talks and asks questions. He annoys me with his constant candy eating."

Aime rings the bell at the front gate early one evening and asks to talk to Clement. In Clement's office, he asks for Zilda's hand for his son, Maximilien. Trapped, worn out, pushed by her mother to accept, Zilda considers the proposal. She wants to have children, she has already refused two official offers and the advances of a friend, and her first love and fiancé, Victor, has died. She cannot refuse a fourth offer for her hand. She reluctantly agrees to an engagement.

Maximilien begins visiting Zilda at her home in the evening. Her young siblings are boisterous, the family plays many games, but Maximilien does not participate. He speaks very little. At times, the family speaks in patois, the local dialect—they intersperse patois words and laugh. They tell and play jokes. It is all foreign and confusing to Maximilien, an only child.

At nine in the evening, Aime usually rings the bell and, hat in hand, says, "It is time for Maximilien to return home to sleep." One evening, Clement takes out his gold watch on its chain, looks at the time, and says, "It is close to nine o'clock, Maximilien has to go home to change his diaper." The family laughs; Maximilien gets up without a word and leaves. That is the last time his father comes to the front gate to collect him.

Around Christmas time, Maximilien takes Zilda on a ride one evening, stops the car in a secluded spot, places his hand on her breast, and tries to get under his fiancée's skirt. It is the first time that he tries to be physical, and he is soundly rejected. Zilda is brought back home in icy silence. She tells her father of the incident and Clement decides that it is time to set a wedding date.

Clementine, pregnant, is expected to deliver her first child in mid-January of 1934; Zilda's and Clement's wedding date is set for mid-February to give Clementine time to recover from childbirth. Clementine is on schedule; she has come to her parents' home a few days early for the birth of her first child. She allows Zilda to be present at the delivery. With her mother holding her hand on one side, her sister on the other, and a midwife assisting, she has an amazingly easy experience. A healthy boy is delivered. Zilda thinks that the delivery was almost as smooth as sliding a letter into a mailbox; she was reassured by Clementine that marital relationships are delightful, and birthing children is obviously easy. Zilda does not love her husband-to-be, but she will make the best she can of the situation, have children of her own, and be happy.

Her partner at Clementine's wedding dies by suicide shortly after Zilda's wedding date is announced. It is rumored that he died of a broken heart. Zilda is not told for a few months of the loss of her friend, until she asks her mother one day why he and his parents were not present at her wedding.

For their engagement, Zilda offers a tie pin with a large, beautiful clear diamond to Maximilien. Clement had gone to Antwerp and selected two flawless stones, one for Zilda, to be made into a ring, and one for Maximilien's pin. Maximilien gives Zilda a ring with a smaller stone.

Clementine's wedding was a lavish affair, and Zilda's parents are determined to offer the same experience to Zilda.. The day before the wedding is extremely cold. Workers are moving furniture and setting tables for the wedding reception. It is a beehive of activity when Victoire enters the house from the rear entrance. She searches for Lydie and she says: "Maximilien is sick, there will be no wedding tomorrow." Lydie is livid. "What does he have?" she asks. "He has fever and is in bed, too sick to get married." Lydie will not hear of it: she rents petrol heaters for the church, the wedding will take place.

That night, the mother takes her daughter aside; "You may never refuse your husband," she repeats. "You may never refuse him." Nothing else is said.

On February 12, 1934, nineteen years old Zilda enters the church on her father's arm and stops; about to walk down the aisle, she has a premonition of doom, she is uncertain, she has the urge to flee. "What is it?" asks Clement. She hesitates then says, "It is the children, they are pulling on my train," and they resume walking. After the church ceremony, the couple is married at the city hall and returns home for the wedding reception. Wedding photos are taken, the groom and bride barely smiling. Zilda looks forlorn.

Maximilien has not said a word since meeting with her at the church. He declares that he is tired and needs to lie down. Lydie takes him to a bedroom with attached bathroom upstairs, as far from the festivities as possible so that he may take a short nap in tranquility. She takes the key and locks the door. Zilda is left to greet the guests and accept their congratulations alone.

CHAPTER 7

Around seven o'clock on the wedding night, a young guest alerts Lydie to the banging on an upstairs door; she had forgotten Maximilien, who slept for the entire afternoon. He is now hungry and goes to the kitchen to find food, then he looks for Zilda and says, "It is time to leave."

Zilda changes from her wedding clothes to a black dress and coat and they are taken to Brussels by car. During the drive, Maximilien removes his wedding band and hands it to Zilda. "I don't need a wedding band to know that I am married," he says. Except for that exchange, the young couple does not talk.

They arrive at a commercial hotel near the train station. The hotel room is plain, typical of a commercial hotel, and the toilet is in the hallway.

The young bride looks around and decides to undress. Turning around for modesty, she changes into a pretty pink embroidered silk nightgown and sits on the bed near a bedside table with a telephone. She is a little apprehensive but she is also curious. Her sister sang the praises of the marriage bed, and she is ready to experience the same pleasure.

Maximilien undresses above the waist, flexes his arms, and says, "Look at my biceps, I exercised a lot at university." He takes poses, then changes into a striped pajama. Turning the light off, without saying a word, without any foreplay, he swiftly couples with Zilda, turns on his side, and goes to sleep. He snores.

Zilda had seen her little baby brother's penis, but she had no idea that the organ got so big. She was totally ignorant. She is in pain, physically torn, raw and bleeding, she is shocked and feels violated, she curses the sister who told her that lovemaking is delightful. She is emotionally shattered and bewildered; she is silently crying.

At two o'clock in the morning, the telephone rings. It is her mother calling. How does she know where we are? wonders Zilda. "How are you doing, is everything okay?" asks Lydie. Zilda only says, "He is asleep." She is too ashamed to share details with Lydie, who told her that she could not refuse her husband and did not prepare her for the experience.

The hotel does not offer breakfast and the young couple goes out in the morning. Conversation is limited; "What should we do?" asks Maximilien. "Should we go to a movie?" They wander around the neighborhood and take the train to return to Aimeries, heading to their respective homes late in the afternoon. Maximilien wants to sleep in his bed, Zilda returns to her parents' home and also sleeps in her own bed. Then start a few strange days, Maximilien sleeping at his parents' house, Zilda sleeping at hers.

She does not give details to her parents, but they immediately sense that she is hurt and dejected. Lydie takes her aside: "You will have many deceptions and bad days in your life," she says, "things will get better." Clement is troubled. Lydie makes decisions; the young couple will go on a honeymoon to get to know each other better and will temporarily live with the groom's parents when they return. In the meantime, the families will search for a place for Aime and Victoire to move to, leaving their house with the medical office to Zilda and Maximilien. This, also, will be temporary, since Clement intends to build a house for Zilda, as he has done for Clementine.

Clement funds the honeymoon since Maximilien still has very few patients and little income. The couple travels by train to the French Riviera; they make stops on the way and visit a few sights. In Nice, on the English promenade, they meet—by chance or design, Zilda wonders—a group of Maximilien's friends from the university. Introductions are made and a woman in the group, in her late twenties, embraces Maximilien, laughs, and says: "My god, Maximilien, you really robbed the cradle." At first, Zilda thinks it is a compliment, she is young and pretty; but later she realizes that it was mockery, and she feels vulnerable and isolated.

They take a train to Italy; there is snow in Ventimiglia at the border and they have to exit the train. Zilda makes snowballs and throws them at Maximilien, but he is not amused and does not reciprocate. The honeymoon, so far, has seen very little conversation, no tenderness or playfulness. They have their first fight in Marseilles.

Zilda realizes that her life is going to be difficult with a humorless man. She regrets that she did not follow her urge to turn and leave the church at her wedding.

A few days later, in a hotel room, she finds out that she is having her period. She informs Maximilien, who grabs a carafe of water and throws it on the wall. Zilda is afraid. She also discovers that her young husband is not fastidious; he soils his laundry, he stuffs his underwear under his pillow, and she is revolted.

When they return home from the honeymoon, they find that Aime and Victoire have not moved to another house yet, though Clement is offering one to them free of rent. Zilda moves her clothing into Maximilien's bedroom; they share his bed and Zilda is forced to live with her in-laws for a few weeks.

The trio resume their habits; Maximilien waits for patients, plays cards with his parents, eats enormous amounts of candy. Zilda wants to learn to play cards and asks to be included in the games. "It is too difficult for you," she is told. She sits in a corner of the room and knits; she is bored and resentful and retreats more and more into herself. On Sunday, they all go together to a movie. She visits her family, fifty yards away on the same street, as much as she dares. She despises Aime and Victoire and suffers in silence.

Finally, the parents-in-law move to a temporary house nearby and leave the young couple. Zilda has more freedom in the house; her mother buys her a small dining room set and she is free to cook and set her own schedule. But Aime has kept a key to the house, and to Zilda's dismay, he lets himself in early every morning, and from the bottom of the stairs, he shouts: "Time to get up! What's new? What's going on?"

To Zilda he says: "When are you going to give us a grandchild?" He has kept his grip on his son's life and Zilda hates him more and more. One day she replies: "Why did you not have more children yourself? Leave me alone"—a rare sign of rebellion. She tells Maximilien that she will no longer tolerate his father's unwelcome intrusions, but it falls on deaf ears.

Clement drives by the house every morning and rings the horn of the car; Zilda rushes out and gives him a kiss, happy to see her father. One day, he finds her in front of the house; they have had a coal delivery, and she is busy scrubbing the sidewalk. "My daughter does not wash sidewalks," he says. He is supporting the young couple, and he wants her to hire a maid. Victoire knows just the right person to hire, a young woman from her village, who is hardworking and needs the work. Soon Zilda discovers that the new maid serves as a spy for her in-laws and fires her. She will find her own maid.

Clement knows how deeply unhappy his daughter is. He always intended to build her a house as he did for Clementine. He believes that she might benefit from some distance from her parents-in-law and that Maximilien would have a better chance to prosper if his practice were in Brussels, near the big hospitals. He proposes to find a property in the capital; he offers to build a polyclinic where Maximilien could open a clinic for babies and young children and stay in close contact with his mentors at the university. Maximilien categorically refuses. He wants to stay in his small community, near his parents. The search for a suitable building site or an already built house goes on; Maximilien does not like any of the choices.

One day, Clement calls Zilda. "Get ready, I am picking you up," he instructs. "Do you remember the large, wooded property next to our old house on the main street? It is for sale; I want to go look at it with you." Zilda remembers Sleeping Beauty's park, and they go visit the estate. The huge property is shaped like a rectangle with many centuries-old majestic trees. The main house, at the back, with adjacent stables, is fronting a narrow side street. The house is old and very big, with two-meter-high windows and Zilda thinks of all the work needed to renovate, clean and keep the house. She is hesitant. There is a small gate on the opposite side of the property opening to the main thoroughfare of the town. That gate is surrounded by small old houses, two of which Clement already owns.

Maximilien does not want to establish his practice on a small side street; he already has difficulties attracting patients on Alliance Road. It would be repeating the same mistake. He refuses to move to that property. Zilda, too, has reservations about the house.

But Clement is resourceful, and he has a fortune: he offers to buy the property, telling the seller that he would divide the land following the purchase and sell the house separately. Now the owner refuses to sell: "I will divide the property myself," he says, and he offers a large part of the land to Clement. A new house could be built, fronting the main street, after acquiring and razing two small row houses on each side.

Maximilien warms up to the idea but the side of the property on the main street slopes down steeply from the thoroughfare. It would have to be filled and leveled. "No problem," says Clement, "the town is building a tramway line and enlarging the street. We will offer to take the soil from the roadwork and use it as landfill to level up the land."

A large section of Sleeping Beauty park is acquired, leaving the main house, the stables, the hothouse, and the pavilion in the back as a separate lots. Maximilien would have liked to include the lot with the side buildings, but it is not part of the deal.

Work starts on the property. The small houses are razed to make a wide front with a gate, while the sloping section is landfilled and terraced with central steps and a narrow side road to the park behind. One of the sacrificed adjacent small houses has a large forge behind it, three meters high, with a pigeon coop and a fruit cellar. The forge will serve as a garage; it is large enough to house six cars.

Zilda is not adjusting to married life with Maximilien. Maximilien hardly talks to her. The physical relations are brief and unpleasant; she is passive, inhibited, resentful.

Her in-laws interfere in her daily life, they show up on her doorstep every day.

Clement realizes that the marriage is in peril and thinks that the young couple would benefit from spending some months in England while the work on the newly acquired property goes on. He has business interests in London and Newcastle, and he believes Maximilien could officiate as his representative. He wants to distance Zilda from both her own family and her in-laws. Maximilien could visit the pediatrics department in London and attend conferences there, possibly make good contacts. The young people, finally totally on their own, might get closer and form a bond.

Zilda and Maximilien move to London. Clement is sending a generous check every month and the couple lives in a very nice apartment near Hyde Park with a bedroom, a small living room, and a kitchen. Zilda learns to cook the dishes that her husband likes. He has a sweet tooth; she makes him treats.

The couple walks, discovers London, goes every day to nice restaurants for dinner. They canoe, shop for clothes for Maximilien that are to Zilda's liking, go to the movies and concerts. They journey to Brighton, but Maximilien refuses to go to Newcastle, saying that he knows nothing of his father-in-law's business. Maximilien visits the local children's hospital and joins as an associate in a volunteering capacity. He makes connections, and the young couple is invited for tea at the house of colleagues.

Maximilien still covets the back portion of the land that Clement has purchased for his daughter. Without telling Zilda, he looks for a cheaper apartment to save money and tells her that they are moving. Clement is not to be told; the difference in rent will be saved to acquire the additional land. He already has been in touch with the owner, he says, and he will build a wall at the back of their land to separate it from the original old house. Zilda does not dare to argue; she no longer has a kitchen to prepare meals, so she buys a small alcohol stove. They no longer go to expensive restaurants.

Maximilien has discovered that she is not a proficient writer, that she cannot spell properly, and he is furious. "I have married an inferior woman, I have an inferior wife," he rages. "Money has to compensate for my sacrifices. And you are not getting pregnant!" Zilda cries secretly, she is terrified and misses Victor and her father. Her husband is a brute, she thinks, he is messy, cruel, and unfair. She works as a slave; ashamed, she washes his underwear by hand before sending it to the laundry.

A visit to the zoo is planned. They take several buses to get there and Maximilien walks fast ahead of his wife; he does not turn around to make sure she follows. Zilda, resentful, stops a couple of times and hides behind people to see if he will slow down. Maximilien forges ahead and Zilda turns around and decides to return home. She is not stupid, contrary to what Maximilien believes; she may be uneducated, but she is quietly observant, and she has memorized the numbers of the three different buses they took to the zoo. Near the apartment, there is a lovely park; she walks and sits there peacefully for a couple of hours.

When she returns home, she finds Maximilien, who has been crying. He is frantic, he has searched for her everywhere, and he tells her to never do that to him again, but he is more restrained and does not yell at her. She thinks: ha, he cares a little bit after all!

They have been in the United Kingdom for six months; they know each other better but have not developed love and affection. They have not adopted the French-language familiar way of addressing each other, the "*tu*" used between friends, lovers, and family. They will forever address each other formally, and Zilda sometimes addresses him as "doctor." She thinks of him as "the doc."

Maximilien is not attracted to his wife, he finds her passive, unexciting. He is too selfish and self-centered to spend time trying to initiate her to the pleasures of lovemaking—it does not even occur to him. Zilda, who needs nurturing, tenderness, and patience, is too insecure and inhibited to make a first move, to try to explain to her husband that she too has desires. They are hopelessly wrong for each other. They decide that it is time to return home.

CHAPTER 8

The building of the new house begins in early 1935. The property includes the back lot with the stables, pavilion, and hothouse that Maximilien coveted, and it covers almost three acres.

It takes two years to finish the construction of the house and the initial work on the park. Clement suggests using the services of the architect who designed his own house. Maximilien refuses. Instead, he hires a newly minted architect, a friend from childhood, an artist. The young man makes mistakes, mostly in the choice of materials, but produces a grand design.

Clement insists that the foundation be laid out properly. He supervises and brings his own people and material for the pouring of the cement. He insists that a bomb shelter be built under the main stairs. He demands that the front door and the framework be dismantled and redone properly. He has many heated arguments with Maximilien, who is inexperienced but wants his own ways, in spite of the fact that Clement is covering all the costs.

Zilda is never consulted by her husband in any of the decisions. She would have liked marble in the grand entrance but is overruled. It is tiled, and to her, the colors are ugly. The doors are plain and painted red, and she hates them. She wanted closets in each room; there are none in the plan.

The house is massive and full of light with large double-paned windows overlooking the park. Toward the street, there is a cavernous two-story-high central entryway with a grand staircase. Behind it and overlooking the park is a large formal dining room opening to a living room with a fireplace. A smaller dining room is separated by a wall and communicating door to the living room.

At the front of the house, there is a paneled private office for Maximilien on one side and a three-room medical office at the opposite side of the front hallway. Maximilien can enter his medical offices directly from the hallway. Patients enter and leave the waiting room from a separate outside entrance.

Four bedrooms and a huge green-and-black tiled bathroom are on the second floor, with a balcony facing the street and circling the entryway below. The third floor consists of an enormous attic with servant's quarters. The basement is a maze of ten rooms, including a large kitchen below ground level with a dumbwaiter to bring food to the smaller dining room above. Half bathrooms are built on all levels.

The park is heavily wooded, and many mature trees are felled to create a large central lawn around the pond. Maximilien consults with arborists, and they keep the most majestic trees —a colossal beech, a fifty-meter-high ancient cypress, horse chestnut trees, linden trees, poplars, and magnolia trees. The park is connected to the upper level and the house by a narrow road circling the central lawn. A second, smaller lawn is surrounded by a path and is adjacent to a dog kennel and a chicken coop. Except for the iron-gated front, the entire property is surrounded by brick walls obstructing the neighbors' view. Most of the walls are hidden by bushes and trees. It is a very private property.

At the back of the land, near the pavilion, Maximilien fences in a large kitchen garden. He plants climbing roses on trellises and trains pear trees to grow along the brick walls. He plants peach, nectarine, and cherry trees and improves the soil to plant vegetables. It is a colossal project, and he hires help, throwing himself physically into the work alongside the hired men.

The glass hothouse is repaired and found to contain ancient grapevines. The grapevines are fertilized with blood meal, and they start producing the next summer. The huge kitchen garden is seeded with all types of vegetables. Posts are erected and lines installed to dry laundry. It is a fair walk from the main house to bring heavy baskets of wet laundry, but a perfect unshaded location shielded from the main house.

Zilda and her husband move into the house in 1937. At first, it is empty of furniture except for the most basic items: a dining room table and chairs, a kitchen table, the marital bed. The huge house resonates with emptiness. Lydie buys drapes for Zilda; it helps to make it a little more comfortable.

Aime and Victoire are intrusive, they come and go as they please; unannounced, they bring acquaintances to visit the house. "Here," says Victoire, "is my son's office, look at the beautiful built-in oak bookshelves." She crosses the hallway, uses her hip to open a door and says, "Here are my son's medical offices." She takes visitors upstairs: "Here is the master bedroom, look here, and here, here."

Zilda is furious. Her own parents are barely tolerated by Maximilien and when Lydie visits, he retreats into his office, closing the door.

She attempts to push her in-laws outside through the front door; they come back at the rear of the house through the kitchen door.

Her only support is her faithful maid, Albina; the house is too big for Zilda to keep up by herself. A full-time gardener is hired. Part-time help is engaged—an older woman comes to do the laundry, another does the ironing.

Zilda has been married for three years and she is not pregnant. Maximilien makes love to her like a parched man who drinks water; swiftly, almost desperately, but he remains unaffectionate. He does not like to be touched. Zilda now tries to make advances, she wants to be a good wife, but she is rebuffed. "I don't do it on command," says Maximilien. She asks, "Do you love me?" He turns toward her, stares, and after a pause says, "You should know by now what you got."

The young wife is desperately unhappy and feels trapped. Her father arrives one evening and says: "I have come to get you, I am taking you back home." She gets into his car, and they drive a short distance. They stop. "Is this what you want?" asks Clement. "Do you want to come back to live with us, get a divorce?"

She stays silent for a while; she thinks, I am married before God, maybe I will have children soon, my mother does not want me to live in her house, and she tells her father: "Turn around and take me back." Maximilien has gone to bed and is asleep.

A couple of gynecologists are consulted. Zilda is found to have a long narrow cervix and the uterus of a twelve-year-old. Her periods are irregular. The specialists advise time and patience.

Maximilien considers getting divorced, but he loves his new property, and he keeps his thoughts to himself. The medical practice is finally taking off. It is well located on a main thoroughfare with public transportation, Maximilien holds regular clinics and starts to make house calls. He works five days a week, reserving Wednesday and Sunday for himself, and he spends hours working in the park and the vegetable garden.

Zilda serves as the medical practice receptionist; she takes phone requests and makes a list of patients for Maximilien to visit. He accepts all calls, except for baby deliveries, which he does not like to perform, and he drives to several communities, going from house to house. He goes out during the night for emergencies. One day, he comes home with fleas after visiting a poor house; it will not be the last time. Zilda picks fleas from the waist of his pants.

Maximilien gives free care to people who can't afford to pay. These clients sometimes show up later with money in an envelope or with a chicken for payment. Aime is worried that Maximilien is not having sufficient income; through his political connections, he finds work for his son, teaching at a nursing school. He argues that it will bring secure, regular income and provide Maximilien with a pension when he retires.

Aime himself is running for a political position; he is well liked and likely to win the election. His opponent, a professional politician, has a proposition: he will secure a second, permanent, well-paid position for Maximilien at another school with a guaranteed pension if Aime steps down as a candidate. The deal is agreed on and the young doctor now teaches classes twice a week. He also becomes the official physician at Clement's factory. He is paid by the visit and goes to treat workers when needed.

Between these various sources of income, the family is finally financially self-sufficient.

The young couple has found a rhythm, in a life devoid of love. She prays and asks God to send her a child. Each month is a disappointment. Maximilien sulks and turns silent for days each time.

After visiting patients on house calls, he does not come directly to the house. He goes to his garden and waters the plantings, or sits outside until dark, until it is time for the evening meal.

It is mid-1939, and preparations for war are ongoing. Ferdinand, a French citizen, is called to join the army. He already has three sons, with another child on the way, and he is the director of the French factory. Clement decides to travel with him to Paris and plead at the French war ministry to cancel or postpone his son-in-law's service in the army.

Clement has a chauffeur, and they usually travel by car, but there is a new model of train, and Clement, who has always been fascinated by trains, wants to experience the new ride. During the ride, a fire starts under the car where the two men are sitting. The asthmatic Clement is the first to detect the smoke and he shouts to the other riders that they all have to get out. They ring the alarm, but the train is in the middle of farmland, so the driver continues until the nearby station where there will be help.

The passengers are trapped, they cannot open the doors from the inside, the windows are unbreakable. Panic ensues and people climb over each other. Clement is smothered and dies. Ferdinand is slightly injured.

Lydie is now a forty-seven-year-old widow; she still has three young children at home, and no experience in running a large business. Despite her immense sorrow, she finds the strength to care for her children, she relies on her brother-in-law who is an administrator at the factory, she promotes reliable people.

Zilda falls apart. Heartbroken, weeping, distraught, she is listless and despondent; she has already lost Victor, and now, her father, her guardian angel and protector is also gone.

She finds herself to be pregnant the following month. It is the emotional shock, says the doctor. But she is deeply convinced that her father made a deal with God and gave up his life so that she would become pregnant—he sacrificed himself for her. She hates Ferdinand who did not protect and save his father-in-law.

Clement is buried in a large marble mausoleum. According to Belgian law, Lydie inherits half of the interest in the factories and the family's fortune, while the other half is divided equally among the seven children. Lydie has custody of the shares of her handicapped daughter and of her three youngest children.

Zilda is getting income from her shares in the enterprises and the balance of power with Maximilien is shifting.

At seven and a half months of her pregnancy, Zilda experiences sharp back and side pain and is taken to a hospital in Brussels. She has some blood in the urine but the pregnancy is otherwise progressing normally. The doctors are baffled; they recommend bed rest. They do not recognize that Zilda passed a small kidney stone.

Clement had bought an large apartment in Brussels in an upscale area close to the hospital where Zilda will deliver. The mother and daughter are together every day. It is a peaceful time for Zilda, and her mother tells her of the difficulties she has with Zilda's eighteen-year-old sister who is promiscuous, drinks and smokes; the child she so much loved and favored.

With her mother at her side, six years and one month after her wedding, Zilda delivers a healthy baby girl of eight pounds in March of 1940. The baby is almost bald, with a few wavy pale blond hairs. Maximilien arrives in Brussels the day after the delivery. He holds his daughter and cries and laughs at the same time. He does not thank Zilda; he has no words of love.

At long last, Zilda is happy. She has a lovely, healthy, placid baby; her life has changed. She decides to name her daughter Marie, after the Virgin Mary.

The young family returns home and Maximilien immediately proves himself to be an anxious father. He hovers over the baby; he thinks that her chest is too narrow. Zilda chides him, "Our daughter is perfect," and she enjoys her newfound happiness.

CHAPTER 9

The happy period is short and ends abruptly. The German invasion of Belgium starts on May 10, 1940. France is already at war. The German army advances rapidly, and Wallonia, the southern part of Belgium where the family resides, is bombarded relentlessly. Bombs have fallen on Aimeries. The population leaves and tries to find refuge in France.

Zilda, Maximilien, and Victoire hurriedly pack what they can, mostly clothing and diapers for Marie, and they head south to the French border. Aime stays behind to guard the houses. Lydie requisitions a large truck from the factory and also heads to the border. The vehicle is filled with her mother Laure, her children, her remaining sister, her niece, and everyone's luggage. Another vehicle transports all the documents from the factory. Clementine, in the north of France, has already evacuated with her children and Ferdinand's mother. Ferdinand has been drafted and is an officer in the French army.

In Belgium, the queue of cars is interminable—traffic is very slow. It is nighttime and headlights cannot be used. There are bombardments on the roads nearby, people try to find refuge in houses. The family finds shelter for the night in a single bedroom where they all sleep. During the night, Zilda helps a young mother whose face is embedded with glass shards after the windshield of the family car was shattered. Maximilien heads back to get his father. Near their hometown, Maximilien narrowly escapes a bomb explosion, and he rejoins his family without his father.

They resume driving toward France the next day but are soon ordered to abandon the car and travel on a refugees' train. They are not told the train's destination. The train stops for long hours on sidetracks; passengers are not allowed to leave. Roads are bombarded but the Germans need the rail tracks and spare them.

Passengers have run out of food and water. Zilda has not been drinking for hours and her milk is now insufficient for the baby who cries. She sees a railwayman on the tracks, and through the window, she begs for water. "I will help you, hand me the baby," the man says. "Get off the train and move to the opposite side of the tracks." He is poor but generous; he takes the small family to his wife and home where they stay for two days. Their hosts share the little they have. Zilda does not know the name of the locality; in their confusion, they forget to ask the name and address of these generous people and she regrets it for many years.

The family finds transportation and heads to Clermont-Ferrand, in the southwest of France, where a daughter of Victoire and Aime's neighbor is living. They are received warmly, but these people have five children and very little means. The wife takes Zilda in town so that she can buy clothes for Marie and some necessities. On the square, there are tents to receive and help refugees and a Red Cross center.

Maximilien is the Red Cross president of his community. He introduces himself at the Red Cross center and is told to go talk to a local viscount, who asks Maximilien to consult on, and treat, a sick relative. The viscount and his wife are elderly and kind. They live on a magnificent estate to which they invite the young couple to stay. After two restful weeks, they decide to try to rejoin Lydie, who has bought a vast property in the countryside, an ancient vineyard near Bordeaux, in the Gironde. The house is huge, fully furnished, and comfortable. There already are nineteen people there, adults and children, including Clementine, her three boys and mother-in-law, other family members, and family friends - Victor's parents - who also showed up.

Victoire is a constant irritant to Zilda: she snores loudly at night in the room they all share, she is critical and complains about everything. Lydie, too, barely tolerates her, and Zilda walks on eggshells, trying to keep the peace. The young mother walks with her baby in her arms, sings to her and tries to distance herself from all the activity in the big house jammed with people.

Victoire repeatedly demands that Maximilien travel back to Belgium to find Aime; they do not know if he is still alive or where he has found refuge. Zilda is opposed. "The German army is advancing rapidly, all the roads are getting bombarded, it is too dangerous," she says. Over her objections, Maximilien returns to Belgium and finds Aime at a farm. He had narrowly escaped death, he is disoriented, unrecognizable. They return to Lydie's property.

The situation at the estate is tense—there are too many people living too close to each other. Maximilien tells the children to be quiet while his baby daughter sleeps, an unrealistic demand of Clementine's energetic young boys. The young children run and shout below the window where Marie is sleeping and Maximilien slaps one of them, angering Clementine and Lydie.

A couple of days later, Ferdinand, in uniform, on a short leave from the army, makes a visit. At the evening meal, a dish is empty by the time it reaches Maximilien. He makes snide remarks. The next morning, Lydie tells Zilda and Maximilien that they and Maximilien's parents have to find other lodging. Aime and Victoire find a room in a bakery. Maximilien rents a tiny, rudimentary, one-room house with one bed, a small wood table, and two chairs under the window. Soldiers lived there before, and the whitewashed walls are covered with graffiti and drawings. Zilda prepares baby bottles on a small alcohol stove; she does the laundry in a shallow stream running behind the cottage. There is no toilet, only an outside barrel with a plank and a hole.

Again, her mother has shown preferences; Zilda is deeply humiliated that she and her family were the ones made to leave the comfortable estate. Her mother pushed her to marry Maximilien and now she cannot tolerate him. It is another slight against her, one that will stay with her for a very long time. She escapes in her memories of happy times with her fiancé, Victor, and she tries to soldier on.

CHAPTER 10

Maximilien takes his family back to Aimeries in September. The area is fully occupied by the Germans, and the bombing has stopped.

The two family houses, Maximilien's and Zilda's, and his parents', have been broken in but are structurally intact. Maximilien resumes his medical practice; as a physician and the president of the local Red Cross, he is allowed to move freely. Everything is rationed and each person receives food stamps. The kitchen garden provides fruit and fresh vegetables. Belgians are allowed to have chickens but no livestock.

Winter is approaching, the family receives some coal from the factory, but the house is large, and they do not have sufficient supply. In exchange for free medical care, he gets small bags of coal from miners. The coal is hidden in a corner of the park, under old leaves.

German collaborators visit; they have information that the family is hiding coal, but they do not find it. Two days later they return: "You have been denounced again," they say, "we now know where you are hiding the coal," and they head directly to the cache to confiscate it. Zilda and Maximilien are lucky they are not fined or imprisoned. They are convinced that the new owners of the old mansion at the back of the park have denounced them. They are the only people who can see into the park from their second-floor windows, and they are angry that Maximilien built a brick wall very close to their house.

The family survives by bartering and buying on the black market. Maximilien comes home with butter from a farmer's wife he has treated. She believes that he has saved her life, and she hides butter for him, but the price is exorbitant. When Zilda can find grain, she brings it to the mill and has it ground to make bread.

Zilda is pregnant for a second time and the pregnancy is again easy; she gains more weight than the first time. She is due in February.

Jean, Zilda's younger brother, is eighteen; his girlfriend, twenty years old, is also pregnant. She comes from a poor family and her parents demand that Jean marry their daughter. Jean protests that he was trapped, that he was seduced, but Lydie insists that he must marry. The baby, born two months after the wedding, is stillborn.

Jean is sent to the factory in France for training. When he returns, the twenty-year old is installed as the Belgian factory's director. He finished high school but failed the first year at a technical school. Lydie enlists the help of two former associates of Clement to work alongside the young man for a year, and coach him on how to run the business.

Zilda's seven-year-younger sister has broken an engagement. She likes to dance, and she goes to Brussels where she frequents bars, drinks, and flirts. She meets a young Jewish-Hungarian refugee in a bar, a civil engineer and talented piano player trying to raise sufficient money to join his parents in the United States. She is smitten.

The young man visits Lydie, brings her a gorgeous bouquet of flowers, kisses her hand. Lydie is enchanted with the courtly young man and gives her blessing to the marriage. She offers the groom a well-paid position at the factory. The young bride immediately gets pregnant. Zilda cannot help to reflect on how warmly Lydie treats her new son-in-law, and she is jealous. She has the wrong husband.

CHAPTER II

The weather is extremely cold in early February. It is decided that Zilda will go to Brussels and again stay with her mother to wait for the delivery of her baby.

This time, the relationship is strained; Lydie, unerringly close to the truth, accuses Zilda of being jealous of her sisters and her brother. An unhappy, resentful Zilda anxiously waits for the delivery, to be away from her mother and her accusations. The second baby girl is delivered with forceps. She has a full head of thick black hair. She weighs a pound less than Marie at birth, but she is a beautiful, healthy baby and Zilda rejoices.

Maximilien arrives the next day; the trip to Brussels was difficult, the roads almost impassable with ice and snow. When he sees the newborn, he is stunned and says very little. There are no congratulations for Zilda, no words of tenderness, he does not thank her. He believes that this infant cannot be his, she is too different from the first one with her thick dark hair and long eyelashes.

In wartime, with restrictions, the room at the hospital is very cold and the new mother holds the baby against her under the covers to keep her warm. Zilda is focused on her daughter, cooing and trying to nurse; she is happy, and she fails to notice Maximilien's reaction. Zilda has learned not to expect affection from her husband.

She names her baby Marguerite. Like her sister, the baby is baptized and Victoire and Jean are asked to be the godparents.

The frigid weather continues; Maximilien works hard at finding supplies for his family. He visits farms, gets some food on the black market. He has brought home about a hundred eggs. Zilda and the maid, Albina, are busy in the kitchen, rubbing the eggs with vinegar to place them in a vat with gelatin to preserve them.

As they often do, they chat and laugh. Maximilien, who likes to spy, stealthily comes down the kitchen stairs, hears the laughing, and imagines that the women are mocking him. He becomes very angry and breaks all the precious eggs on the floor. Incensed, Zilda calls him crazy, says he always imagines that he is the center of attention, that he knows what Zilda is thinking, that he does not tolerate for her to have fun. They have a huge fight, and he is told to clean the floor.

Since she has had children, Zilda feels stronger, less afraid of her husband's wrath and temper. Her shares at the factory bring income to the family, though it is Maximilien who keeps the budget, and he does not give her much money at a time.

She has realized that, in addition to being cold and unaffectionate, her husband has complexes, that he is impulsive, that he can be insecure. She thinks over his reaction at the birth of Marguerite, that he did not demonstrate the same joy as at the birth of Marie. Maybe, she wonders, he was disappointed that we did not have a son.

She has evolved physically from a pretty, thin, fragile woman to a stronger, beautiful, mature, and more secure one. She can be imperious, cutting lines, asking for special treatment by invoking Maximilien's name: "I am the wife of doctor…"

Maximilien has said that he does not want more children, but Zilda gets pregnant five months after the birth of Marguerite. She loves being pregnant; babies make her feel wanted, fulfilled, and happy, they are not critical. This time, she does not want to leave her two little girls and deliver in Brussels. She will have the baby in her home.

Zilda wakes up with contractions one night in July 1943; she gets up and the waters break in the early hours. She tries to wake up Maximilien. "I need to sleep," he says, "we have time." He turns over and goes back to sleep.

She is alone in the kitchen, walking back and forth between the contractions, when the maid comes down in the morning.

Together, the maid and Zilda manage to bring a table and supplies to the second-floor bathroom where she will give birth. The midwife is called. Maximilien, now awake, calls his parents. Albina is occupied with the children.

Maximilien has gone outside to talk to the gardener. He does not come to check on his wife and the progress of the delivery. Birth is imminent, the midwife calls him to assist at the delivery, but he tells her to call another doctor. Just at the time when the baby is being born, Aime, with little Marie in his arms, enters the bathroom without knocking. Outraged, Zilda and the doctor scream for him to get out, and she delivers a third baby girl.

The new baby is just over six pounds, smaller than the first and second ones, but healthy. She has the first child's thin, pale blond hair. Zilda thinks her ugly, that she has a round, red farmer's face. She looks like my mother-in-law, thinks Zilda; each of my babies is smaller than the previous one, she muses.

Told that he again has a daughter, Maximilien takes a long time to come up from the garden to see the newborn; he does not hide that he is disappointed. He sulks for several days, categorically says that he will not have a fourth child.

As a peace offering, the new baby is named Maxine. She cries and tries to feed immediately, but this time, Zilda's milk is slow to come. "Put her in the bathroom," says Maximilien, "she will wake up the others." The mother takes her newborn to the kitchen and against orders from her husband, gives her sugared water, which calms the baby down. The infant is greedy and latches on the breast ferociously at each feeding; she is demanding. This one is different, thinks Zilda, maybe because she was smaller at birth?

"Clementine gets a piece of jewelry from her husband every time she has a new baby," says Zilda to her husband, "and you never gave me a gift." Maximilien offers a large aquamarine pendant set in a gold horseshoe but says a week later: "The jewel was very expensive, I would like to return it and get the money back. I will tell the jeweler that my wife did not like it." Zilda does not like the jewel very much, and she knows that she will rarely wear it, but she is outraged and hurt. She refuses to hand it over.

Maximilien has a mistress. He fell in love with a younger married woman just after Marguerite's birth, and he justifies the affair to himself, thinking that he is not Marguerite's father. Zilda would not dream of looking at another man, and all three children are his. Her husband is difficult, demanding, quick to anger, but she has convinced herself that she has some love for him and that there is hope for her marriage. She tries to please him, to make him love her.

He is out of the house all day, making house calls, teaching at two schools, goes to the factory when needed; he spends time at the Red Cross. He comes home for two regular weekly consultations at his office, to eat, and to sleep. He is free to come and go as he pleases, stopping at the house to get the list of patients to visit.

His mistress likes sex: she is inventive, uninhibited, and he returns to her every day. When he comes home, he directly heads to the kitchen garden, crouches, balances himself on his haunches, holds the water hose, and stares at his garden for hours. Then he heads to his office and closes the door. He visits his parents briefly twice each day. Zilda keeps dinner warm for him, but he often eats at his parents' without telling her not to wait for him.

Zilda, entirely unaware of the affair, fully absorbed in the care of three young children, believes that he stays away from her because he does not want to have more children, and she believes him to be cold and uninterested in sex. She knows that he is busy and works hard, and so she carves a life for herself and the three small children. She is occupied with feeding them, walking them, playing and singing, making dolls' clothes. She cooks all their food to Maximilien's exact instructions.

She and the children spend a lot of time in the park behind the house. She pushes the baby carriage around the small road circling the property and sits on the grass with the baby and the toddlers. Overall, Zilda is happy. I have three beautiful children, she thinks, and she is proud to take them out and parade them to family and neighbors.

CHAPTER 12

Maximilien constantly scrutinizes his children. He still frets over Marie's chest, thinking that it is too narrow. Zilda is so annoyed that she demands he take the child to the Brussels' pediatric hospital where she is examined and declared by the chairman of the department to be perfect.

One day, Zilda gives a bath to the newborn in a bassinet in the bathroom. Marguerite, who just started to walk at thirteen months, is sitting on the bathroom floor near Zilda. The rim of the big sunken bathtub is at ground level, behind a closed curtain. Marguerite gets close to the bathtub and falls in it. She is bleeding heavily; it seems as if blood comes from the eyes. The child screams, Zilda is terrified; Albina runs into the room carrying Marie, and she takes over the baby while Zilda rushes with Marguerite to a nearby doctor. The child has a bleeding scalp cut, which the doctor cleans and bandages.

The child recovers quickly but Zilda is fearful of Maximilien's reaction when he gets home. When he sees his daughter with a bandaged head, he swears, yells and screams at Zilda. The ever-present Aime opines that she is obviously unable to take care of the three children. "You would not be able to raise a litter of rabbits," he says. The two men decree that Marie should be raised by Aime and Victoire in their house.

Cowed, and feeling guilty, Zilda is unable to fight back, but she insists that Marie return in the evenings and sleep at home. She soon wants her child back during the day as well. Aime and Victoire, with Maximilien on their side, refuse to hand over Marie until Zilda, resolute and ready to fight, goes to bring her back a few weeks later. The child belongs to her.

Marie, back home for a couple of weeks, develops rubella. Out of fear of contagion, her bed is moved to the grandparents' home. It is winter, it is hard to get around, the two younger children develop rubella as well, demanding a lot of time and care, and the battle is lost for Zilda; Marie will be raised by her grandparents. Aime brings her to her parents' house regularly, and Maximilien sees her on his daily visits to his parents' house, but the child is now living on Alliance Road.

On days when Marie is visiting with her mother and sisters, she fights over toys and refuses to share them. Zilda tries to control her and make her share, but she cries: "I want to go back to Grandpa and Grandma, where I am the favorite and I do not have to share."

When the child starts elementary school, she has difficulties learning. Aime tutors his granddaughter. He patiently spends hours helping her. She grows up as a spoiled child who never plays with her sisters. Marguerite and Maxine, sharing the same bedroom, constantly play with each other.

Zilda had made modifications to the house in order to child-proof it. The banister of the stairs and around the second-floor balcony had large gaps between the horizontal bars and she already had it modified, but she had not realized that the sunken bathtub was also dangerous. It is a very big bathtub, now raised from the floor, creating a hiding space, and surrounded by removable Bakelite panels. Maximilien makes Zilda practice removing and reinstalling the panels faster and faster so that he can slip under the tub if he needs to hide in a hurry. It is the war after all, one must be ready for any occurrence. Zilda wonders, he would be hidden, but what about the children and me?

CHAPTER 13

An agent for the factory has lost his house in a bombing. Together with his wife and son, he finds lodging near Zilda's house, and she meets them at her mother's house. The son is twenty-four years old. When the twenty-nine-year-old Zilda sees him for the first time, they gaze into each other's eyes. It is love at first sight for both. She has never known such desire. Her love for Victor, her dead fiancé, was sweet and gentle; this is passion, and she burns for the young man. She does not have much free time, but she often walks at night to her mother's house, when the children are in bed and Maximilien is ensconced in his office, with the door closed.

The young man watches for her; they walk together in the dark. They kiss, embrace, tell each other their feelings. Zilda is too religious to sleep with the young man, nor do they have opportunities to do so. But she is consumed by the burning foreign emotions; she cries and loses weight; she becomes depressed. Maximilien is oblivious to the changes in his wife and her depression. She loves but cannot be with her loved one; it is torture. She blames Maximilien: if he loved me, she thinks, I would not have fallen in love with another. I thought that I loved my husband, but I do not.

One day, tormented, confused, she tells her husband: "I love another man."

"Who is he? I will kill him," says Maximilien. He has a German gun and ammunition; he takes the gun and leaves the house. Zilda knows that her husband is full of bravado but has no courage. He comes back and declares: "He is lucky; I did not find him." Zilda learns that he did not go to the young man's house, and she is not surprised. Time eases the feelings of passion. Zilda knows that she is a beautiful woman, men often compliment and propose to her, but she hides behind her children for emotional protection.

The Americans cross the Belgian border in September of 1944, and the Allies liberate the country; the war ends in February 1945. Life slowly returns to normal. Two young American officers posted in Aimeries ask Zilda at the front gate if they may come in, and Maximilien agrees. They have fresh eggs; they ask Zilda to cook them. The young people strike up a friendship, they manage to understand each other and have fun. The Americans come visit almost every day, they play with the little girls and bring candy. One day, Maximilien asks one of the men if his wife could send chocolate from the US. She sends filled chocolates and Maximilien gives the American the beautiful diamond pin that Zilda gifted him at their engagement. She is outraged; Maximilien says: "It belongs to me, I don't wear it and I never will. I can give it away if I want." Zilda detaches herself a little more from her callous husband.

The Belgian coast has not suffered from the bombings. Lydie reopens her property on the boardwalk and invites her children to visit. Maximilien wants his children to vacation at the coast and be exposed to iodine. Most of Lydie's family is there, and there is no room for Zilda to stay at her mother's apartment. She rents a couple of rooms at a nearby hotel; she visits with her family but has lodging and meals at the hotel.

Zilda spends a couple of weeks at the seacoast with Marguerite and Maxine while Marie is at school and lives with her grandparents. Maximilien plans to bring the oldest child on the weekend. The little girls are rosy cheeked, they run on the beach, visit with some of their cousins; they fall asleep immediately at night.

Each night, as Zilda and her little girls have dinner at the hotel, they are served by the son of the owners, an elderly couple. The waiter, twenty-six, is the most beautiful man Zilda has ever seen and he too has noticed Zilda; he joins her several times on the beach after he finishes his work, helps build sandcastles for the children, makes small talk.

Maximilien arrives with Marie for the weekend. Zilda wants to be close to him. The children are asleep in the next room. Maximilien is undressing in the bathroom. She approaches from behind, kisses his neck, and tells him that she wants him. He looks at his wife in the mirror and says: "The children," and moves away.

Maximilien has left with Marie at the end of the weekend. Hurt and rejected again, Zilda goes for a short walk after Marguerite and Maxine fall asleep. She has given some money to the chambermaid to keep an eye on the children's room. On the boardwalk, she sits on a bench and cries. The waiter has followed her and takes her in his arms. He hugs and kisses her, soothes her. She returns to the hotel and goes to bed. She is half asleep when the young man comes into her room and simply says, "I want you"—the words she has been waiting to hear from her husband. She lifts the covers, and they make love.

So, this is what Clementine had been talking about. The lovemaking is slow and tender, the pleasure is intense, something she had never known with her man. She has only one night with the young server. She has no regrets, but she asks herself why is she so unlucky? She is bitterly jealous of her sister Clementine.

CHAPTER 14

Zilda is pregnant. She has not told a soul of her night of love. She believes that the child was conceived at the North Sea and that the young dining room server is the father. She is afraid, heartbroken; she knows that she cannot keep the child. "I do not want another child," says Maximilien, and Zilda, heartbroken, conflicted and relieved at the same time, agrees.

Maximilien performs an abortion in his medical office. He has few sexual relations with his wife; he tries to remember when they last made love. The marriage now exists and endures for the sake of their three children.

Zilda's younger sister has abandoned her husband, the Hungarian jazz player, and two children; her baby boy is barely six months old. Lydie asks Zilda and Maximilien to go find the young mother in Brussels and bring her back. They find her with a man in a cheap hotel room. She has no money, asks her sister to give her some; she refuses to return to her family.

Driving back after that encounter in Brussels, Maximilien taunts Zilda; "At least," he says, "your sister has the courage to leave a bad marriage," but Zilda does not take the bait. Her sister has a good husband, steadfast and honest, an excellent father to their children.

Lydie, ashamed of her daughter, intervenes in the lives of her little grandchildren. They live next door to her, and she is a constant in their lives. She sings them lullabies, gives them affection. She is now overweight and has a beard; she shaves every few days and often has stubble. When he grows up, the little boy calls his grandmother "grandma who pricks."

In peace time, life returns to normal. Marie, Marguerite, and Maxine are five, three, and two years old. The family settles into a rhythm. Marie comes and visits but goes back to her grandparents after a couple of hours. She ignores her sisters. For Marguerite and Maxine, it is a wonderful time. They are too young to notice the tension and lack of affection between their parents.

Their mother is loving and attentive; she cooks wonderful food, she invites little cousins and organizes wild hide-and-seek games in the house and in the park. Zilda makes chocolate treats on a whim at midnight, to surprise the children in the morning. She buys fake turds, and to the kids' great amusement, she leaves them around the house for Maximilien to find. He is not amused; the children laugh. One day, she makes waffles, threads string in a waffle as it cooks, and offers it to Maximilien. She has told the children in advance of the joke, and they are having a difficult time keeping it a secret. Maximilien bites into the waffle and throws the entire platter through the open window before storming out.

Grandfather Aime is devoted to his granddaughters. He is at the house every day and takes the three children for walks and buys them candy. He is patient, and for years, he teaches them about plants, flowers, and trees. Zilda does not like him and resents him, but she knows that her three daughters love their grandfather. She is careful not to communicate her feelings to her children. They would not understand, and they would be confused.

Victoire, too, loves the little ones. She makes stacks of waffles and pancakes that Aime brings over; she sews flannel pajamas for the children's birthdays. The grandmother buys cakes of pink embossed soap called Baby's Dew. To Marguerite, the soaps smell divine; they are wrapped in thin pretty paper and Victoire makes a ceremony of opening a drawer in her dresser and handing over a bar of soap on special occasions.

Sometimes, Zilda brings her children to visit her mother, though she most often visits by herself in the evening. Lydie is a stern, formidable woman, always surrounded by other people. She is not affectionate to Zilda's children; they are not her favorites and Marguerite does not like her.

Laure, Zilda's beloved grandmother, sometimes comes for tea. Lydie's driver brings her, she stays for a while, admires her great-grand daughters but says little.

Laure is always dressed in black, she is very old and wrinkled like an old apple. She is tiny and quiet with snowy white hair in a bouffant style. After a while, having sat peacefully, she returns to Lydie's house. There, one evening, she says: "I am tired, I am going to bed," and she dies, gently, as a candle that flickers and goes out.

CHAPTER 15

Once a month, Maximilien makes the children sit in a row in the bathroom and trims their nails, he inspects the ears and throats, weighs the children, charts their progress. He cares for his children, but he never kisses nor hugs them, "A perfect way to transfer germs," he says to Zilda. He is business like, it is almost as if the children are a clinical project to him; he wants them to be healthy, and he wants them to be well educated. Those are his responsibilities, and he takes them very seriously. He does not vaccinate the children against smallpox or tuberculosis but takes their temperature regularly. One day he thinks that one of them has a slight temperature. "She has been running around," says Zilda, "she is fine." He makes the other two run around the house and takes their temperatures before and after the run to test Zilda's theory, which proves right.

Maximilien has digestive issues and he projects them unto his children. Bowel habits are scrutinized. "Has everyone had a bowel movement?" he asks. "What did it look like?" He continues this as they grow up, embarrassing his daughters. "For god's sake, Maximilien, stop this questioning!" chides Zilda.

At the slightest scare, he brings the children to the university hospital in Brussels and they are examined by the chairman, who never finds anything amiss. Penicillin, discovered in 1928, is now commercially available for injection; Maximilien makes liberal use of it. At every cold or suspicion of a cold, every bleeding scratch of the knees, he gives penicillin injections. Every time one of the girls has an injection, he gives her a fifty-franc coin.

The children have to stick their tongues out for inspection. "Your tongue is loaded," he says to Marguerite. Loaded with what? she wonders. He smells her breath. "We have to keep an eye on Marguerite's liver, a loaded tongue may indicate liver problems," the father tells Zilda. She rolls her eyes. Maximilien is really paranoid when it comes to his children.

The large basement kitchen is the house's center of activity. Zilda, who does not have any close women friends, likes to work, chat, and laugh with the maid, the washerwoman, and the woman who comes to do the ironing. As she grows older, Marguerite likes to spend time there when the women work and chat.

Marguerite, six-year-old, watches her mother work; how the irons are heated up on the coal stove, how one irons a shirt, a complex task. Zilda shortens her husband's shirtsleeves on the pedal-activated sewing machine, and Marguerite asks to be taught to use the machine.

The door to the adjacent laundry room is open. She observes the washerwoman pump water from the cistern, heat it in a huge vat, wash the clothes by hand with big cakes of yellow Marseille soap. When she needs help, the maid helps carry and empty the water from the vat into a big floor drain. The water clings to the holes of the drain, and against the dark background of the water below, the droplets look like eyes before they blink and disappear. Watching the water "eyes" in the drain captivates Marguerite for a long time.

In the earlier years, the women twist the wet sheets together to wring them, but Zilda acquires a centrifugal spinner, which fascinates Marguerite and Maxine. It has large rubber feet to stabilize it, but it still moves along the floor if not held in place. The children hold it down and laugh at the vibrations. Zilda and a maid bring a heavy basket of laundry to the drying lines in the garden kitchen. Together, they snap the sheets before hanging them on the lines. Sometimes, there is running back to remove the laundry when it starts raining. Marguerite likes to help.

Much is learned in the kitchen; there, Marguerite hears for the first time about women's menstruation. She learns of hunger when the laundry woman who emigrated from the south of Italy tells of surviving by eating stolen grapes. The woman is not married and has two children by different men. How can that be possible? She hears gossip. She remembers what the women talk about. She hears of different countries: there are a lot of immigrants in Belgium, many from Italy and Poland. "Italy is a beautiful country," says Zilda.

Maximilien has hired a young woman, Louise, a protégé of Aime, trained as a physical education teacher, to come exercise the children in the park. The young woman is energetic and always in a good mood. She is also very pretty, olive-skinned with almond-shaped eyes, and Zilda wonders what is the relationship between her and Aime? And is Maximilien interested in the young exotic-looking woman?

She finds her answer when she catches Louise kissing the much older Aime on the mouth one day. She is stunned. Aime is old enough be her father, and all of this under the nose of Victoire. It troubles Zilda, but she stays silent and is relieved that Maximilien is not involved.

There are regular trips through all seasons to the North Sea, where Zilda now rents an apartment. Marie joins her mother and sisters when she is not in school. Maximilien stays behind; he needs to take care of his patients and does not like to leave his parents for long.

At the coast, mother and children take long walks on the beach. In December and at Easter, the wind is fierce, and the children are bundled up. They thrive, they run races, have sand-castle-building contests, collect shells.

They love to watch the large Friesian horses slowly walk in the surf, pulling nets to catch small gray North Sea shrimp. Zilda buys shrimp right there on the beach from the fisherman, and with a bucket of sea water, they go to the apartment and boil the small tasty shrimp; it takes forever to remove the shells. They visit the fish market and eat fish caught a few hours before.

Zilda is relaxed and playful when away from her husband. She is not a timely person and there is no strict daily schedule: they eat when they are hungry and may have breakfast for dinner. She is a wonderful mother to the young children; she reads to them before bedtime and they are introduced to the world of Tintin, the Belgian comic book hero with adventures in foreign lands, and his dog Snowy.

Back at the family home, the atmosphere changes—a cloud descends on the family.

Marguerite, the eight-year-old middle sister, starts to sense the discord between her parents. Her mother changes from relaxed and laughing to being tense, on her guard. When her parents fight, Marguerite imagines herself to be in a small boat, on a raging sea. She is at the bottom of the bare shell of the boat, helpless, curled up, waiting for the storm to calm down, a grain of sand in a walnut shell, bobbing on the water.

During the summers, Maximilien takes a vacation with his family. They go to the Atlantic coast of France and to Switzerland. Maximilien wants the children to be at high altitude; "It builds red blood cells," he says.

On a trip to Arcachon, the sea resort in France with the longest European sand dune, Maximilien insists that Louise accompany the family. "She will help take care of the children," he says, "and exercise them." Zilda is not pleased. She demands that Louise find her own accommodation and not stay with them in their hotel.

Back from a long walk with her children, she finds Maximilien lying down in bed, Louise is massaging his belly, slowly up and down, then in a circle. "I am constipated" says Maximilien, "I had belly pain and Louise is helping me." Zilda is intensely jealous; Maximilien does not let her touch him. She tells Louise to leave and return home on her own. It is true that Maximilien has a congenital inversion of his colon, a situs inversus and often has digestive problems and belly pain. But it does not excuse the familiarity with another woman.

CHAPTER 16

Lydie had filed a lawsuit against the French railway company after her husband's death in the train accident. The lawsuit lingered during the war but after several years of depositions and testimonies, the family is awarded damages for the loss of the father and husband. Lydie and each child receive compensation, but the French President Charles de Gaulle, decrees that French currency must be spent in France.

With the windfall, Maximilien and Zilda take vacations in France for a couple of years. They visit the area of Bordeaux, proud to show their three children to the old couple who had given them refuge during the war. The next year, they decide to go to the French Riviera. Maximilien writes to the chamber of commerce of a few cities and is directed to a family who owns a large property in Saint-Jean-Cap-Ferrat. The secluded property is located on a spit of land near the sea. It is difficult to find the place; frustrated, Maximilien almost turns the car around, but they finally arrive there. They discover a luxurious property and gracious hosts.

They are the only guests. They go to the beach, they visit nearby towns. The food is exquisite, the hosts are discreet and kind, though the wife tells Zilda that she has never in her life seen a couple so poorly matched.

The children participate in the Nice carnival, wearing clothes that the owner rents for them. Zilda falls in love with the French Riviera and hopes that one day, she can afford to have a property there.

Another vacation is spent at Clementine's summer home at the Touquet-Paris-Plage, a seaside resort town in the north of France. Clementine and Ferdinand are very wealthy, and they have acquired a big property. They now have seven children. Clementine is happy to host guests, but they have to pay a significant sum of money, as if at an upscale inn. For the children, it is a wonderful place to be, though their rich, sophisticated cousins ignore them.

During that vacation, Zilda and Maximilien's children go to the pool every day and learn to swim. They are bought tennis racquets and are given tennis lessons. They take horseback-riding lessons in the forest and canter up a hill. Marguerite never forgets her first magic canter.

Initiated to swimming, tennis and horseback riding, the girls now need to experience skiing, decrees Maximilien. Each child gets ski pants, a parka, winter boots, and a pair of après-ski lighter boots. Zilda has thought of everything and spent a lot of money to outfit her daughters. The entire family goes for a two-week vacation in St. Moritz in Switzerland. The children get skiing lessons; all three declare that they do not like it. Ice skating is a little more successful, but again the children are not very interested. There will not be another winter vacation in Switzerland.

Maximilien has his daughters' blood counts checked regularly. He continues to be obsessed with their health. Marguerite is discovered to have a low count of white blood cells called lymphocytes and a low platelet count. The father panics and brings the child to the university's Pediatrics Department in Brussels. Nothing amiss is found: the child is energetic, but he is told that it could be a sign of early leukemia and that Marguerite should have regular blood checkups. Thus starts a monthly ritual that lasts for many years. The father takes the child to a nearby clinic, a half hour drive away, and she has blood drawn. After each painful experience, he gives the child a coin that she saves in her piggy bank.

They usually ride in silence to and from the clinic but get used to each other's company in the car. She sits in front next to him. Maximilien is anxious and frets for a few days until he gets the results of the blood test. Ah, good, the cell count has not changed, he can relax until next time. The white blood cell counts remain steadily low over the years. The regular checkups are spaced out when Marguerite is a teenager. She is an outlier, healthy, but with blood counts outside of those of the general population, and she remains so for her entire life.

Maxine too is found to have a health problem: she has proteinuria, abnormal amounts of protein excreted in the urine. Panic ensues again. This could be the sign of a serious disease that might progress to kidney failure, or, as it happens in some children, it might correct itself and disappear in a few years. The outcome is unpredictable. There is nothing to do but keep a watch and wait.

Zilda, who does not fully understand the implications of the abnormality, is not as worried, but Maximilien instructs her to take extra precautions with Maxine. She should not exert herself too much, she needs to be protected, driven around instead of walking. Maxine grows up coddled; her mother drives her everywhere.

She becomes Zilda's favorite. On the way from school, they stop at antique shops, they have fun. Maxine soon feels entitled to the special treatment.

Maximilien does not spend much time playing with the children, but one summer day in the vegetable garden, in a rare playful mood, he decides to play catch with Maxine and Marguerite. He starts running toward the hothouse and closes the glass door shut as Marguerite reaches to push it open; her hand goes through the glass. She has a large gash from the base of the right thumb to the tip of the finger. A slab of skin and muscle hangs over and bleeds profusely, the bone visible. Maximilien grabs his daughter's hand, holds it high, and makes her run with him to the house. Pale, sweating, he cleans the wound and sutures it while Zilda holds her daughter. It is not easy to do—it is in a difficult curvy spot. Marguerite ends up with a thick, uneven scar limiting the amount of stretching she can do with her thumb.

That summer is eventful. As they always do, against strict orders, Marguerite and Maxine climb the brick wall behind the cherry trees. The trees are full of ripe cherries the children love to eat. Maxine falls from the wall and breaks her collarbone.

Bicycling has become Marguerite's favorite pastime. She is allowed to leave the house and goes to her paternal grandparents to visit frequently. One spring day the next year, she bicycles with Maxine and a friend of her sister into the wood near the community. It is not far from the grandparents' house; Aime used to take the children there for walks. The wood is beautiful, a favorite destination for local people, with nice trails for bicycling. It has a small, very old chapel, and it is full of daffodils in the spring. The children want to pick up daffodils for their mothers. The wood is largely empty of people on that weekday. Maxine and her friend are just ahead of Marguerite; the three children hold their bicycles and walk slowly to find the best place to pick the flowers.

A man approaches from behind and tells the children that he knows where the best flowers are to be found. He tells Maxine and her friend to go that way, he will go the other way with Marguerite who gets suspicious; she tells the other two children to get on their bikes and pedal away, she mounts her own bike when the man grabs her skirt from behind and tries to stop her. She turns around to hit him and shake herself free, and she is lucky to hit him in the eye. He lets go for a moment and she too pedals as fast as she can as the man runs after them. Nearby, at the edge of the wood, there is a farm. Marguerite yells to enter the farm's courtyard and they see the farmer there. They tell him what happened; he calls the police and Maximilien, who, livid, comes to pick up the children. Maximilien is furious, shaky. He is told that there has been reports of a suspicious man.

Two weeks later, the family's young maid, going home at night, is raped in a field. The man is apprehended; Maximilien testifies that he tried to rape his daughter.

Marguerite again has a similar incident a year later. Bicycling back from an evening visit to her grandparents, she is almost at her house, in a small dark side street. Two men try to stop her, but she escapes. She becomes wary of men.

CHAPTER 17

Lydie sells her wartime property in France, the vineyard near Bordeaux, and buys a small chateau with a large park near Namur in Belgium. She intends to use the castle for family reunions and vacations. Zilda offers a large antique bijar oriental rug as a housewarming gift for her mother's castle.

Maximilien, Zilda, and the children visit just once. Maximilien does not get along well with his wife's family, he refuses to return to the castle, but he starts thinking that he, too, would like to own a property in the countryside.

Lydie revels in her fortune; she has a luxury car, always the latest and biggest Mercedes model, and a chauffeur. She travels frequently to Portugal, Spain, France, and Switzerland to buy handmade embroidered linen and embroidered silk shirts. She makes regular pilgrimages to Lourdes and distributes little Virgin-shaped glass bottles of holy water to family members.

The matriarch is generous to her family: she holds a big Christmas party every year where she has thoughtful gifts for her twenty grandchildren, daughters, son, and sons-in-law. For the women, she travels to Cartier in Paris and chooses expensive pieces of gold jewelry. At Cartier, she sits in an armchair and selects from the pieces the jeweler reverently presents to her.

Soon after Lydie buys her castle, Maximilien meets an older, wealthy hunter who invites Zilda and Maximilien to join him. They hunt with hunting dogs, and local farmers beat the bushes to raise the pheasants. A babysitter is hired to watch the children at a nearby farm, but they get to see the ferrets, the excited dogs, the tally of the hunt, rabbits and pheasants in rows, an occasional deer or boar.

Zilda is a better hunter than Maximilien; she likes the genial atmosphere and the enthusiasm of the hunters. At the end of the day, the family comes home exhausted, with their share of the game, which Maximilien hangs to ripen in the cellar. He shows the children how to skin a rabbit and pluck a pheasant. Zilda cooks the game a few days later. Game meat is delicious; Zilda is a great cook.

Maximilien ate pigeons when he was young; the family now has pigeons in a coop in the old forge. He is the one who cleans the coop and feeds the birds. He selects young birds to eat and wrings their necks. The family eats young pigeons from time to time as well.

Next to the coop, there is a fruit cellar where Maximilien stores the apples and pears from the garden on wooden slats. He likes the ritual walk to the fruit cellar after dinner to select fruit for the family dessert. The cellar smells rich and earthy and he inhales deeply. The family eats homegrown fruit and root vegetables well into the winter.

The father does not like to see cats and dogs on the property. There are hedgehogs at the back of the park, and he wants to protect them, though they are well able to protect themselves. If a roaming dog finds its way into the park, he shoots it with salt pellets; he clubs and kills the unfortunate cats venturing onto the property. His children are very upset, and he shrugs. The animals should not come here he says.

Both parents like the area where they hunt, near the border with France. They decide to look for a property there; there is a foreclosed one coming up for auction.

They visit the property, a tall, turret-like home next to a small lake. The lake empties into a stream close to the house, there are fields and a small wood. Maximilien likes the property, Zilda does not. She finds the house to be damp, too big; she thinks of the upkeep of such a property, which would fall upon her, but Maximilien is entranced and determined to bid at the auction.

Zilda points out that they do not have the money to buy the property. Maximilien says: "We will borrow from your mother." Zilda feels used and does not intend to do so.

On the day of the auction, the bidding starts at four hundred thousand Belgian francs. A few local farmers, a restaurateur who wants to open a restaurant on the site, and Maximilien bid against each other. The farmers soon stop, but Maximilien and the restaurateur keep bidding. The price has more than doubled and Zilda is frantic. At eight hundred and fifty thousand francs, Maximilien finally listens to his wife and abandons the chase.

There is another property nearby, one hundred and fifty acres, with an ancient farm, for sale for four hundred thousand Belgian francs. It has been on the market for a while but is not selling because the farm building is old, needs extensive renovations, and is still occupied. The lease terminates in two years.

The farm is a low, long building on a windy plateau with land and pastures sloping down on both the front and back sides. It is locally known as *Hurlebise*, "howling wind," as the wind can be fierce on the plateau. The building's stone walls are one yard thick. There are two small streams on the property, crossing the fields, one on each side of the plateau. There is crayfish in the deepest of the two streams.

The farm building is reached by a steep, narrow winding road along a small wood. On the opposite side from the access road and the plateau with the farm building, there is an upward-sloping dense wood. The property extends across the border with France. The pastures are in Belgium, and the big wood with the stones marking the border lays mostly in France. Maximilien loves the property, Zilda gives her approval, and they use all their savings to acquire it.

Since the farm building cannot be used for a couple of years, Maximilien has a one-room cabin with a little woodstove built, at the end of the big wood on the French side. He throws himself into the process of cleaning up the neglected wood, creating and enlarging trails, and with help from local farmers, he plants thousands of seedlings—larches and pines. He buys an additional section of land when it becomes available and transforms it into a tree nursery. He rents the pastures to farmers. With rich grass and streams, they are easy to lease, and he collects the rents.

He goes into his woods every Wednesday and Sunday, often hiring local help. Over the weekend, if the weather is nice, he brings Marguerite and Maxine to play around the cabin while he works; Marguerite prefers to read. She sits on the front steps of the cabin with her book. Maximilien returns home dirty and exhausted but happy.

CHAPTER 18

Maximilien says one day: "Marguerite looks pale." Zilda counters: "She looks fine to me." Indeed, Marguerite has pale skin, and it contrasts with her thick black hair. She looks like a doll with her fringe and moss-green eyes.

"Still," says Maximilien, "I think that we should send the children to the mountains in Switzerland; I read about a wonderful summer camp in the Valais. The children are twelve, ten and nine, old enough to stay at the camp by themselves." The decision is made; the parents will drive the children to the summer camp. They will drop them off, take a few days of vacation by themselves in the mountains, and return in one month to pick up the three girls.

It is the middle of the summer and hot. They take a few days to drive to Switzerland, making a detour to Strasbourg, in Alsace. The little girls get their first pair of sunglasses in Strasbourg. They arrive at the camp in the middle of a party for the departing group of campers. All the doors are open; the children wear costumes and are running around, noisy, excited and happy.

The three sisters cannot wait to stay at the camp. It looks like a lot of fun! But Maximilien notices air drafts; all the doors are wide open. His children will catch a cold. Zilda ventures in the refectory; it has long tables and benches that remind her of her childhood boarding school. In a rare moment of agreement, they look at each other, and because of temporary air drafts, and wood benches bringing back bad memories, they unite and decide that their children will not stay at the camp.

The girls are heartbroken, but the parents are not swayed. The family finds lodging in a nearby inn and then starts what is to be the best vacation in Zilda's life. She is away from her tormentors, Aime and Victoire; there is a truce between her and Maximilien; they spend the days watching their healthy children playing in small streams, building stone dams, jumping from stone to stone. They visit small towns and climb mountain trails. Maximilien, away from his mistress, is amorous, delighting Zilda.

Zilda makes many changes and improvements to the family house over the years. She repaints all the doors and decorates them with moldings. Her mother, Lydie, has gifted tasteful, excellent-quality furniture at every childbirth. The living room is fully furnished, the large formal dining room as well. The couple is buying artwork and antique furniture; it is an area where they find common ground. They like figurative art, portraits, landscapes, and they accumulate a valuable collection under the guidance of an old art expert, a friend of Aime. They acquire large paintings for the hallway and the formal living room. They slowly decorate the house with porcelains, bronzes, and sculptures. In the living room, they have a glass cabinet with carved ivory and miniatures.

Some of the artwork is bought in France, and to avoid paying customs taxes, they travel at night along lesser roads where there is little scrutiny of cars and car trunks by the border agents. When they buy a painting, they put it on the back seat, cover it with blankets, and tell the small children to lie down and pretend to sleep. They are never caught.

The couple subscribes to a glossy art magazine called *Connaissance des Arts*. They have every monthly issue ever published, and they read it avidly. It adds to their knowledge of antique paintings and furniture. Except for the art magazine, neither one reads books.

Marie had her First Communion at eleven. She is now twelve, and after the vacation in Switzerland, Zilda wants to bring her daughter home for good after years of living with her grandparents. The bedrooms are reassigned: Maxine stays in her childhood room, communicating with the parents' bedroom. The next communicating bedroom is prepared and furnished for Marie, and Marguerite is given the fourth bedroom, which is farther away and separate from the other three, on the other side of the landing. That room faces north, the main street, and is gloomy. Marguerite requests bright yellow curtains. They make her room appear sunny in the morning.

Marguerite does not like the house where she lives; her new room is noisy and cold and the large resonant hallway is forbidding, she always crosses the hallway as fast as she can, especially at night. Even during the day, it takes a while to find her mother when she needs her; she could be on any of the floors, somewhere in the maze of basement rooms, or in the large attic where there are hanging closets and clothes are stored. Even in her own bedroom with the yellow draperies, she is not comfortable in the house; her bedroom opens outside to a large decorative balcony facing the busy main street. Someone could climb to the second floor and try to open the balcony door to her room. It is a little scary.

Zilda invites the house architect, to discuss transforming the balcony off Marguerite's new bedroom into a small storage room. There are no closets in any of the bedrooms; she would like space to store the linen, and it would insulate and separate Marguerite's bedroom from the noisy street. When the man comes, she invites him into the small dining room and offers him a drink. Aime tries to enter the room, and annoyed with the interference, Zilda firmly pushes him out and closes the door.

Aime reports a couple of days later to Maximilien that Zilda was privately entertaining the young architect, laughing and drinking champagne with her guest. Maximilien returns home with anger on his face. Zilda braces herself for a fight.

"Why did you not tell me you had the architect here a few days ago?" he asks. "Why did you lock yourself in the dining room with him and offer him champagne? You must think that I am an idiot, that I am blind? You closed the door in my father's face!"

Zilda replies, "Yes, the architect was here, I closed the door because I am tired of seeing your parents use my home as a public place and without respect for my privacy." She gets worked up and adds, "We do not have champagne in the house, and my mother is not received here with courtesy, and your father is losing his mind and…" She is unable to say more. Maximilien slaps and hits her and brutally pushes her against the dining table. It is the first time he has physically attacked her. She is used to verbal abuse, but she will not tolerate physical beatings.

Zilda has bruises and she is angry, incensed. She leaves the house immediately to report the abuse to the police and she shows her bruises, the tracing of a hand on her face. The officer on duty happens to be one of Maximilien's patients. He is embarrassed, unsure of how to proceed. He takes Zilda's deposition but tells her that if she wants to file an official complaint, there will be an inquiry. Maximilien and his father will be called to testify. It will be her word against theirs. Zilda asks him to register and file her complaint, but she will not take it further right away. "You have today's deposition," she says. "If this happens again, I will mention my first complaint, the date of the incident, and you will be a witness."

When she returns home, Maximilien is in ambush at the gate. As soon as he sees her approaching, he gets back into the house and goes into their bedroom.

Marie is visiting her parents' house that day. The three children have witnessed the fight, they are scared, and they surround their mother in the hallway. A gunshot is heard. Marguerite cries, "He killed himself!"

Maximilien gets out of the bedroom, bends over the banister, smiles, and says: "I scared you, no?"

This angers Zilda even more. "Idiot, imbecile, you could have killed one of the children." Maximilien shot the gun into the bed, thinking that the bullet would stop there, but it went through the mattress, the floor, the ceiling below; it damaged an expensive piece of furniture in the formal dining room and lodged into a windowsill. Zilda retrieves and keeps the bullet as evidence.

Soon after the incident, she goes to Alliance Road. She has come to get Marie back. There is a lovely, rearranged bedroom waiting for her. Victoire cries, Aime insults her, but she grabs him by the collar and pushes him against the wall; "Try to stop me," she says, and takes her daughter back home with her.

At first, Marie is unhappy to be living at home. She does not allow her sisters in her bedroom, and she spends a lot of time there by herself. She does not befriend her sisters, does not share her toys; she does not like her father, but she eventually warms up to her mother.

CHAPTER 19

Zilda is a shareholder in the Belgian and French family enterprises. There are quarterly shareholder meetings in both countries and a big annual meeting where a statement of accounts is provided to the family members. It is when Zilda learns how much of the profits she will receive for the year. The meetings run for hours and are followed by dinner, and Maximilien does not want her to come home late at night from France; he wants her to stay home with the children. Zilda gives him power of attorney for the meetings. Maximilien is the one keeping the family budget anyway.

Lydie, the majority shareholder, chairs the meetings. She dreads them. The family is not united, she braces herself for recriminations. Maximilien and the husband of the youngest sister, who has named his dog Ferdinand to rile the brother-in-law, have formed an alliance; they both want more money; they are aggressive and vocal. They have learned of the princely sums Jean and Ferdinand receive in salary; they are incensed, there are inequalities, and they debate why such-and-such man earns more than he deserves. They argue that Jean has no education and that he should not be the director of the Belgian factory. But he is Lydie's son, and she favors him; he stays as the director. Ferdinand is only a lowly electrician. Lydie is not swayed, and she is getting angry.

Maximilien is paid by the visit for his caring of the factory workers, and he complains that he is not being paid enough—he wants a regular salary. He is granted a small salary with benefits, but, says Lydie, "You must come and spend at least a half hour in the medical office at the factory every day."

"What if there are no people to treat?" he asks.

Lydie responds: "It is now forty-five minutes, read cartoons for all I care"

When she hears that Maximilien has demanded a salary, Zilda is ashamed. They already receive countless benefits: the coal for the house; the full-time gardener; all work done at the house is performed by factory employees, at no cost to her family. She apologizes to her mother.

Maximilien is careless with money, with his car. It was left out of the garage, with windows open, on a couple of nights with heavy rain. A few warm, humid days followed, and mushrooms are growing on the floor carpet and the seat cushions. Maximilien decides to replace the old car with a new one. It is taken to the factory for demolition.

Jean calls his sister: "You have to come and see this," he says. Stacks of moldy French currency have been found under the car seats of the demolished car, the proceeds of the last shareholder meetings at the French factory. Maximilien forgot it there—it is too damaged for redemption.

Zilda revokes the power of attorney she had given to Maximilien. She attends all the business meetings going forward, and she takes charge of her own finances. She is a careful manager of her own money; she now has more freedom to do what she wants. She buys herself a car, a small Morris.

The couple, now with separate accounts and control of their own funds, agree that they each will pay 50 percent of the family taxes.

Maximilien brings home the cash his patients pay him, carelessly stuffed in his pockets. He has a loose, imprecise system for tracking his earnings; his accountant chides him and has a hard time making sense of it all.

As the children grow up, the father sometimes asks them to come into his office in the evening. He empties his pockets of the daily stash of paper currency and loose change on his desk. He asks the girls to identify and separate the coins, to add them, and he lets them keep the loose change.

The families are not united, but they have rituals, and they pretend to get along on specific occasions. On the Day of the Dead, all the families dress up, go to church, visit Clement's grave, and bring enormous wreaths of chrysanthemums to his tomb. The wreaths are surreptitiously compared. Who brought the biggest one?

At Christmas, there is a celebration and a large meal for the entire family at Lydie's house. This is when Lydie distributes gifts. The women dress elegantly and compare jewelry. All except Zilda have mink coats and designer clothes from Paris. Zilda's family has less money at its disposal than Jean and Clementine, who spend freely.

At the Christmas party, there is a lot of food and heavy drinking. Lydie, who instigated the union and pushed Zilda to marry him, barely tolerates Maximilien. There is palpable tension. Maximilien finds his in-laws arrogant, empty suits. To Zilda, he crudely says, "They fart above their ass"—they behave above their station, and all because of money they did nothing to earn. He is the one who is the most educated, but he is considered to be a peasant, and he is mocked. He intensely dislikes Lydie, Jean, Clementine, and Ferdinand.

On occasion, arguments and fights break out. At one Christmas party, some of the men, including a drunk Maximilien, get into a physical fight. The fight has to be broken up and Zilda's family is told to leave. Zilda and the children are deeply embarrassed. They are the outsiders.

On New Year's Day, there is a complicated choreography of visits to each house to give and receive wishes for the New Year. It is a very important day for all the children because the parents and uncles distribute money. They give coins to each child. Marguerite adds the money to her piggy bank. With the coins she gets from her father every time she has blood drawn and the loose change from Maximilien's pocket, she is accumulating a tidy sum. She asks to open a savings account at the bank.

CHAPTER 20

A new tradition is started around 1952 by Jean, Marguerite's godfather, who announces that he will make a gift, every year, to the family child who has the best grades at the end of the school year.

In Jean's mind, it will be a nice competition between the cousins, it will prompt the young ones to work harder. Maybe he is thinking of himself and how little he was motivated as a child. He has to be given each child's report card at the end of the school year, and he will determine the winner. He always chooses a very nice gift: a scooter with thick rubber wheels the first year, an expensive tennis racquet the next, and so on.

All three of Zilda's girls are in elementary school. Marie, though still tutored daily by Aime, is an average student. Maxine, the youngest, is intelligent, and she has an excellent memory. But she does not like to study and apply herself; she wants to play. She is like mercury, cannot be corralled to do her schoolwork.

Marguerite, ten years old, is different. She is at the head of her class; she loves school and is naturally disciplined. She has figured out that it works best for her if she does her homework as soon as she gets home from school. She is then free to play and to read, to ride her bicycle. She does not bring school friends to her house. She is now fully aware of the tension and disagreements between her parents. She often finds refuge in her imaginary small boat on the raging sea, her mental escape. Hers is not a happy, welcoming house.

Maximilien's goal for each daughter is to be healthy and educated; each has to have a profession, be able to make a living when she grows up. And he pushes his children hard. He hires tutors when one struggles with a subject.

Zilda intervenes when he is too harsh. "We have plenty of money," she says, "my family is rich, the children will always have money." Maximilien does not agree, and they fight. On the subject of education, Maximilien does not yield. He let his wife choose the names of the children, he did not interfere when she wanted them to be baptized, he does not object that they are raised to be Catholics and have First Communions. But education is essential and not open for discussion.

Marguerite resents Maximilien's interference. She has self-discipline, she does not need his help, his constant badgering about her schoolwork. She is doing well on her own. "Have you done this?" he asks; "Yes, I am done, I finished," she replies. "I want to test you," says Maximilien. "It is not necessary," replies Marguerite.

One day, frustrated at her resistance, he throws a book at her head and narrowly misses her. He threw a book at Marie a few days ago and she has a black eye and a small wound at the edge of her eyebrow.

Marguerite, defiant, stands up, looks at him, holds his stare. "Do not dare throwing books at me," she says, "I do not need you. Leave me alone." And he does.

Every year, Marguerite wins her godfather Jean's competition for best student in the extended family with twenty cousins. She won a scooter, her favorite toy ever and she cherishes it; she has an expensive tennis racquet. After a few years, she eventually tells her godfather, "Give me the prize at the beginning of the school year; I will have more use of it that way." She does not mean to be sarcastic or mock her godfather. To her, it is logical, she wins every year, it is not going to change. Jean stops the competition.

As a young teenager, Marie is tested for competence in Brussels. She relates to her mother and sisters that: "I was taken into a room and shown cards with spots and dots on them, and asked what I was seeing."

Maximilien is told that she is unlikely to succeed at the university, that a different path should be chosen for her. Marie resented the testing; she guessed its purpose. She is deeply hurt that she was singled out, thought to be deficient. She holds that day's humiliation against her father for her entire life.

No education is complete without the ability of playing a musical instrument, decrees Maximilien. He hires a piano teacher, a bald, older, gentle man he has known for a long time, who needs the income. A piano is brought into the living room.

The teacher comes to the house for two hours every week, to tutor Marguerite and Maxine. They are told to practice daily. Neither child is interested; they do not practice enough. The piano teacher tries the best he can, but the lessons are cut to a weekly half hour for each child due to lack of talent and interest. Zilda offers the man tea and cookies and sits with him for a chat after the lessons, embarrassed by her daughters' lack of enthusiasm.

Maxine starts to hide in the park when the lesson is about to start; she does not respond to calls to return to the house and misses several of her lessons. One day, while Marguerite is at the piano listening to the teacher's instructions, Maxine hides behind the heavy velvet draperies and, in her little voice, she mockingly repeats all the instructions the teacher gives to her sister. Too polite to complain, the piano teacher soldiers on, needing the income and afraid to offend the parents by telling them that their daughters have no talent whatsoever. The mother continues to offer him tea at each visit, until, one day, Maxine pours salt in his drink, and he declares defeat.

Zilda deeply believes in God; she has been to church and to mass her entire life. When she is distressed or fervently hopes for something, she prays to the Virgin Mary; she asks her dead father and Victor to come to her aid.

When the children get older, she starts taking them to mass with her. She likes to go to the late Sunday morning mass in the next town where important local citizens gather and chat after mass. She dresses herself and the children in their best clothes, puts on makeup; she always wears a hat. She buys new hats regularly. The mother and children are routinely late; she is not naturally punctual, she likes to be noticed and makes a grand entrance.

She is a beautiful woman but has many insecurities. When walking behind another woman, she often asks, "Is my behind bigger than hers?" "No, of course not," say the children. "Stop asking that stupid question," says Maximilien.

He often ridicules his wife's poor writing skills. She cannot conjugate properly, she misspells words; she is embarrassed and humiliated that he brings it up in front of her daughters.

He also makes fun of her hyperacute sense of smell; she has hyperosmia. Marguerite has inherited the same trait. Zilda cannot stand the smell of eggs, she remarks on how people should bathe more frequently. On a drive to the North Sea, on a road they have never traveled before, the car windows are open and she says: "We are approaching a cemetery, I can smell it." Maximilien scoffs. "You are unbelievably stupid"; they pass a cemetery.

After the Sunday mass, Zilda takes the children to a pastry shop; if the shop is busy, she pushes to the front and asks to be served first. The family has tea and pastries in the afternoon in the living room. Except for meals, when Maximilien is often absent, it is the only time during the week that the family is together. The atmosphere is often strained. The children are wary of their father and escape as soon as they can. Sunday tea in the living room is the time and place of memorable fights between the parents.

Maximilien likes to take Marguerite unto his lap; he holds her by the hips and she does not like it. She reaches for a pastry and wiggles free after a few minutes.

One day, at the Sunday afternoon tea, in a particularly bad mood, vindictive, spoiling for a fight, the father, who has Marguerite on his lap, declares: "Marguerite is not my daughter." Zilda is stunned; the young girls do not understand.

"Maximilien, you are Marguerite's father!" "Not so," says Maximilien, "she has a different father." Zilda cries and swears that it is not true. She is beside herself. "You are Marguerite's father," she insists, and she turns to Marguerite, tears streaming down her face; "I swear that he is your father."

The children escape from the room. Marguerite is strangely untroubled by the declaration. She is upset that her mother is upset, she resents her father for hurting Zilda, but she does not dwell long on the possibility that, maybe, she has a different father. Who would he be? Does he have dark hair like her? She lives here, in this house with this family; she senses that Maximilien favors her because of her good grades. She does not want to think about this.

The young girl has concrete, factual thinking. If there is a problem, one should fix it.

She tells her parents that they should separate, divorce.

When she gets older, she reflects that she has Maximilien's thick knees and strong calves, his short arms and stature. She is the shortest of the three children. She has narrow hips as he does. Her two sisters have their mother's feminine build, with generous hips and slender legs. She puts the idea that she may not be Maximilien's daughter to rest. It makes no sense to dwell on it.

Another Sunday afternoon tea is ruined when the parents start arguing about which one of them is tallest. The children are bemused; they are about the same height, and Zilda is tallest when she wears high heels, but Maximilien insists that he is a few centimeters taller. They segue into saying that they hope the other will die first, leaving the other to live his or her life in peace.

That is a frequent topic of conversation. The tone gets more and more heated, and challenging each other, they ask their children to decide which parent they want to live with if they divorce. Marie and Maxine immediately slide in next to their mother, Marguerite leaves the room. She thinks that neither parent is an attractive choice.

CHAPTER 21

At home, most of the daily meals are tense. Maximilien, who drinks Pepto-Bismol at every meal, wants to eat lunch and dinner at exactly the precise time he decides. "I cannot wait," he says, "I have to eat right now." It is stressful for Zilda to have each meal ready exactly on time.

At lunch, the father likes to listen to the midday stock market report. He and Zilda own shares of gold mines in the Belgian Congo and everyone has to be silent while he listens to the news. The price of stocks is recited one by one in a long litany. If the stocks that the family owns are down in price, he swears profusely. "We are going to be ruined," he says, "we are going to be poor."

The children have to clean their plates of the food they asked for because there are starving children in Africa. The next day, the starving children have moved to China. It is very confusing—leftovers cannot be sent to Africa, and the dog eats the table scraps anyway.

After a long battle of will with her husband, Zilda has managed to claim the largest room of the medical suite, and the kitchen has been moved from the basement to the first floor, next to the smaller dining room where the family usually eats. The three-room medical suite is reorganized into two rooms.

The maids now work in the first-floor kitchen; they bring dishes to the table and hear the conversations.

Often, for days at a time, the spouses do not address each other directly.

Sitting across the table from her husband, Zilda says to the maid, "Tell the doctor that…," and Maximilien responds, "Tell Madame that…" The children leave the table as soon as they are able. They recognize the ridiculousness of the situation. The maids sympathize with Zilda.

Marguerite is eleven years old. She has gone to catechism after school for one year and has her First Communion.

She is uncertain and confused about god and religion. She has to go to confession and the old parish priest asks her strange, irrelevant questions. "Do you have impure thoughts?" What are impure thoughts? she wonders. "Do you touch yourself?" "Well, I wash my body." "Have you lied?" "Yes I have, doesn't everyone lie now and then? Sometime, there is no choice but to lie." "Say ten Ave Marias and God will forgive your sins," instructs the priest.

Her godfather Jean is rumored to have a mistress; Marguerite has overheard her mother say that Jean's wife and the mistress have the same mink coat and the same Mercedes car. How can he be unfaithful to his wife, which is forbidden by the Bible, and be a good Catholic? He goes to mass every Sunday! Does God give him absolution for the same sin every time he goes to confession? He must be saying a lot of Ave Marias. Another uncle also has a mistress, and there is talk of divorce, but at least he does not go to church.

Uncle Jean's wife is always at Lydie's house. She knows of the mistress but does not want to divorce; she likes her lifestyle very much, and Grandmother Lydie protects her. It is confusing. The uncles, and sometimes her father, drink too much. Is this not a sin?

The local church has after-school activities for children who have had their First Communion. Marguerite is interested; there are sports, games, she can go by herself to the playground behind the church and she asks to join. There, a young energetic woman leads the group of girls in the games. One day, Marguerite sees her and the young parish priest embrace and kiss on the mouth in a secluded corner. Marguerite tells the other children what she has seen, and the news spreads.

The old parish priest, and the younger priest she saw kissing, summon Marguerite and her parents for a meeting. Marguerite has to publicly declare that she lied and invented the kissing story. She refuses. She is adamant that she saw the pair kiss. She would be lying if she retracted the story. Lying is a sin, the priests have been emphatic about that at catechism, and now they want her to lie? The hypocrisy! She decides that she is not a Catholic, she doubts that God even exists. It does not make any sense.

CHAPTER 22

Hurlebise, the old farmhouse, is vacant. The lease ended and the tenants have left. There is much work to do to make the house habitable. Maximilien plants a cotoneaster at the corner of the farmhouse; "I love this plant," he says, "its glossy dark leaves, the small red berries in the winter." He checks and waters the plant at every visit before he goes into the house.

The building is about ninety yards long, most of it being sheds, a cavernous hangar, haylofts, animal pens. The habitable part is small, consisting of a wide central corridor with two rooms on the right and two rooms on the left. There are four small bedrooms upstairs. Each daughter is assigned a bedroom.

Space for a tiny half bathroom is carved out of the hallway upstairs. A huge metal bathtub is installed in the middle of an otherwise empty, cold, poorly lit, backroom on the first floor. It is weird to bathe there. Mother brings buckets of hot water, the tub is emptied with a hose hanging out of the window.

Zilda plunges headlong into renovating the habitation and making it comfortable. She buys furniture for the large kitchen and a den. Everyone loves the ancient brick, build-in, bread oven in the corner of the kitchen. The house is heated by woodstoves, and the den has an open fireplace. Maximilien cuts and stacks wood in an alcove near the fire.

Though small, it is now a comfortable, cozy place. With its yard-thick stone walls and deep windowsills, it stays cool in the summer and is easy to heat in the winter; the heat rises from the first-floor woodstoves to the bedrooms above through ceiling vents.

Marguerite likes the farm a lot more than the huge family house in Aimeries, and Zilda and Maximilien, working side by side, usually manage to be civil to one another or even have a good time.

Isolated on a plateau, the place is very quiet. The only noise is that of the wind, and on some nights, the lowing of cattle illegally brought through the wood in France to the pastures in Belgium.

In the beginning, when they first have access to the farm, Marguerite chooses to stay in the car and read books, to Maximilien's great annoyance. She has been reading books voraciously for several years. Eventually, she joins on long walks in the woods with her parents and younger sister. The appeal of the small, fragrant, wild strawberries is too hard to resist in the summer. Marie refuses to spend the weekends with them; she goes to her grandparents instead.

Marguerite's best times with her family are spent at Hurlebise. On the way, they stop at a small town to buy fruit pies and food to cook on the open fire. At the village a mile from the farm, they buy hot French bread at a small bakery, and they all start eating the bread right away in the car.

The woodfire at night in the den is peaceful and smells wonderful. At the farm, both Maximilien and Zilda work hard, she inside the building and he in the woods, and both are tired in the evening. The family has never played games together, but there is quiet talk about the work accomplished that day. The woodfire is lit and soothing. Marguerite reads a book. They almost look like a normal family.

Maximilien decides that it would be fun and profitable to raise sheep at the farm; the family will eat grass-fed lamb in the spring. He buys six ewes and a ram from a farmer. The next spring they have several lambs and Zilda stuffs a mattress with sheared wool. But Maximilien finds that raising sheep is not as easy as he thought; there is no one to watch the animals for days at a time. He sells the sheep but butchers a lamb; he is out of sight for a long time. Zilda and the children go looking for him. He is in one of the sheds, the slaughtered lamb suspended on a hook from the ceiling; the pelt and the organs have been removed. Maximilien and the ground are bloody. Maximilien has cut a long thin strip of meat and is eating it raw.

CHAPTER 23

Zilda has a kidney stone. She is taken down the stairs of the big house on a stretcher, pale, in obvious pain. The children watch from the hallway, they are mute and afraid. Their mother is at the hospital for days. It is the first time they are left at home alone with their father for an extended period of time. The mother returns with a huge crescent-shaped scar on her flank and is slow to recuperate.

Zilda is not shy with her children. The family has only one bathroom, a hard-to-heat huge bathroom tiled in green and black, and she and the children often share the space. Her daughters see their mother naked. She has stretch marks on her belly and breasts; "I do not mind them," she says, "it is the price to pay for having children." She washes herself on the bidet and imparts the knowledge that sex is dirty and messy, it is not pleasant, and one should douche and wash right after intercourse.

The mother takes great care of her appearance; her hair is permed and dyed blond. She puts on makeup: foundation, face powder, lipstick. She uses expensive Lancôme creams, for the day, for the night, for around the eyes. She applies Chanel Number Five or *L'air du Temps* perfume. Marguerite prefers Aunt Clementine's perfume, Shalimar.

When the bathroom is occupied, Maximilien uses the toilet down the hall. He walks the hallway naked except for an undershirt that he pulls to hide his genitals, his hand cupped in front. His narrow buttocks are plain to see. This troubles the growing girls, and when the mother is absent, they lock themselves in their bedroom.

At thirteen, Marguerite has not had a period yet. Marie and Maxine had theirs at twelve and eleven respectively. Maximilien is concerned and he is badgering Zilda.

"I had my first period when I was sixteen," says Zilda, "there is plenty of time, stop bothering me and the child." "You were not normal," says Maximilien, "something very serious could be going on."

Maximilien asks the question every day to Zilda: "Has Marguerite menstruated yet?" When Marguerite finally has her first menstruation, she takes advantage of her father's relief and asks if she can learn how to drive. The park has a narrow road circling the big lawn. There is no risk in teaching her there, and Maximilien obliges. She soon is proficient enough to drive, illegally, on the street. Traffic is not heavy in the rural community; there is a lot of open land with fields and wood, and when not in school, she drives her father to some of his patients' houses.

Maximilien is not talkative, they drive in silence. She takes him many times on his medical rounds. She waits in the car and reads while he visits his patients. He never divulges details of his patients' illnesses.

Some rules are not made to be obeyed. When it suits him and shortens his route, Maximilien directs her to drive down a set of wide, shallow steps joining streets. They go on one-way streets in the wrong direction; "No one is coming, it is much shorter," says the father, "hurry up, go fast." They are never caught and stopped by the police. Maximilien would claim a medical emergency if caught.

CHAPTER 24

Italy, West Germany and France establish the European Union in 1955. The Warsaw pact, the military assistance between Communists members, is signed the same year. The Suez crisis and the Soviet invasion of Hungary occur in 1956.

But there is peace in Belgium; the world's events barely register in Zilda's mind, and the children are oblivious to them.

The three sisters are all in high school. Marie goes to a girls' school about two miles away, Marguerite is enrolled in an academically demanding girls' school a half-hour drive further in the same direction. Maxine is enrolled in another school in the opposite direction.

Maximilien drives Marie and Marguerite to their respective schools in the morning; he hurries them to get ready, he has a full day of work ahead of him. Marie is dropped off first, and Maximilien continues to Marguerite's school farther away. The two girls return on their own by tramway in the afternoon.

Zilda takes Maxine to her coed school in the opposite direction; they are often late. Zilda picks her up at the end of the school day. Maxine still has proteinuria, she must be sheltered. The mother and her youngest daughter are alone together for long stretches of time.

Marie, fifteen, has met an eighteen-year-old boy, Jacques, and she is in love. The boy walks to a college on the same route as the one Maximilien takes in the morning to drive Marie and Marguerite. Marie always sits at the back of the car, on the right side; she is glued to the window as she hopes to catch a glimpse of the boy she loves. She urges her father to slow down so that she can watch for the boy. Maximilien scoffs—he has information, he says. "The father is an alcoholic, the boy is a heavy smoker, he drinks a lot of beer, he is a devout Catholic." How Maximilien has that information is a big mystery. He must have an army of spies, guesses Marguerite. If Marie sees the boy, she perks up and has a good day. If not, she blames her father for driving too fast and they both are in a bad mood.

High school is not as easy as elementary school. Marguerite is enrolled in demanding courses; it is preordained that she will be going to medical school. It is what her father wants, and it is fine with her. She does well in the humanities course; trigonometry and algebra demand much more work and attention. For the first time, she welcomes a few tutorials from the old mathematics teacher, Aime's mistress. She is competing for first place in her grade with another girl, Nicole, the daughter of a local surgeon who went to medical school with Maximilien.

When she complains of being overwhelmed by the amount of schoolwork, the mathematics teacher, a diminutive Russian teetering on high heels, tells Marguerite in a heavy accent to divide her tasks into manageable parts, to attack one part at a time. "Do work on a task," she says, "ignore the others; when done, work on another part." It is advice that Marguerite remembers her entire life.

Face one task or problem at a time, solve it and take on the next problem. It works very well.

She is a very good student, polite, she observes the rules though she gets in trouble once when a teacher she does not like, orders her to carry her heavy load of books and she refuses, an instinctive reaction; she did not like the way she was ordered. The teacher demands a parent-teacher meeting. The school director is also present. Marguerite says that she is not a mule; she will not apologize. When she decides not to budge, nothing can make her change her mind. The incident is smoothed over.

There is a boys' high school next to the girls' school. The girls can hear the boys play and shout at recess. The boys' school is putting on an end-of-the-year play. They need a well-behaved girl for the play, and on the recommendation of the teachers, the school director selects Marguerite. She is trusted to represent the girls' school with honor.

It is interesting to be around boys. Marguerite finds some to be attractive. She studies her lines, goes to the rehearsals after school for several weeks, behaves well. She overhears some of the boys say that she is good-looking but she has dark hair in her nostrils and on her legs; her mother has not talked to her about shaving her legs; Zilda does not pay much attention to Marguerite. The boys laugh at her. She acquits herself decently at the play. She is merely adequate, does not have a future as an actress.

Marguerite has two passions, reading and bicycling. After school, when finished with her homework, she takes her bike and heads out by herself when the weather is nice. She pedals out of the community and rides along the fields and through the woods.

She is often gone for hours. She does not ask permission from her parents; she has learned years ago that if she asks, one will say yes, and the other will say no. She is sure to displease one of them.

They are strangely indifferent to how Marguerite spends time. The father cares about health and education; the mother, often unhappy, pays less and less attention to her growing daughters. Zilda is distancing herself.

The three sisters have nothing in common, they do not spend time with one another. Marguerite and Zilda, each a middle sister, are totally different in looks and temperament. The only similarity between them is their heightened sense of smell.

Marguerite is a solitary young girl. When she comes home, she reads. She lies on her bed, eats chocolate, and she reads. Since she was little, as soon as she learned to read, she has asked for books as gifts. Birthday? "Books." Christmas? "Books, please." Her parents have always obliged and generously. She started with stories and legends from around the world. She read all of the Countess of Segur's children's books. Jules Verne's Twenty Leagues Under the Sea; Michael Strogoff's adventures. In her teens, she is reading Balzac, Cocteau. *Les Parents Terribles,* The Terrible Parents, written in 1938, resonates with her, Proust is boring, she does not finish reading his books. Dickens, Prevert, Colette, very interesting. Agatha Christie, Arsene Lupin's books, romance books. Everything and anything at random. She has a subscription to the publication of contemporary plays. As soon as she gets the text of a new play in the mail, she disappears in her bedroom. She has to be called for meals. She reads late into the night.

Zilda is closest to Marie and Maxine, who need her support against their father and are interested in makeup, hairdos. The mother is jealous of Marguerite as Maximilien favors the second born, she feels inferior to the academically excelling child. It may be that Marguerite is so independent and self-sufficient that the mother feels unneeded; the result is that she largely ignores Marguerite, who does not become aware of it right away. Zilda thinks that her middle daughter is arrogant. She has forgotten that her own mother, Lydie, had favorites, and how it affected her emotionally.

The mother now absents herself from the house frequently. She goes to Brussels to visit her mother, saying that she will be back at dinnertime and bring food for the meal. The three daughters wait for her and for dinner, but she does not get home until very late, well past bedtime. The children wait for hours at the second-floor window, watching for the lights of their mother's car to come through the gate. Maximilien paces downstairs and is in a foul mood.

Zilda sometimes leaves for a few days. The young girls do not know where she goes or when she will come back. They do not like being left alone with their father. Maximilien does double duty of driving all three girls to their schools. There are loud fights when Zilda comes back.

She goes to Spain on a long trip with her mother and is absent for two weeks. Then on another trip to Portugal, also a few weeks long.

Marguerite still regularly visits her paternal grandparents. They do not come to her house anymore, but she likes to see them. Aime had a stroke, he has aphasia, but he recognizes the children. He tries to talk, tears run down his cheeks, and he caresses the face of his grandchild. Victoire spoon-feeds him *lait de poule*, hen's milk, an egg yolk beaten in warm sweetened milk. It is heartbreaking.

Victoire openly criticizes Zilda, and Marguerite defends her mother. "If you criticize my mother," she says, "I will no longer come visit you."

One day, Victoire says to Marguerite: "I am your godmother, it is time to buy you some items for when you marry." She is generous within her means; it is rare to come from her house without a small gift. "You like this?" she asks, "Take it, I want you to have it."

They walk to the hardware store where Victoire buys a set of red enamel cooking pots and a small paring knife for Marguerite. On the walk back, Victoire says that she needs to pee. "Look if anybody is coming," she says to Marguerite. "I don't see anyone," replies Marguerite. Victoire locates a storm drain in the street, she is wearing a long black skirt, she spreads her legs and, standing, she urinates over the drain. She is not wearing underwear, thinks a stunned Marguerite, and this is why she smells.

Marguerite is not fond of her grandmother Lydie; she knows that Lydie is not fond of her either, but she asks if she can go and spend a week at the apartment at the North Shore at Easter. Lydie says yes. She hosts Marguerite but barely interacts with her. Marguerite does what she likes, takes long walks on the beach and on the boardwalk. She sits and has coffee by herself, watching people go by, she watches the waves. She is peaceful.

She is sixteen; a young man, twenty years old, asks if he can sit with her. It is safe, there are a lot of people around and the young man is entirely proper. He just wants to talk. They meet for coffee a couple of times, two loners on the boardwalk.

The young man says something that Marguerite remembers for a long time. "I am not interested in people who are not interested in me," he says. "I would never love a woman who does not love me. I would be wasting my time."

Life's lessons are learned at random, from family and strangers. Marguerite absorbs it all.

CHAPTER 25

Zilda never forgot her family vacation on the French Riviera. In 1955, she takes her children for a monthlong summer vacation in the south of France. She has no firm plan; they take the train to Paris, and from there the overnight train to Saint Raphael. She finds a hotel, then rents a studio in a small community near the beach.

She scouts the area and reserves half of a house for the next summer. The third year, she rents the entire house. On that third vacation, she visits a real estate agency and on impulse, she puts a deposit on a sloping piece of land with a view of the sea, halfway up the hill rising from the coastal road. She does not have sufficient money to buy the land, and Lydie gives her the necessary amount. Maximilien joins the family for a few days; he cosigns the purchase agreement of the land. Many years later, she will rue the day Maximilien co-signed the document.

This is Zilda's project, her dream house. She consults with an architect and builds a two-story villa, using her own money and funds from her mother. The living space with a kitchen, two bedrooms, and a bathroom are on the second floor, at street level, with a large terrace that looks out to the distant sea. The ground floor, at the level of the garden, has three bedrooms, a bathroom, and a large garage with laundry and storage space. She now has her own garden, to plant as she wishes. She grows lemon trees, lavender, lilies, roses.

Zilda is happy on the Riviera. She loves the weather, the relaxed atmosphere, she is away from Maximilien, his demands, criticisms and bad moods, she feels close again to her daughters. My daughters are really pretty, she thinks. They go to the beach, go shopping at the local open-air food market, eat well, take naps. They listen to music; she loves opera, Maximilien does not tolerate it. She laughs, she starts to tell off-colored jokes to her bemused daughters, revealing a side of herself they did not know about.

Back in Aimeries for the school year, the family falls again into the same pattern. Each person has a different schedule; there is no time shared as a family except for brief dinners. Sunday teas are forgotten. Maximilien is almost always at the farm on the weekend, and he works hard during the week.

Zilda still disappears and reappears without notice. When she is around, she facilitates romantic encounters. She regularly drives Marie to see her boyfriend. Maximilien is very much against the affair, but Marie has decided that she is going to marry Jacques as soon as he graduates from engineering school and military service.

Marguerite, at sixteen, has met a boy at the North Shore. He lives in Brussels, too far away for her to meet with him on her own. Zilda drives her to the 1958 World's Fair near Brussels, and she lets the two young people spend the afternoon by themselves. Maximilien hears of the encounter and is furious. "The boy has had tuberculosis," he says. How does he know, wonders Marguerite. Is he making it all up?

At seventeen, Marguerite meets another boy. This one lives in the town over, and she can go to his house by walking or by tramway. The boy too belongs to a troubled family. They are well-to-do, but the father is an alcoholic, which, of course, Maximilien discovers right away. How the father finds information on the young men his daughters like is a big mystery.

The boy is a year younger than Marguerite, tall, a brooding young Marlon Brando type; she likes to look at him. He is not a good student, does not talk much, but he is quiet and peaceful, and a gifted musician. His house has a door to a side street at the back of the walled garden, and there, he has a small studio where he plays the clarinet, the windpipes, the trumpet. He opens the back door to his studio for Marguerite and she listens to him play.

When his parents are not at home, he brings her into the house. His father has a safe where he keeps gold bars—the boy knows the password of the safe. He opens it, takes out a gold bar. Pure gold is soft; he gently scrapes gold from the bottom of a bar. Always a different bar. "I like to do experiments, my father has not noticed," he says.

They go upstairs in his bedroom and kiss and caress each other, giving each other tenderness and pleasure, but never have intercourse. Marguerite is willing, but the boyfriend tells her that he promised his Catholic mother that he would wait for marriage.

Zilda buys lipstick and silk stockings for Marie. Marguerite hears her mother and sister talk about the correct way to put the stockings on. She hears something about the need to be careful with fingernails; curious, she approaches. She wants to participate in the conversation. "It is not for you," says Zilda, "this is between Marie and me."

Marguerite is often excluded from her mother and sisters' conversations. She feels like an outsider, she is different. Maxine who has now been nicknamed *moustique*-mosquito- for her pointed barbs, tells her sister that she looks like a huge salami with her narrow hips. She says: "Your calves are too big; mine are much nicer, slenderer." Breasts are compared: Marie's and Maxine's breasts are perky, Marguerite's are not, hers are rounder. Perky is best. The sisters have blond, wavy, and fine hair, the nicest. Marguerite's thick black hair looks like a thatched roof according to Maxine, who can be gleefully malicious. Maxine proclaims that she is the prettiest sister, and Marguerite is made to feel physically inferior. Her mother does not come to her defense.

CHAPTER 26

In fact, boys find Marguerite attractive. They are very drawn to her, she is quite pretty in a different way than her sisters. She can hold a conversation, she is serious but she can be funny and irreverent. Older men notice her too and she is on her guard, wary. An uncle makes an improper sexual joke to her; she gives him a blank stare and walks away.

Marie finishes high school. She did poorly. Her grades in French class are good, but in spite of constant tutoring by the old mathematics teacher, she failed in that subject. Maximilien, ashamed of his daughter, furious, goes into Marie's bedroom and breaks her record player, her radio; her cartoon books are shredded, the favorite small objects decorating her dresser are smashed. Marie hates him.

She is sent to a school in Brussels to get a teaching certificate for elementary school. Zilda finds her a small apartment near Lydie's own place; she lovingly furnishes it and sets everything up for her oldest daughter. Marie, unlike Marguerite, likes Lydie and she visits her grandmother frequently but finds that she does not like to live alone. After a few months, she asks to transfer to the school's dormitory.

Marguerite tells her father she is taking the tramway to see a movie in the next town. She will be back at a reasonable time.

Maximilien, who has been acting like a jealous lover, forbids her to see her boyfriend. Ignoring the order that she deems unfair, she goes to the movie with the boy and he brings her back home on his scooter, cautiously stopping out of sight a hundred meters from her house. Maximilien has been in ambush near the cinema and has followed in his car. He saw his daughter get off the scooter and kiss her boyfriend. He arrived at the house first, and is now waiting in the hallway. When Marguerite walks in, he hits her so hard that she falls and slides on the floor. Zilda is away from home that evening, Marguerite has no protection. She gets up from the floor and rushes up the big stairs to her bedroom. Projectiles follow her. Maximilien is carefully choosing Zilda's favorite porcelain objects and throws them at his daughter. He misses and dents the wall. Marguerite locks herself in her bedroom. Maximilien is sullen the next day, Marguerite ignores him for a long time. Zilda is furious that some of her favorite things were destroyed, she is not concerned about Marguerite.

Marie intensely dislikes her father, she is afraid of him and avoids him at all costs. Marguerite is not afraid. She defies him, and in a way, he seems to respect her. She excels at school, and he is proud of her success. Maxine is hard to pin down—she laughs and disappears. She still has some proteinuria, she must be treated gently, and she takes full advantage of it.

Marie failed the last semester at her school in Brussels. She has to repeat the tests at the end of the summer. She has been studying at home, and Zilda drives her to Brussels for the tests. When results are announced, she finds out that she has passed. It is late in the day; Zilda has waited to drive her back home. Her fiancé, Jacques, who is doing his military service, is posted a short ride away and Marie wants to go tell him that she has now graduated. Zilda refuses, and Marie is mad at her mother.

Zilda knows how important this is for Maximilien, she does not want to make him wait for the news. Marie sobs in the car. When they arrive home, she is still crying; she bangs the door of the car and runs into her bedroom. Maximilien believes that she has failed. Zilda says, "No, no, she passed, she graduated, she has her teaching certificate, she is crying because I refused to drive her to see Jacques." What should have been a joyous day has turned into a disaster.

Marie and Jacques are about to be married. Maximilien is still strongly opposed to Marie's chosen fiancé, a devout Catholic, smoker, and beer drinker, all grave sins in his eyes. But Marie is determined. She cannot wait to be free of her father.

Zilda and her daughter have ordered a wedding dress in the north of France, about a one-hour drive from the house. They are driving there to pick up the dress; Maximilien is told that they will be home in time for dinner. On the drive home, the gas pedal of Zilda's car gets stuck. The car is accelerating dangerously on a long straight segment of road. Zilda turns off the ignition, gently brakes until the car stops. They have to walk a long way to find a garage and Zilda calls from the garage to say: "We have a car problem; the mechanic says he can fix it, but we will be home much later than expected." "Where are you?" asks Maximilien. "We are at the border with Belgium, do not worry, we will get home on our own."

Without telling his wife, Maximilien gets in his car and heads to the border. Meanwhile, the car repaired, Zilda and Marie cautiously make their way home.

Maximilien calls home from the border: "Where are you?"

"We obviously are at home, I just answered the phone here; where are you?" says Zilda. When he gets back, Maximilien is terribly angry. "But I told you we were coming back on our own," says Zilda, and Marie adds: "Why are you so angry? We are not dead!"

"That would have been better," he replies.

He strikes the glass-covered dining room table with his fist and the glass shatters. Past the point of self-control, he grabs a bottle of beer, throws it at Marie's head, and narrowly misses. He gets up from the table and tries to hit Marie. Zilda swiftly moves in front of her daughter. She is not afraid this time, she threatens to throw Maximilien on the street and she lets out all her resentment and anger. They have the most ferocious, angriest fight of their life. Zilda is not holding back; she has become a fury. Marie, in tears, leaves the house and walks in the dark to her future in-laws' house. It is a long walk; she is getting married in two days. She flies from one cage into another.

CHAPTER 27

Marguerite is different. She seems strange to her sometimes disorganized and untimely mother and sisters; Zilda thinks again that her daughter is arrogant. The young girl just knows what she wants; forced from an early age to make her own decisions—after all, her parents never agree on anything—she goes her own way.

But she has some traits that baffle people. She does not like fussiness; all the little bows and decorations on her clothing are immediately removed. She does not want to have her hair curled at the hairdresser, she refuses to wear lipstick. Everything in her room is orderly and clean; tilted wall frames are straightened. She loves pretty objects, but she does not want to own many. Clutter bothers her.

She thinks concretely, does not grasp metaphors and circuitous thinking readily. Abstract thinking requires mental gymnastics that are not easy for her. She cannot deal well with "what if…" scenarios. She does not always understand sarcasm and occasionally does not read body language properly. She is direct in her own speaking and sometimes says things that she regrets later.

But she is focused on her goals, systematic and organized. She is self-confident. She once finished a sewing project of her mother, as a surprise, and it was perfectly done.

She has a savings account at the bank. She has saved all the money she was given over the years, from each blood test, each penicillin injection, each birthday and New Year's gift. All the loose change her father distributed at the end of his workday. Her parents buy her everything she needs; she likes to see her bank account slowly grow.

At eighteen, she is headed to the seven-year-long medical school training in Brussels, and she has sufficient money to buy a small car. She goes by herself to the dealership. The man recognizes her, he knows Maximilien. If he is surprised to see a young girl buying a car by herself in 1960, he does not to show it. She buys a *Deux Chevaux,* a "two horses," Citroen. It is the most basic, cheapest car one can buy.

Maximilien gives her money to go enroll at the medical school in Brussels. The tuition is cheap, most of the cost being subsidized by the state. She is given money to rent a room. Neither Zilda, who found and furnished an apartment for Marie, nor Maximilien offer to help her enroll and find housing.

She goes to Brussels on her own, enrolls at the medical school, and finds a room in a boardinghouse within walking distance of the campus. The room is not a welcoming place, but it is clean and safe.

She breaks up with her boyfriend after being in Brussels for a few weeks. He is still in high school, she is in medical school, and she does not have time to see him. They are apart academically. She sees his scooter under her window, at night, but she does not go to him.

There are over four hundred students enrolled in the first year of medical school. They fill the large auditoriums, it is very chaotic. In the first year, the curriculum includes physics, chemistry, botany. Physics and chemistry are difficult subjects for Marguerite.

She has moved from a small rural community to the bustling capital of Belgium, the seat of NATO. Everything is interesting, different, new. She is free to do as she pleases, and she does. She sees two movies a day, skipping classes. There are streets to walk on, markets and stores to explore, museums. Her schoolmate from high school, Nicole, has also enrolled. Marguerite can ask to copy Nicole's notes when she misses a class.

There are as many girls as boys in the class. It is clear that many have enrolled to find a husband. Pairs form quickly. Marguerite is surrounded by interested boys, but one is particularly persistent. The young man attaches himself to Marguerite. As soon as she comes to a lecture, she finds him at her side; he keeps the other boys away. His name is Lucien. He is Jewish, intelligent, charming, very self-confident. He is a short man, barely taller than Marguerite, and one year younger. They have long conversations. He tells Marguerite that his father, a Polish Jew, died in the Holocaust when Lucien was just a few months old.

Lucien had sex for the first time when he was thirteen years old. He is a physical young man, always kissing, hugging, and they have sex after a few weeks of dating, the first time for Marguerite. Lucien is experienced and prepared, he has condoms with him.

They have intercourse in Marguerite's room before going to a lecture. As they walk on the street toward the campus, Lucien asks, "Are you okay? Do you have pain? How do you feel?" "I am fine," responds Marguerite. It was not a big deal, she reflects, not earth shattering as I have read in romance novels but definitely better than what Mother described.

After a few months, Lucien takes her to his home, where she meets his mother and stepfather, a diamond cutter. The mother is not pleased that Marguerite is not Jewish. When Marguerite introduces Lucien to her own parents, they are very displeased that he is Jewish. They claim that they are not antisemitic, but, in reality, it disturbs both of them greatly.

Many classes are missed; Lucien likes to make love frequently, too much, thinks Marguerite. He would have sex three times a day if given the chance. "I study better after," he tells Marguerite. When the time comes to take the first-candidacy's end-of-the-year oral tests, they are not prepared.

All testing is done one-on-one with each individual professor. Lucien and Marguerite are bright, but they have not studied sufficiently, and both fail the examinations.

"What do we do now?" they ask each other. The university allows students to retake the tests at the end of the summer a few weeks later, and if they fail, they can re-enlist to repeat the year, but will get only a third chance. There is not much time to study; they are in love and want to be with each other. If one of them graduates to the second candidacy, but the other does not, they will be separated. The first-year classes are held at a campus at the edge of town; the subsequent years, classes are held faraway in the center of town, near the teaching hospitals.

They decide they will tell their parents they failed the second round, and they re-enlist for the next academic year. Marguerite reassures her parents she certainly will pass the tests next time; Nicole, the high school friend, moves on to the second year of medical school, the second candidacy.

The second time around, the young lovers attend all the classes and study hard. At the end of the year, the students sign up for the examinations, pay a fee, and there is a lottery system allocating dates for oral tests with each professor. The lucky students have tests at the end of July; they have a much longer time to study. The unlucky students take the tests right after the end of the academic year classes, with hardly any time to prepare.

Lucien and Marguerite have been so absorbed in their studying that they miss the deadline to sign up for the testing. When they realize their mistake, they go plead with the officials at the medical school to be allowed to enlist anyway, and are told that they may, but will be the first two to go in front of the professors and be tested. Testing is random, the professor asks a question or two, and the student has to know the answers. Luck has a big role to play.

This time, they pass all of the subjects handily. Marguerite aces botany. The botany teacher is an acquaintance of Maximilien, and he is vocal and passionate about ferns. First there were lichens, then moss, and then, ferns appeared about 360 million years ago, before the dinosaurs. It was the first plant to appear on planet earth. Any student who cannot identify a fern is automatically disqualified, even if they can answer all the other questions. The botany professor makes no exception.

The academic year started with about four hundred students. One hundred and fifty pass on to the next grade. Many young women fail or quit. Some have found a fiancé; they had enlisted to meet eligible young men.

Marguerite has been going home fairly regularly on weekends, though she spends some of them in Brussels. At home, her parents are still fighting. Maximilien now claims that he has not fathered any of his three daughters. Zilda fights back.

When Marguerite returns home on the weekend, Lucien attends the synagogue with his family. They observe the Sabbath. Their medical school class has a fair number of Jewish students. They form a tight group and spend a lot of time together.

CHAPTER 28

Maxine graduates from high school and starts university the year her sister repeats her first year of medical school. The parents pushed her toward the humanities, and Maxine is enrolled in a program of archaeology and art history.

She was a mediocre student in high school, but she likes her university courses and is applying herself. She completes the first year without difficulties. In the second year, she is singled out by a teacher who becomes her mentor.

She becomes involved with a law school student, and they move in together. Augusto is from a family of minor Spanish nobility and Maxine is impressed by the connection. She has to push him to study, a reversal of sorts for her.

Maximilien and Zilda are supporting Marie and her husband while he finishes his military service. Helped by Maximilien, Marie has found employment at the local elementary school, where she teaches French. Her salary is insufficient to support the couple, but she likes her teaching job. Maximilien is fretting that she is not getting pregnant.

Maximilien gives money to his daughters while they are at the university. Marguerite receives a check every month, sufficient money to pay her rent, buy food, and cover other modest expenses. She never has to ask for the money, Maximilien is always punctual. And she is thrifty, careful of how the money is spent. She does not wonder where it comes from; she assumes that both parents probably contribute, but she never gets her stipend from her mother. Her parents always seem to have plenty of money, she does not give it a second thought.

Starting the second year, until graduation, Marguerite's classes are held in town, near all the large hospitals. She has to find different lodging.

As she did the first time, she consults bulletin boards, and she walks in the smaller streets around the bustling center. She sees a "Student Room For Rent" sign in the window of a large brick row house and she rings the bell. The room for rent is on the top floor of the large house and is lovely. It overlooks a small garden, and it is quiet and cozy. She could be comfortable and happy here.

The landlady, Madame Leonce, is friendly; she lives on the first floor with her husband. The rest of the spotless house is divided into studios and students' rooms. Marguerite rents the room. The lodging is within walking distance of the medical school campus and the hospitals, on a side street with a small grocery store. It is perfect. Her grandmother Lydie lives a ten-minute walk away.

Lucien's parents have friends in Paris, Jews, survivors of the Holocaust like them. The prosperous family has a large apartment near the Seine and the Isle Saint-Louis. Lucien and Marguerite, now engaged, are welcome to visit. They stay in separate rooms of course.

Lucien and his parents have asked that Marguerite convert to Judaism. She is not keen on the idea but is willing to explore and learn. Maybe Judaism is different from Catholicism, less hypocritical? Lately, Lucien has become more domineering, he has made her cry a few times. He has Napoleon's complex, thinks Marguerite, just like my father. She is disturbed. Maybe this will pass.

The young lovers are in the second candidacy at the medical school. They apply themselves. Lucien is the better student, but he has difficulties with anatomy and Marguerite helps him.

All the medical students have to dissect cadavers. Each student, in a white coat and gloves, is assigned a corpse and directed to dissect specific areas of the body. The leg, abdominal organs, the foot, the neck. It is unpleasant work, the large dissection laboratory is very cold to preserve the corpses, and it reeks of formalin and other noxious smells. Surgery residents supervise and coach. One of them forces the female students to perform rectal examinations on the cadavers. He finds it hilarious, the girls do not.

The students have all year to finish dissecting their assigned cadavers. All the dead people were old, they were sick, many are skeletal. The poor sell their bodies to the university in exchange for money while they are alive. The dissections make Marguerite think of Leonardo da Vinci, but his cadavers were fresh, they did not smell of formalin.

At the end of the academic year, Marguerite gets the highest grade in anatomy. Lucien gets a passing grade, and although he did better than her in the other courses, he is very angry that she bested him in this one course. They are in Marguerite's lodging, and he is furious, jealous that she did better. He makes her cry. He advances with his fist raised and she grabs a letter opener from the table, stabs him in the thigh. There is a hole in his pants, he is bleeding, but it is not a deep wound. "What will I tell my mother?" he says. He immediately deflates, as a punctured balloon, and apologizes profusely. "This will never happen again," he says. "I am so very sorry, I love you, I am sorry."

Lately, Lucien has been increasingly argumentative. When they argue, he taunts her: "Say it, I am a dirty Jew, you think that I am a dirty Jew." Marguerite is silent, she never would tell him that he is a dirty Jew, it is total nonsense. He now pushes her hard to say the phrase, he is fixated on making her say it. He is paranoid, thinks Marguerite.

They are going to Paris for a week; they stay at their friends' apartment. Marguerite has met a couple of times with a rabbi in Paris, who has mapped out a program of steps and studies that she has to undertake before converting to Judaism. What am I doing, she reflects after meeting with the rabbi. She has been with Lucien for almost three years, he is a very bright man, but he now tries to dominate her, the relationship has shifted. He has become more and more difficult and demanding. He wants frequent sex. She does not want to make love twice a day. She does not want to convert to Judaism. I am making a big mistake, she realizes.

Back at the apartment of their friends after a meeting with the rabbi, Marguerite tells Lucien that she is breaking up with him. Lucien pleads and cries, Marguerite is unswayed. "I have decided," she says; "this is not working for me."

Lucien opens the big living room window and steps on the windowsill. "If you leave me, I will kill myself," he cries. The apartment is on the third floor, he certainly could die or be badly hurt if he jumped, but Marguerite retreats deeper into the room.

She turns around and leaves. She packs her bag and heads to the train station.

When told of the breakup, Zilda is upset. "It was difficult to accept the relationship at the beginning," she says, "but we got used to him, he is a bright young man. Are you sure that it is the right decision?" Maximilien is silent. "I am certain," reassures Marguerite. "It is the right choice for me, I will be fine."

Madame Leonce, the landlady, has taken Marguerite under her wing. She has no children and loves to come out of her apartment and chat with Marguerite when she gets back to her lodging. Marguerite is her substitute daughter, and she tells her landlady of the breakup. "You made the right decision," she is told; "my husband beats me sometimes, you will find a better man."

Lucien was a frequent visitor, well known to Madame Leonce, who he had easily charmed. But she is firmly on Marguerite's side. She relates that Lucien has come several times asking about Marguerite. "I say that you are well, that there are many fish in the sea," she says, "he will find someone else too."

Marguerite ignores Lucien in the classrooms and auditorium. He sits with his Jewish schoolmates. Occasionally, she sees him outside of the university; she feels that he is spying on her. Over the next few months, she spots him near the farm and near the villa on the Riviera.

Marguerite is in the third year of medical school. She meets young medical students. The ones she likes happen to be Jewish; she dates some of them, but does not form a serious relationship with any.

She meets a few young men with different occupations. Of the men she meets, some talk about themselves for the entire date, one tells her that she should lose weight. She is not overweight; she refuses to meet him again. Some are just interested in sex. One, an engineer, takes her on a car ride, it is winter, and he insists on keeping the car windows open for the entire ride. "It is healthy," he says. She is frozen, she refuses to go on a second date.

She passes the end-of-year examinations without any difficulties. Her high school classmate Nicole, who was a year ahead, fails and they are reunited. Of the four hundred students in the first year, only about one hundred remain.

Marguerite goes home less and less often. When she does, she visits Aime and Victoire. Aime is now bedridden, Victoire still gets around. She keeps giving things away. She has gifted most of her antique oak furniture to Marie, her favorite granddaughter.

The sisters rarely see each other. Maxine is in another part of Brussels; Marie is teaching, and her husband, an engineer, has found a job at a large steel factory.

Marguerite assumes that her parents are fighting as usual, but she is not there to witness it. What type of life do they have now that their three daughters are out on their own?

Zilda regularly visits her own aging mother in Brussels, near Marguerite's lodgings and the university, and Marguerite has met her at her grandmother's apartment a couple of times, by chance, but her mother has never seen either of her rented rooms, or asked to meet for coffee in Brussels since she started medical school. They see each other when Marguerite returns to her parents' home. Zilda is not interested in spending time with Marguerite.

At Christmas, Marie announces that she is pregnant; the baby is due in the summer. Maximilien is overjoyed. Zilda too is delighted, both she and Maximilien want grandchildren. Marguerite is happy for her sister; she too will have children someday, but it is years away, after she finishes medical school; and she is not even dating at the moment.

CHAPTER 29

Belgium is a country made up of different parts and very different people. The northern region separated from the Netherlands in 1830 after a rebellion, and the present state was artificially created by joining that section with part of France after Napoleon's defeat, becoming an independent and neutral state in June of 1831. There are three official languages in Belgium: Dutch, French, and, in a small section of the country, German.

At the medical school in the capital, courses are taught in parallel in both French and Dutch. The curriculum is identical, and the students use the same facilities but have different professors and schedules. There is a large French-speaking contingent of students and a smaller group of Dutch-speaking students. They do not mingle though they are taught in the same buildings.

Marguerite sees the Dutch group of students of the same grade exit the auditorium. She notices a tall, dark-haired, handsome student in animated conversation.

It is easy to learn his name, Pieter, and find information about him. He is the star student of his class; he graduates every year with the highest honors. He drives a small red sportscar and heads home every day. She wants to meet him. She easily catches the eye of the young Dutch man, and she smiles; he stops and approaches; they introduce themselves; he is fluent in French, immediately interested in getting to know her. They make a date.

They are very attracted to each other; they both love reading and they discuss books for hours. They talk about their families; he is an only child, raised at a Catholic boarding school. They find agreement about the Catholic religion. He is as anti-religion as she is, but he is fond of a Catholic priest, Father Thierry, a mentor in high school, and he has kept in touch with him. Pieter is twenty-one, Marguerite is twenty-two.

The young man is engaged to the daughter of friends of his parents. He breaks up with his fiancée a week after meeting Marguerite; "She is not as interesting as you are," he tells Marguerite. "My parents are very upset" he adds.

They first make love within two weeks of meeting. It is the end of the school year, they both graduated for the year, him, first of his class, with highest honors, she in the middle of her own group.

Pieter invites Marguerite to come and meet his parents in his hometown. His parents, both heavy smokers, are cautious when meeting her. The mother, Adele is still quite upset that Pieter broke up with his fiancée; she is polite but reserved. The father, Frank, is more welcoming. Frank manufactures slippers, he has a small workshop and one employee.

Marguerite, whose Dutch-speaking ability is poor, can barely communicate with Adele whose French is also very limited. Adele does not appear to be very bright. Pieter is very short with his mother and often ignores her. Marguerite wonders how such a brilliant, gorgeous young man could have been born of such a drab woman. Frank is more open and friendly, and Marguerite likes him.

Marguerite introduces Pieter to her parents. They are dazzled by the tall, handsome, and very bright young man. This time, Marguerite seems to have made a good choice.

Pieter does not use condoms; "It does not feel the same," he says. He and Marguerite want to make love, and nine days after having her period, she thinks that she is safe from getting pregnant. She is not, and she is with child two months after having met Pieter. She is overcome with the desire to have this baby. Waves of fierce new feelings wash over her. With the insouciance of the young, they both are delighted. They will get married, have the child, continue with medical school. If their parents continue to give them the same amount of money as they are receiving now, they can make things work. Otherwise, they will take a loan. After all, they both will be physicians and earn good incomes. They met three months ago, they barely know each other.

Marie gives birth to a boy in August of 1964. The same day, Marguerite announces to her parents that she too is pregnant and will have a baby at the end of March of next year. Maximilien, still very happy to have seen his first grandson, hesitates a few seconds, then tells Marguerite that he is happy about her news too, and that he will support her. It takes a little longer for Zilda, but she loves babies and rejoices as well.

Pieter and Marguerite drive to his parents' house. Pieter sits down, pulls Marguerite onto his lap, and tells his parents that Marguerite is pregnant, they are getting married. Adele bursts into tears. "How could you, how could you have done this?" "The usual way," says Pieter. The mother does not stop crying and sobbing; "Enough, stop this," orders Pieter. "It is done." Frank gets up and embraces Marguerite. "I am very happy to welcome you as a daughter," he says, "let's pick a nice pair of slippers for you." He is a sweet man.

"We do not have much time to find you a wedding dress," says Zilda.

"I do not want a wedding dress," replies Marguerite, "I find them to be a waste of money."

Zilda is speechless; her oldest daughter married in a beautiful white lace wedding dress made to order. She knows that Marguerite, her strange daughter, will not change her mind; she relents. But she wants her daughter to have a nice wedding and good clothes, and they go shopping together in Brussels. Marguerite selects an off-white wool suit, a gray suit, and a gray dress made to measure. "Very practical," she tells her mother, "I will wear them with colorful scarves, grandmother Victoire's pearls." It is the most time they have spent together in a long time.

Marguerite meets Pieter's extended family. Frank is one of thirteen children. The visit is brief, and Marguerite never sees these people again. They are not invited to the small wedding.

Adele and Frank are shy and impressed when they visit at Marguerite's house. There is a huge contrast with their own station in life. And for Pieter, it seems that he wants to leave his old life behind, make a clean cut with his extended family. He has many cousins, but Marguerite is never introduced to them.

Maximilien and Frank agree to support their children while they are in medical school. If it is a burden for Frank and Adele, they do not mention it. The soon-to-be-married pair rents a small apartment in Brussels. They are looking forward to their wedding, their life together, the birth of their child. They are getting married soon, before their classes resume.

CHAPTER 30

The wedding ceremony is performed by Father Thierry in the church of Aimeries, where Marguerite was raised. Zilda and Pieter's parents insisted on a church wedding. Marguerite and Pieter argue with Father Thierry about what he and they will say, making it as short and simple as the priest would allow. Marguerite does not say that she will obey her husband, but they promise to love each other till death do they part.

It is late-August, and hot. She is two months pregnant. She lets her mother talk her into going to the hairdresser to set her hair. She thinks she looks ridiculous—her hair has been curled and brought up on the sides. It is not her, but it is too late to change it.

At the church, just after the priest declares them man and wife, she faints. The church is hot, her suit is made of wool. She comes to her senses outside, lying down on a bench in the shade of the church's garden. She soon is well enough to walk out the church front steps where pictures of the couple are taken.

There is a small wedding celebration; only close family is there for the catered lunch: Pieter's and Marguerite's parents, Marguerite's two grandmothers, her sisters and brother-in-law. Her friend Nicole is there. After the meal, more relatives arrive for dessert, they spread out in the park, they mingle. The newly married couple leaves Marguerite's parents' house in Pieter's little red car in the early evening. Marguerite is very tired, she is nodding off.

Classes for the next medical school year start in less than two weeks.

Marguerite receives free care from the Gynecology and Obstetrics Department chairman at the medical school. When he examines Marguerite for the first time, he tells her that she is built like a boy with narrow hips. "Delivery may be long and difficult," he predicts. The pregnancy proceeds well. The obstetrician watches her weight carefully; she is not gaining much.

The students at the university are now aware that there is a pregnant woman in their midst. She is the only married person in the class. Medical school is not the time to marry and have children. There is a full schedule of classes, much to study, laboratory work. The other students squeeze in fun parties between studying, but Pieter and Marguerite never join them. They are in different classes, have different schedules.

Marguerite bears her baby way in front, she wears a tent-like dress; she does not look pregnant from the back, but in profile, she looks huge, distorted. It becomes difficult to squeeze into the narrow seats of the auditorium. She faints during a lecture of internal medicine. Lucien is watching.

Marguerite goes for a checkup at the end of March. "The baby is coming soon," the doctor says. "Next time I see you will be in the delivery room."

"I am close to delivery," she tells Pieter. "No more stepping on the scale."

Late that evening, she starts having contractions, it is almost midnight. They head to the clinic, her physician is called, and he breaks the waters.

"I will see you in late afternoon or in the evening," he says. "For the first baby, it takes a long time, and you have those narrow hips." But the contractions are close together, it is very painful. Marguerite has not been checked for about an hour; she feels a heaviness between her legs. Pieter calls the nurse; "I think my wife is progressing fast," he says, "please check her." The nurse examines Marguerite and says: "I am calling your doctor." She pushes twice, the baby is born in record time at three thirty in the morning. It is a girl, and they call her Eve. Marguerite just turned twenty-three; Pieter will be twenty-two years old in a month.

Zilda and Maximilien visit at the clinic the day Eve is born. They are very emotional at seeing their second grandchild. "Do you plan on baptizing Eve?" asks Zilda. "We had not planned on it," replies Marguerite. Zilda's face shows disappointment. "Mother, if you want, you can have her baptized. There is a chapel at the clinic." Zilda arranges for the ceremony.

The end of the academic year is just two months away. Marguerite has missed some classes, her friend Nicole shares her notes. It is a stressful time; Marguerite starts breastfeeding, but her milk dries out after just two weeks. She has lost a lot of weight. She needs to go to classes, she needs to study for the end-of-year examinations.

Zilda offers to take the baby for the next couple of months. She is madly in love with the little girl. Zilda is truly happy only in those times when she has a baby in her arms, when she feels needed. Eve gives Zilda a new lease on life. Marie brings her own baby boy to visit from time to time, but never leaves him at her parents' house.

Marguerite and Pieter agree to Zilda and Maximilien's proposal. If Marguerite fails the year of medical school, she will have to repeat it. The young parents drive to see the baby a couple of evenings a week, but Marguerite is able to attend her classes and study. It is a big sacrifice and heartbreaking for the young mother, but it is a rational decision.

Aime has passed away. He died three days after Eve's birth, and Marguerite, with her newborn in her arms, visits before the funeral. Her grandfather is lying on a bed in the living room, a shadow of the man who was so devoted to his grandchildren. She says goodbye to him and thinks, a death, a birth. She holds her baby to her chest. Marguerite loved her grandfather, the calm man who cared so much for his granddaughters, who patiently taught them so much.

Baby Eve stays with her grandparents for a couple of months; Marguerite passes the end-of-year tests; she has now completed four years of medical school, there are three more years to go. Pieter, as usual, is at the top of his class, he again graduates with the highest honors.

They call Zilda and Maximilien to tell them that they are coming to get their three-month-old daughter and take her back to live with them. Zilda is incredibly upset. "She is doing so well here, she has a quiet room, fresh air from the park. I am taking such good care of her, she loves me, recognizes me. I have all the time to be with her, you cannot give her the same attention. You cannot take her back to Brussels, to your little apartment." She goes on: "What will you do when classes restart after the summer? This is too much commotion for the baby." Zilda has forgotten her own sorrow when Marie went to live with her paternal grandparents.

Pieter and Marguerite leave the baby with Zilda for a few additional days.

"We are coming to get her soon," they say; "you will see Eve quite often, we will bring her to visit; it is summer, school is over for now, we can all stay at the farm for a vacation." Zilda refuses to listen to reason. Pieter and Marguerite go to the grandparents' home and have to forcibly remove the baby from the arms of a sobbing Zilda. They move to a bigger apartment with a small room for Eve, and by the end of the summer, they have found a babysitter. They plan on bringing the child to the babysitter's home in the morning and pick her up after classes. It soon becomes clear to Marguerite she is the one who will drop off and pick up the baby. Pieter dashes out the door in the morning. He has started working in a laboratory and doing experiments, an extracurricular activity. It is up to Marguerite to take care of the child.

The baby often cries with colic, though she is thriving. Eve cries when she is put in her crib; she stops when Marguerite picks her up, bounces her and walks around in the apartment. One evening, she does this a couple of times; Pieter is studying, he is irritated that Marguerite walks around in the small apartment with Eve in her arms. "I cannot concentrate," he says. He takes the child from the mother, puts her in her crib, and locks the door to the baby's bedroom. "I forbid you to go take her," he says, "she will eventually stop crying." The baby cries for hours, Marguerite cries as well. She is resentful and never forgets that evening, how she could not comfort her child. There is a crack in the relationship.

Pieter is Dutch. Dutch people have the reputation for being unsentimental and stubborn. Marguerite discovers that her husband can be hard and unfeeling. He is physically attracted to her, and he says that he loves her, but he is not tender, he is impatient. His studies come first, and he wants a quiet apartment. She also finds out that he is quick to spend any money they have. He likes to go eat in good restaurants. From time to time, she receives a gift of extra money from her parents. Pieter finds a way to spend it right away. Marguerite would prefer to save it.

The next year, Father Thierry invites the young couple to lunch. It is a hot early summer day, and Marguerite is wearing a sleeveless dress. They enter the restaurant, greet Father Thierry, who looks at Marguerite in a strange way. A few minutes after sitting down, the priest starts chastising Marguerite for wearing the sleeveless dress. "You should not show your arms, you are indecent," he says, "it is very improper." Pieter takes his wife's hand and says, "We are leaving." He does not engage in arguments. He has done the same thing at Marguerite's parents' home. They were having dinner and Maximilien criticized something the young couple had done. Pieter threw his napkin on the table in the middle of the meal and forced Marguerite to leave the table. There was no discussion, they left the house with their baby.

Now, Marguerite discovers that Pieter is masturbating. She sees the evidence in a handkerchief under his pillow while making the bed. She is stunned, upset, she feels sullied, insulted; she never refuses to have sex. She knows that masturbation is normal, and that she probably should leave the subject alone, but she is uncapable to let things simmer. She would like to be able to get advice from someone older and wiser, but she has no one and it is a difficult subject to talk about. If she does not talk about it, it will fester in her mind and weigh on her.

She goes to Pieter and asks, "Why do you need to masturbate, don't we have enough sex? Is there something you would like to do? I would like to talk about this." Pieter looks right at her and says, "I blew my nose in the handkerchief, there is nothing to talk about," but she knows that Pieter is lying. He refuses to engage in discussions and his way to deal with difficult subjects and controversy is to turn around and leave. Emotions, fears, doubts are things that Peter does not wish to deal with, talk about. Marguerite is young, inexperienced, she made a mistake in asking Pieter about masturbation, she made him defensive, embarrassed. They are not dealing with each other well, their problems and misunderstandings are accumulating.

CHAPTER 31

Maxine has graduated from the university. She has a degree in art history and archaeology. Recommended by her mentor, she finds a position as art history teacher at a high school. Her boyfriend, Augusto, graduates from law school the same year. Maximilien is pushing Maxine to get married; she has reservations. Augusto was struggling at the university, he has not been able to find a position yet; but they have been together for almost four years now. Maximilien is insistent, and Maxine relents.

Meanwhile, Marie is pregnant for the second time; she has a second son a few months after the birth of Eve. Her husband, Jacques, often travels to Italy for his job. He drinks a fair amount; "It is expected in my position," he says, "there are meetings with clients, alcohol is served. After we complete negotiations, there are dinners I have to attend, and everyone drinks."

Victoire has gifted her house to Marie and Jacques. With two young children, their apartment was too small.

Marguerite receives the last small parcel of farmland that Victoire still owned, and Maxine gets a sum of money, to compensate for the gift of the house to Marie. Maximilien knows of a farmer who is interested in buying the land parcel, and Marguerite sells it right away. They need the money.

Pieter is working in a laboratory at the university after his classes; he is already publishing in medical journals and is considered to be a rising star. He likes to travel. They go to Switzerland to visit a laboratory; Zilda takes care of Eve while her parents are away. They now have the money from the sale of the farmland, and Pieter wants to visit Amsterdam; later, he wants to go to London for a week. Each time, Marguerite hesitates to leave Eve, but it is hard to resist Pieter; she wants a harmonious marriage. Zilda is always begging to keep the child as much as possible. Eve is in good hands—both Maximilien and Zilda adore the lovely little girl. It is a time of relative peace for both of them.

Maximilien has started coming to Brussels once or twice a month, to take his daughter and her husband to lunch. They meet in good restaurants between classes. Maximilien is very much taken by Pieter, admires his intelligence. He does not like his two other sons-in-law. The two men get into long conversations over lunch and Marguerite sees a different aspect of her father, one that she likes. Zilda only visits when she can see her granddaughter.

Maximilien says that Zilda is difficult. Zilda says that Maximilien is impossible to live with. "Is it me or is it him?" she asks, "Which one of us is crazy?" She has consulted a psychiatrist who told her that there is nothing wrong with her, the problem lies with her husband, and he prescribed medication for mild depression. She occasionally tells Maximilien, "I need a Valium, can you write the prescription?" "My legs are swollen, I need some Lasix." Maximilien gives her what she asks for. She has a stash of antidepressants.

In the last two years of medical school, the students start working at the hospitals as interns; they rotate through different departments, and during the last year, they are on call at night at emergency rooms. The rotations include a stay at a sanatorium near the beach at the North Sea. It is one of the earliest rotations for Marguerite. She has to live at the sanatorium for six weeks, make rounds with an attending physician, learn how to treat tuberculosis. Her rotation is in the summer.

Zilda embraces the opportunity to babysit for Eve. She rents an apartment close to the sanatorium and takes Eve to the beach every day to play in the sand; Marguerite escapes when she can and briefly sits with them before she has to return. The child is two years old, and the grandparents declare that she has superior intelligence. They are besotted with the sweet, pretty little girl who starts talking early and is very curious and engaged.

Marguerite is bored at the sanatorium. There is nothing much to do and she does not learn anything useful. When it is Pieter's turn to be at the sanatorium, Marguerite manages taking care of her baby and working at the hospital. She enjoys her rotation in surgery. There is a lot of camaraderie among the surgeons, the nurses, and the students. She has an affinity for physical and technical work, she enjoys assisting and observing. I could become a surgeon, she muses. It is what Nicole has already decided.

Her friend is getting married. "My fiancé puts cocoa powder in his coffee," Nicole tells Marguerite, "that's when I knew that I was falling in love." Her friend fell in love because of cocoa in the coffee. Maybe as good a reason as another. Marguerite is not sure her own marriage has a good foundation.

During internal medicine rotations, Marguerite starts having doubts about her chosen profession. She falls in love with some patients and would hold their hands for hours if allowed. There are patients she does not like, finding it difficult to interact with them. Pieter is emotionally detached, more efficient, more abrupt. He is by far the better clinician, thinks Marguerite. He is more knowledgeable, how does he know what to do? He has a photographic memory, retains a lot of information.

I am not emotionally equipped to deal with sick people, realizes Marguerite. I do not have the knowledge and assurance that Pieter already has. She is troubled about what the future holds for her. When both are on call the same night at the emergency department, they leave Eve with the babysitter. A senior physician is there to supervise the students; Pieter confidently takes on the patients with heart attacks or complicated metabolic conditions. Marguerite has a hard time reading electrocardiograms; she deals with the drunks who need suturing after a fall.

The students assist at the clinics. They are assigned patients to examine and triage before a senior attending takes over. Marguerite is told to examine a young woman.

"What can I do for you, why are you here?" she asks. The woman, in her twenties, says, "I have abdominal pain when I drink alcohol." Marguerite examines her thoroughly; the physical examination is entirely normal, the woman appears in good health. Marguerite communicates her findings to the senior attending, who gives a cursory examination. The young woman is sent home, told to return if she develops more symptoms.

It is not until a lecture a couple of months later that Marguerite learns that some patients with abdominal Hodgkin's disease experience pain in the affected lymph nodes when they drink alcohol. She is crestfallen. She hopes the young woman returned to the clinic and was properly worked up and diagnosed. The attending should have known.

Maybe Pieter would have read about abdominal pain in patients with Hodgkin's disease and realized what the patient had.

Marguerite is suffering from impostor's syndrome. She knows that she would be an inadequate physician and she is deeply disturbed. Over the years, she has a recurrent dream that she needs to repeat medical school, that she is inadequate, cannot treat patients; she always wakes up feeling anxious and unhappy after the dreams.

While on call overnight at a teaching hospital, Marguerite often eats in the evening with an eccentric elderly physician. He comes to work at his laboratory in the middle of the afternoon and works through the night. He singles out and engages in long conversations with Marguerite, a young, inexperienced woman, and they have deep discussions. Men of all ages like Marguerite.

She can be irreverent, likes to laugh, speaks her mind. She has widely read. She and the old man find subjects of common interest and he invites her to visit his laboratory. There, he shows her an electron microscope, an instrument that Marguerite has never seen before.

Dr Albert Claude wins the Nobel Prize in physiology in 1974.

CHAPTER 32

Both Zilda's oldest sisters have already died of colon cancer. Lydie is in poor health, obese, and no longer travels. Zilda is frequently in Brussels with her mother. She tells Marguerite: "Your grandmother made me empty and reorganize her closets. I counted eighty pairs of bedsheets." Lydie is hoarding; her vast apartment is cluttered with paintings, oriental rugs, antiques, linens, hand-embroidered clothing she can no longer wear. Zilda, who felt unloved by her mother when young, has stayed close to her; she is the most devoted of Lydie's children. She still tries to earn her mother's love.

Marguerite, in her last year of medical school, becomes pregnant in the fall. She hopes to have another girl. The baby is expected in July; the timing is unfortunate. She will have the second baby during or right after the last year of medical school's final examinations. It is a difficult time for her; she has a two-and-a-half-year-old little girl, classes to attend, overnight stays at the hospital. Pieter is doing research after his classes and is not sharing childcare equally.

Marguerite has decided to apply for a residency in pathology; it is a specialty with no on-call night duties, and she will not interact with patients. She hopes that it is a good choice. Pieter has already been recruited to join the Internal Medicine Department at the cancer institute affiliated with the university.

The couple prepares for the arrival of their second child. The children will share a room, and a twin bed is bought for Eve. "Ask your grandmother for a pair of sheets for the twin bed," says Zilda, "remember I told you she has eighty pairs of sheets?" When she sees her grandmother, Marguerite asks if she could have some sheets. Lydie replies: "I cannot spare any."

At eight and a half months' pregnant, Marguerite is taking her final tests. She is interrogated by the pharmacology professor. As with all the tests in the Belgian medical school in 1968, it is a one-on-one oral examination. She hopes that he will ask a question she can answer. She did not have the time or energy to study everything.

The professor looks at the heavily pregnant woman and says: "Tell me about alcohol." It should be an easy question. She skipped the subject when she studied, reasoning that it was not of much interest. "I do not know anything about alcohol; I hope to become a pathologist," she says, defeated. Each student is usually asked only one question. The teacher takes pity on her and asks another question and this time, she can answer; he gives her a passing grade.

She has finished medical school, she has graduated; the traditional photo of the graduating class with all the teachers from the seven years of school is scheduled for a few days later. "I will not go to the ceremony," tells Marguerite to Pieter. "The baby has descended, I feel that the delivery is near." Pieter is in the class photo, one of the nearly one hundred new young doctors. Only Marguerite is missing.

Pieter is scheduled to report at the army barracks for a mandatory three-day stay and he leaves immediately after the photo. Zilda comes to watch Eve in case Marguerite goes into labor before he returns, and Marguerite delivers a second little girl the next day. The first contractions occur in the early morning hours, the baby is born two and a half hours later. Marguerite has always been efficient. My babies come out like bullets, she thinks. In spite of carrying her two babies in front, with a huge belly, she does not have stretchmarks as her mother did.

The baby is perfect, Marguerite wants to call her Anne. She likes short, soft names, unadorned, uncomplicated names. Pieter meets his new daughter a couple of days later. Marguerite is exhausted, very skinny, she has again lost a lot of weight; this has been a difficult year. Anne is baptized at the university hospital's chapel. Zilda has taken the baby down to the chapel, and Pieter's father accompanies her.

Marguerite has been offered a position as resident in the Department of Anatomic Pathology at the same hospital where Pieter will be working in internal medicine. They are hoping to have the entire summer off. They just became physicians and parents of a second child. The chairman of the Pathology Department demands that Marguerite start working as a resident on August 15. "We badly need help here," he says. "You may have a month off, not a day longer."

The little family drives to Zilda's villa on the French Riviera for their month of vacation. They drive from Brussels in a single day, a twelve-hour trip. Marguerite breastfeeds baby Anne in the car. They stop to find a bathroom, get gas. After her first baby, Marguerite went back to classes after ten days. This time, she has four weeks of rest. She badly needs to recuperate.

The two children thrive; away from the hospital and the laboratory, Pieter is more engaged and participates in the care of his children. The young parents adore their two daughters. It is a healing time; they had differences and misunderstandings in the last couple of years.

Pieter is working as a resident in internal medicine. He is part of a small cadre of excellent physicians, several of whom, including the chairman, have trained in the United States. He is happy and confident, he has resumed doing research. He takes turns being on call and staying overnight at the hospital.

Marguerite's position is not rewarding. The Pathology Department has three senior attendings and a fellow, all males. They do not seem to be very busy. They show up at work only a few hours a day, work at the microscope, and disappear. They do not teach the new hire, who immediately finds out that she is relegated to performing autopsies and to the handling of organs and biopsies obtained at surgery. A senior attending shows her once how to do an autopsy, and after, she is left to her own devices. She learns a lot more from the experienced diener who assists in the autopsy room than from the senior pathologists.

Pathologists make diagnoses from biopsies, tissues removed at surgery, organs from autopsy—all are described and samples are taken, processed, and made into glass slides. The slides are examined under the microscope and diagnoses are made. Alone, Marguerite reviews the glass slides of the specimens she processed, writes her findings, and later tries to correlate her own diagnoses with those of the senior attendings. She is not taught, she is not invited to review the slides with the senior pathologists. She feels taken advantage of and she is not learning properly. She is very frustrated and unhappy.

Pieter, busy with his own training and research, is not inclined to empathize with his wife. Discussing emotions and feelings is not in his character.

The director of the laboratory contracts to do autopsies at other hospitals, and Marguerite is ordered to go perform an autopsy on a baby found dead in his crib. She has never done an autopsy on a child, and she refuses the assignment. Threatened to be laid off, she relents. At the other hospital, she is directed to a small, poorly equipped room. The baby is a beautiful six-month-old male child. Marguerite holds the cold, perfect baby on her lap for a very, very long time and she desperately cries. She is all alone without emotional support. She cries for the baby, for the parents, for herself. She eventually starts the dissection with tears running down and does the best she can. She finds no abnormalities, but is untrained and could have missed important findings.

CHAPTER 33

Pieter wants to go to the United States for training. His chairman is encouraging him to apply to some hospitals in Boston where he, himself, trained years ago. Pieter discusses the idea with Marguerite, and he finds her to be receptive. She would love to leave her current post.

There are many obstacles. It is daunting to uproot to another country, leave her family. Zilda provides a lot of support with their two young daughters. She is always willing to take care of them on short notice, and she is a loving grandmother.

Both Pieter and Marguerite would have to find positions in the same city; they would both have to pass the ECFMG examination required for foreign medical students; they would have to find childcare, lodging.

Pieter is fluent in English, Marguerite is not; she can decipher English medical textbooks, but she hardly speaks the language. "We would train for a couple of years in the US and return to Belgium," says Pieter, "I really want to go." They both sign up to take the required ECFMG examination and they both pass.

Pieter is offered a fellowship in internal medicine at a Harvard University–affiliated hospital in Boston. He will participate in patients' care and do research.

One of the attending physicians in pathology also trained in Boston, and he has stayed in touch with the chairman of the Pathology Department at Boston University, the head of a well-known teaching department with a large staff and a structured training program. He writes a strong recommendation letter for Marguerite; she is given credit for one of her two years of previous experience and is offered a position as a second-year resident.

Pieter and Marguerite rent a house from a couple of academics going to the UK for a sabbatical. They find a young nursing student who is interested in being a paid au pair in Boston; she agrees to a one-year contract.

When Zilda hears that Marguerite, Pieter, and their two little girls are leaving for the United States, she is devastated. She blames Pieter for taking away her beloved granddaughters, but in truth, Marguerite is also eager to escape from her current position, a dead end.

It is a huge emotional blow for Zilda. She has five other grandchildren; Marie now has three boys and Maxine has two boys as well, but she is closest to her two granddaughters. She has taken care of five-year-old Eve for long periods of time; Anne is an endearing two-year-old. Zilda does not have the same love for her other grandchildren. Marie keeps a distance and is not fond of her parents. Maxine has grown difficult and demanding and is often at odds with her parents.

Zilda falls into depression. Marguerite tells her: "It is for two years only. Why don't you and Father come visit in a year? We could spend a vacation in the States together." She adds, "This is good for Pieter and me. We need to train and specialize, it is not possible here."

They leave Brussels on June 27, 1970. Pieter is twenty-seven years old, Marguerite is twenty-eight. They are moving to the United States, which has suffered many political events in the past decade and is in the middle of the Vietnam war. Marguerite vividly remembers hearing about the death of President Kennedy in 1963, when she was in medical school. But on that day of departure for Boston, Marguerite's thoughts are of their own difficulties and challenges ahead, how they will settle in Boston, will she like her new position, will the children adjust?

The family and the au pair arrive in Boston on a hot rainy day. It is over ninety degrees, the clothes immediately stick to the skin. It is oppressive, unpleasant. The owner of the rented house meets them at the airport and takes them in town to a narrow, brick row house with four floors, behind the train tracks, which was omitted in the description, but there is room for everyone, it is air-conditioned and comfortable, and there is a tiny backyard.

It is fairly close to the hospital where Marguerite will work, within walking distance to the Boston Common, the Charles River.

Pieter immediately starts shopping for a used car. Marguerite visits the local A&P supermarket and is dismayed at the soft, mushy bread, the tasteless butter, the processed food. It will be a while before they discover better stores farther away, the good bakeries, the open markets in the North End on the weekend. For now, the A&P has to do. Pieter and Marguerite start their respective fellowships and residencies on July first.

CHAPTER 34

The seventy-seven-year old Lydie is diagnosed with colon cancer, the same malignancy that already claimed her two oldest daughters. The cancer has spread, and she can be offered only palliative care. She has a long, painful course. When Marguerite calls home, Zilda breaks down and tells of her own mother's cries and suffering. Maximilien is not supportive. He visits Lydie once, never removing his hat, shocking Zilda even though she is used to his callous ways toward her own family. He says, "Well, Lydie, you are causing a big commotion." It is a difficult period for Zilda, she is at her mother's bedside until she dies; she sorely misses her two granddaughters. She again falls into depression; her relationship with Marie and Maxine is not easy.

Maxine and her husband are living in a rented old farm with their two little boys. Augusto works irregularly. The farm needs renovations, and Maxine and her family move into her parents' house for a few weeks. They sleep in Marguerite's old room, the room where Zilda had large closets built years ago.

One day, Zilda is looking for Augusto who has not come down for lunch. She finds him curled up in a closet, his arms around his knees, and he is crying. Maxine is abusive; she taunts and insults her husband. She is very difficult with her own parents as well. She is always demanding money, orders her parents to renovate the farm. She criticizes everything. Zilda pours out the news to Marguerite in long phone calls. "I am powerless," says Zilda, "I do not know what to do, your sister is a bully."

Jacques, Marie's husband, wants to have a daughter. Marie has already given birth to three sons in a short period of time. She teaches in elementary school and has a full schedule. "I do not want another pregnancy," she tells Jacques. "I do not want to raise another baby." "Then, we will adopt an older child," decides Jacques. They have heard of a Catholic foundation that places Indian children with Belgian families. Zilda and Maximilien are both very upset at the idea, but Marie and Jacques are adamant. "It is not your decision," they say, "you should not try to interfere." Zilda feels that Marie's children are already not receiving the care and attention they need. She is worried about them.

Jacques and Marie adopt a young dark-skinned Hindu girl of uncertain age, about two and a half years old. The child finds herself in the midst of a family with three boys. She does not speak French, of course. She attaches herself like a barnacle to Marie. She wants to be carried or hold hands at all times; otherwise, she screams. The child is frightened, and she requires constant care for a long period of time. Marie's youngest son is displaced.

Marie's two older sons are in elementary school, the two younger children are enrolled in preschool—they are in the same class. Zilda wonders how Marie is able to handle all her responsibilities.

Marie is not communicative, though she brings her children over for quick occasional visits.

Zilda has a wonderful idea. She will cook food for Marie's family and pick up the younger children at preschool, as a surprise. She goes to the preschool, picks up the two children, and drives them to their house with all the dishes she has lovingly prepared.

Marie has an arrangement with a caretaker to pick up her younger children from school, bring them home and stay there with them until the she returns from her teaching job. The caretaker calls Marie to say that she went to the school, but that the children had already been picked up by their grandmother. "The children are safe, I am now with them," says the caretaker, "and your mother has left; she brought a lot of cooked dishes."

Zilda drives back to her own house unaware of the storm she has created. When Jacques returns from work, Marie, shaking with anger, orders him to go to her mother's house and upturn all the dishes on Zilda's front steps. Jacques drives to his in-laws' house, rings the bell, and leaves all the dishes on the front steps.

Marie communicates to her parents that they are forbidden to interfere in her life. They do not speak for a long time, and Zilda does not see her grandsons for many weeks. She is misunderstood, as usual. She is deeply unhappy. "That was stupid," says Maximilien, "you got what you deserve, you should have talked to Marie beforehand."

Zilda relates all these news to Marguerite in indignant phone calls. I am glad to be far from my family, thinks Marguerite.

At the time of her death, Lydie owned nineteen buildings and rental houses in Aimeries and adjacent communities, the large

MARGUERITE DUVIVIER

apartment in one of Brussels' most exclusive residential areas, and the multi-story apartment building on the boardwalk at the North Shore. Her fortune has to be divided and disposed of.

Zilda and her siblings meet for weeks with lawyers. They gather over long periods of time to decide how to divide and share the estate. The process distracts Zilda from her woes with her own family, her sorrow at the loss of her mother and granddaughters. She puts money away and makes gifts of money and jewelry to her daughters.

Marguerite, in Boston, receives a sizable sum from her mother. "The money is providential," says Pieter. "My parents need money, we will send it to them." Marguerite is taken by surprise, she does not agree; "That money is for us and our daughters," she says, "we do not have any savings, and my mother is not giving me money so that we can give it to your parents." "You do not have to tell your mother," replies Pieter. Marguerite is very troubled; she compromises and is willing to make her parents-in-law an interest-free loan, but she demands a written guarantee that she will be paid back in six months.

Six months later, Marguerite and Pieter have a huge fight. He does not want to ask his parents to repay the loan. Marguerite insists on it. He starts crying; he is sitting on the bed, and he silently cries. Marguerite has never seen him cry and she too is very disturbed and upset. She is wondering if she should forgive the loan.

As usual, Pieter refuses to discuss the issue, why he does not want to ask his parents to repay the loan. Marguerite is in the dark, she does not know why they needed money in the first place. Pieter spends all the money they receive from her parents, they will never be able to save, and saving is important to her, it is prudent. The loan is repaid, and Pieter immediately buys an expensive stereo system. Marguerite wonders for a very long time if she made a mistake.

Marguerite calls home every weekend, she talks to both her parents, tells them how they are doing in Boston, she asks news of her sisters, of her parents' health.

She also calls Madame Leonce, who just lost her husband, regularly. The old landlady is getting hard of hearing, and she says, "I did not understand all you said, can you write to me?" So, Marguerite calls and then she writes a letter with a quick summary of her news.

"The children are doing very well," she tells her parents and Madame Leonce. "I read to them every night, we have outings on the weekends, we go to the beach, we explore the city. Eve has started kindergarten at the local school, she is already starting to speak English. My daughters are so sweet, smart, and beautiful, they are healthy." She passes the phone to Eve and Anne so that they can chat with her parents. Pieter calls his parents too and shares the same news.

CHAPTER 35

The au pair is lonely. Marguerite feels as though she has three children, and the babysitter, still young and immature at eighteen, is the one who demands the most attention. It is not easy for the young woman to be alone all day with two small children in a foreign country. When Marguerite returns home from the hospital at the end of the workday, she is tired, but she needs to give time to the sitter. She gives her attention first, listens to what the young woman has to say, then she is free to give all her time to her daughters. Bath times are lovely, they cuddle and hug. They sit on the bed, and she reads stories. Eve can already read by herself.

Marguerite's English-speaking abilities are rudimentary. She manages to read medical textbooks, but reading, speaking, and hearing are very different things, and initially, she does not understand much of what is said at her new place of work. Many residents and staff have strong foreign accents; it makes understanding even more difficult.

The pathology institute is a teeming place with staff and residents from all over the world. The new group of residents is welcomed in the conference room July first. The training program is very structured with tight schedules, lectures, one-on-one teaching, instructions at the multi-headed microscope where a senior attending teaches eight trainees at a time how to interpret tissue specimens.

It is a raucous and busy place, with camaraderie, rivalries, love affairs, pranks, and much swearing. The residents share a large room; each receives a microscope, a manual, a desk, assigned duties. The chairman of the department is elusive, but there are two hands-on associate chiefs and an administrative staff used to handle residents from different countries. The chief resident is Korean, several residents are from the Middle East, there are Americans, a Russian, a German, a Canadian, an Irish resident. Several fellows and senior staff are from India and South America. A senior attending is from Iran. Marguerite finds him exotic looking and beautiful with his almond shaped eyes and shiny wavy long black hair.

In Belgium, at the hospital, people were all native Belgians, and very formal; secretaries were called Miss or Madam, with their given names; physicians were called Doctor. Here everyone is on a first-name basis; the residents call the attendings by their first name. It takes a while for Marguerite to get used to the familiarity; she is shocked at first. Here she is Marguerite to everyone, not Doctor. She has landed in a different world.

She is assigned to work as a team with a Syrian fluent in Arabic, French, and English. They both came in as second-year residents. Her partner is godsent. They work in the dissection room side by side; she is fast and proficient at handling the specimens, and he helps her with her dictation and her pronunciation with good humor. It takes six months for Marguerite to understand the spoken English, and people often laugh when she gives a presentation. She mispronounces words or uses the incorrect one. All residents have to give talks, regardless of their proficiency with the language.

Marguerite discovers that with the right training, she has a gift for reading pathology slides; she is visual, quickly and easily recognizes abnormalities, and she shines as a resident. She has found the right field for herself, and she learns rapidly. She is also recognized for her efficiency and organizational skills.

Pieter has a different experience; he is not happy at the hospital where he is a fellow. He does not like the other staff members of his department, the rigidity of the system. He went from being a rising star in his department in Brussels to being unappreciated. He is not able to do the research he wants to pursue, and he is talking about returning home to Belgium at the end of the first year.

Marguerite wants to stay for another year. She is learning by leaps and bounds, there is talk of making her the chief resident next year. Could Pieter switch to another hospital, another group? There are three medical schools in Boston, could he find another position?

It is the summer, they are staying another year. Pieter is going across town to another hospital. He will be a fellow in hematology and oncology, treat patients, with a sizable amount of time dedicated to doing research.

Maximilien and Zilda are coming to visit, and the family spends a couple of weeks in Bretton Woods in New Hampshire. The babysitter has gone back home. Maximilien knows another young woman who wants to come as an au pair. "She is mature," he says, "twenty-one years old, dynamic, cheerful." The house rented for a year is no longer available. Pieter finds an apartment across town near Brookline, close to public transportation. Marguerite buys a car.

Maximilien and Zilda are enthralled by their two granddaughters. Eve is six years old, bilingual, Anne is three, both are full of life and joy. The vacation is perfect. The grandparents are happy to be with Eve and Anne, and they seem to get along.

"We now sleep in separate bedrooms," confides Zilda, "your father is still busy with patients. I keep occupied, I go to my villa on the Riviera as often as possible. I am so peaceful there."

Zilda brought jewelry from Lydie's estate to Marguerite, who gets fresh news from home. "Maxine is getting divorced, she kicked her husband out and she danced when he left," relates Zilda. "She wants to build a house and she has bought a small building lot in a bad part of town. She is demanding money to start the construction. She has moved to an apartment. We worry about her two young sons. We feed the boys properly and take better care of them when they visit the farm. They love to come spend time there. But Maxine acts as if she owns the place. "

"We do not see much of Marie," add the parents, "she is distancing herself more and more. The little Indian girl learned to speak French this past year, but she has a speech impediment. She does not seem to be very bright, though she is integrating. Jacques is talking about adopting a second girl; we are very worried."

Soon after Zilda and Maximilien return to Belgium, Marguerite gets the news that her grandmother Victoire had a fall and broke her hip. She passes away a few weeks later. She lived for ninety-two years, and she died with no possessions. She gave everything away in the last few years. "I only need one cup, one plate," she would say to her granddaughters, "take whatever you like."

CHAPTER 36

Marguerite and Pieter start their second year of training in the US. Marguerite has been selected to be the chief resident of the Pathology Department, with administrative responsibilities.

Pieter likes his new chief, his new department, and he is making friends of the other fellows. He does research in the laboratory of a man he admires, and they become close.

Each has a car, they drive across town to their respective hospitals. Eve is enrolled in first grade, Anne goes to kindergarten. The new sitter is indeed dynamic and cheerful, independent, and she explores the city on her own on the weekends, giving some privacy to the family.

Marguerite teaches proper autopsy technique to the new residents. The autopsy dieners are African American. One, a young bodybuilder, offers to sell Marguerite weapons for self-defense. He shows her all kinds of knives, sprays. "The institute is in a bad part of town," he says, "you park in the street, there are drug addicts all around." Marguerite declines the offers.

The other man is older, physically very strong, and Marguerite is wary of him, she finds him threatening. He makes inappropriate remarks and enjoys taunting the young female residents. One day, he and Marguerite are alone in the autopsy room, and he crosses the line. "I could show you a good time, Marguerite," he says "I bet my dick is bigger than your husband's. Black men are well endowed." "Stop this," says Marguerite, and the man laughs.

Marguerite reports the incident. "I cannot work with that man," she says, "he is a danger to the young women here." The associate chief chuckles: "Boys will be boys," he replies. "Good dieners are much harder to find than residents. I am sure that nothing will happen."

Every year, the residents are required to have a physical examination and a chest radiograph. Marguerite has been coughing; she attributes it to her exposure to formalin, a fixative used in tissue processing.

When she meets with a fellow in internal medicine to learn the results of her routine chest radiograph, she finds the young doctor examining the films. "How interesting," he says, "see here." He points to the area of the mediastinum. "Fantastic X-rays. You have either lymphoma, tuberculosis, or sarcoidosis. It needs to be worked up, biopsied. I have to report it to your department."

Marguerite cannot think, she is appalled both at the findings and at the callousness of the young doctor. She thinks of her two young children. What will happen to them if she is sick? She has been very tired; she fell asleep on the beach on a weekend trip, and she slept for two hours on the sand while Pieter and the sitter took care of the girls. She asks to take the rest of the day off and drives home. She cannot wait to talk to Pieter, to discuss her options, make decisions. He is working in oncology, he is knowledgeable, he will know what to do, he can reassure her.

That evening, she tells the news to Pieter. He shrugs. "It is pointless to talk or worry about it until we know what it is," says Pieter. He does not hug her, does not say: "We will face this together." "I had enlarged lymph nodes I was concerned about," he adds, "and I did not tell you about it." He could have as well said: "Do not bother me with your problems."

The conversation is over. Marguerite has to deal with the situation alone. She falls out of whatever love she still had for Pieter.

The chief of the Pathology Department is informed. Marguerite contacts the chairman of the Internal Medicine Department and asks if he could see her as soon as possible and take her as a patient. He specializes in lung diseases and has the reputation of being a thoughtful and thorough physician.

The internist is direct, systematic, reassuring. He is older and kind, grandfatherly, and he proposes a course of action. "How is your PPD test?" he asks. "It is positive, has always been, though I was not vaccinated against tuberculosis," responds Marguerite. "We will repeat the test, do sputum cultures to test for tuberculosis, it is our first plan of action. You will have to submit weekly sputum samples for several months. We will repeat the chest X-rays at two-week intervals to chart any change. And I would like to do pulmonary function tests."

"Now, let me examine you," says the chairman. Marguerite is given a very thorough physical examination. She has a markedly enlarged liver; no enlarged lymph nodes are found. "You cut your toenails too short," gently chides the chairman, endearing himself to Marguerite who is touched by the care and attention. "Your

X-rays are truly wonderful from a teaching point of view," remarks the internist. "I will hide your name of course, but I will use them in my lectures."

The PPD test is strongly positive, indicative of tuberculosis exposure at some point, but the new chest X-rays are unchanged and the sputum cultures are repeatedly negative. Marguerite is scheduled to undergo the lung function tests. She is told to ride a stationary bicycle, she is attached to several machines, and she breathes through a mask. She is asked to pedal harder and harder.

She finds herself on a stretcher, an unknown physician anxiously hovering over her. "You fell from the bicycle," he says, "you had a grand mal seizure. How do you feel? Do you know where you are? You have to lie down for observation for a while. Have you ever had a seizure before?"

"No," says Marguerite, "never."

"We had to stop the testing, your physician will discuss the next steps with you."

Marguerite drives herself home. Pieter again shrugs when she tells him of the seizure. "I have no idea," he says.

On her follow-up visit, her doctor reports that the pulmonary test was inconclusive, it could not be completed. The doctor recommends a mediastinal biopsy.

"I want to think about it," says Marguerite. "I would like to wait, is it really necessary? It is a surgical invasive procedure, there are risks."

Pieter tells Marguerite that to agree to a mediastinoscopy is up to her; an instrument would be pushed into the mediastinum through a surgical cut over the sternum, and biopsies taken. Marguerite would probably be hospitalized for a few days. Pieter is clinical, unemotional. He thinks that there is no harm in waiting for a few weeks. The sputum cultures remain negative; at the next chest X-ray, it seems that the mediastinum may be slightly less enlarged. I want to wait some more before a biopsy, decides Marguerite. The mediastinal enlargement slowly diminishes over the next few months, and the liver returns to normal size.

At the end of the year, the internist tells Marguerite that she most likely had sarcoidosis; chest X-ray should be performed every six months for a few years.

Without a biopsy, sarcoidosis is a diagnosis of exclusion; it is an inflammatory disease of unknown origin, in which the immune system overreacts. Patients may die of the disease, but Marguerite had a self-limited case, she was lucky.

The episode deeply influenced her relationship with Pieter; her feelings of loneliness are intense, she was very afraid.

She is at a turning point in her life. She decides to have a tubal ligation. Pieter does not want to have more children, and she does not want the risk of becoming pregnant again. Pieter is intellectually brilliant, a very handsome man. He has been unfaithful; he had an affair with the wife of a resident last year, he may have been involved with other women. Marguerite does not feel guilty for experimenting herself. She has a brief encounter with a fellow in her department who has been pursuing her, but it is meaningless. Men only want sex, she thinks, there is no tenderness.

There is a younger Irish resident she likes, who is married with a young child. The resident invites her, Pieter, and their children to have lunch at his place, with his family. It is a small party, other young residents are there. Dan and his wife, Mariette, are easy to be with, fun, and Pieter and Marguerite reciprocate the invitation. The two couples become friendly, plan activities together.

At the hospital, Marguerite sees Dan every day; they develop affection for each other. Dan reminds Marguerite of her first love. He is gentle and they talk openly. One day he says, "Why don't we go to a motel together?"

Pieter has been working long hours, he is juggling research and patients' care. He is often on call overnight. On the weekends, he orders Marguerite to take the children out of the apartment so that he can write in peace. The other day, Eve spilled a glass of milk at the table, and he was furious, he sent the crying child to her bedroom. Upset, resentful, Marguerite left the table to go console her child who had just been clumsy. Pieter is unfair, he is hard to live with. Marguerite cannot leave him, he is earning much more money than she is, she would not make ends meet by herself and she does not want to return to Belgium at this point in her training.

She agrees to have an affair; Dan is affectionate. They mostly hold each other and talk. Sex is brief, almost a footnote; it is not why they spend time together. She is not sure why he is unfaithful to his wife; they seem to love each other but he also appears to like Marguerite a great deal. She finds support and peace with him. They spend a few stolen hours together whenever they can. Sometimes, they just sit in the car and hold hands.

The second year of residency is almost over. The initial plan was to spend two years in the United States and return to Belgium where Pieter has a position waiting for him; Marguerite would have to find a new job in Belgium for herself. But Pieter does not want to leave his position in Boston. He is getting his research published in peer-reviewed journals. He has cemented a reputation for innovative ideas and great patient care. His chairman wants him to remain as a fellow until he passes the boards of internal medicine and then he will become an attending, join the senior staff.

Marguerite is nearing the end of her own residency; she is not yet board certified either. In order to take the board in anatomic pathology, she needs to finish four years of training in the US, and she has completed two. She is hoping to remain at the same institute where she is finishing the year as the chief resident. There are fellowship positions available. She is interested in renal pathology, but several other residents are applying for the same spot. The head of the renal pathology section is a very bright man, a great scientist. She has a good rapport with him; they have had great discussions and laughed together.

She is chosen for the position; the fellowship is for two years.

The small family returns to Belgium for a vacation, the first visit since they left two years ago. Marguerite writes to her sisters. Marie responds that she will be away and cannot meet, Maxine sounds happy to see her sister soon. Pieter's parents have not seen their granddaughters in a long time—they are amazed at the changes; both Eve and Anne are bilingual, they are very endearing, lively. Time is spent at the farm with Maximilien and Zilda. Maxine brings her two boys there and it is a good reunion.

Marie and Jacques have adopted a second Indian child. The girl is very dark skinned; the adoptive parents have been told that she is five or six years of age. The Belgian pediatrician who examines the child says, "She is several years older, probably nine or ten years old, she is of very short stature for her age, and she has been sexually abused." When he sees and observes the child, a very upset Maximilien openly calls her the black plague, further antagonizing Marie and Jacques.

He and Zilda do not understand why Marie and Jacques adopted another girl.

It is not working out for the family. The boys are resentful; Marie is barely able to handle the young girl who steals, is defiant, difficult. It is a disaster, and Marie is defensive, she is hiding from her family. Jacques is drinking heavily, and has occasionally been abusive.

Marguerite and Pieter are happy to return to the States and leave the drama behind. They have their own problems.

CHAPTER 37

Marguerite starts her fellowship. The renal pathology service is busy, a referral center handling kidney biopsies from several hospitals. She is expected to start doing experimental research; her mentor proposes some studies, and they decide on a project together.

In academia, there is a saying: publish or perish. To advance in one's career, one has to write papers, submit them to peer-reviewed journals, and see them published. Marguerite has published a few clinical case reports; now she is dealing with mice and rats. She injects them, sacrifices them, harvests their kidneys. It is not work she enjoys, the killing of the animals is upsetting, but it is mandatory at this stage of her career.

She spends a lot of time in the renal pathology laboratory. She learns specialized techniques, the use of machinery, a microtome, an electron microscope; she is shown how to print photos of her research in the dark room, and she personally prepares specimens in the laboratory. She becomes efficient in difficult techniques and spends hours with the technicians.

The laboratory is mostly staffed by young women, and they chat all the time. Three of the girls are having affairs with married fellows and residents. Marguerite is astonished at what is said, most conversations are about sex.

"My boyfriend called me last night," says a young woman. "He said, come now, come as you are. I was naked when he called, so I just wore my raincoat and high heels; the look on his face was priceless. I think he is going to propose." "I am told that I have the softest pubic hair," says another, "I use hair conditioner on it." "Look at my new lipstick," says another. She shows her new lipstick. It is shaped like a penis; she applies it to her lips and laughs.

One of the girls commutes from New Hampshire every day. She drives a small red car and uses a CB radio. Truckers call on the CB radio: "Hey, little red car, do you want to stop at the next exit and meet me?" She tells hilarious stories.

Everyone works diligently, but there is time for conversations. It is possible to work on a microtome and talk at the same time.

Marguerite feels naive, she has never heard such explicit language, of such daring behavior. The girls are happy, liberated. She keeps the details of her own life to herself; she is in awe of the abandon and audacity of some of the young women.

At lunch, residents and technicians often get together in the hospital's cafeteria. An older PhD in the department likes to sit with the young people. He joins several residents having lunch; Dan and Marguerite are there. Nonchalantly, the PhD says: "Men are smarter than women, and I can prove it."

He is looking at one of the young technicians in the renal laboratory. He is trying to goad the gullible young woman, who immediately takes offense. "Women are just as smart as men, this is nonsense," she says indignantly. "Not so," responds the PhD with a straight face; he starts to explain that different regions of the brain are dedicated to specific functions of the body. "For example," he says, "a big piece of the brain is dedicated to the use of the thumb." He goes on to say: "Since women, but not men, have a uterus, and get pregnant, it makes sense that a large section of the brain is dedicated to the uterus and pregnancy, leaving women with less brain space for intelligence and thought processing."

It is utter nonsense, but he says it very seriously. The technician is very upset and argues with the PhD. The residents solemnly nod, appear to agree; they struggle not to laugh. The target of the joke is upset for hours, she keeps talking about that conversation, until Marguerite takes pity on her: "You were being teased, there is no such thing as a brain area dedicated to the uterus."

Life in the laboratory is busy and entertaining; it can also be offensive. The male residents rate the females in the department on attractiveness based on secret criteria. Marguerite does not want to know her rating.

Growing up in Belgium, Marguerite and her sisters were not allowed to swear, though Maximilien swore profusely and frequently. Marguerite is unable to swear in French. It is ingrained. But not so in English. There is much swearing among the men at the institute and Marguerite learns to swear; she is not in Belgium anymore. Swearing can be strangely liberating. But she restrains herself in front of her daughters; she has two different lives, one at home in the evening and on the weekend, the other at the hospital.

At work, she has to fend off men eager to have affairs. Her own boss, married with three children, comes in the darkroom and tries to grope her. She elbows him away, tells him firmly to stop, she is not interested. There is no point reporting his behavior to the chairman of the department. She is not overly bothered by it, she can fend for herself, and she actually likes her boss. He tries to seduce her, it is a game for him, and she makes it clear that he needs to stop. They are good friends, he likes to talk to Marguerite, and she finds him interesting. He is a brilliant man, she learns a lot from him, and she is grateful that he chose her for the fellowship.

The relationship between Pieter and Marguerite is at a standstill. They both work hard; at home, they interact with their daughters. Eve is in second grade and is at the top of her class. Anne appears to be just as smart. I have two very intelligent daughters, thinks Marguerite, at least I got that from my marriage.

The family takes a vacation in Bermuda in the spring of their third year in the States. Pieter and Anne are sitting high on the beach; Eve and Marguerite are at the edge of the water, and they are swept away by a rogue wave, taken to the sea. It is fast, they have no warning. Marguerite manages to grab Eve and swim back to the sand. We almost died, thinks an exhausted and shaken Marguerite, and Pieter did not notice.

The family meets with colleagues and friends, Dan and Mariette often go with them for walks, they have gone camping together at the state park on Cape Cod. That summer, they rent a very large tent to share with Dan and his family, and they go camping to their favorite place on the Cape. At dusk, the young mothers, friends, each beautiful in a different way, go skinny dipping in the lake.

At night, the tired children are soundly asleep in their sleeping bags, each couple in theirs. "We could switch sleeping bags," softly suggests Pieter. Mariette seems eager, Dan and Marguerite look at each other. They are fine with the idea. They have already slept with each other, though Pieter does not know it. Soon, moans and pants come from the sleeping bag shared by Pieter and Mariette; Dan is silently laughing, Marguerite feels his big belly shaking. Pieter has a lot of staying power, Mariette is obviously enjoying the encounter. They exchange sleeping bags again before the children wake up.

The next day, nothing is said, Pieter and Marguerite do not talk of it, Dan does not say anything to Marguerite either. It is as if it never happened.

CHAPTER 38

Marguerite has started doing clinical research and is collaborating with nephrologists at two university hospitals. She gives presentations and conferences. She makes the diagnosis on kidney biopsies and relates it to the patients' attending physicians. Clinicians come discuss their cases with her. Her chief trusts her and she is working independently. She is also teaching pathology at the medical school.

At home, the babysitter takes the children to school and takes care of them at the end of the day, until Marguerite gets home. Pieter usually works longer hours, often overnight. Marguerite know very little of her husband's life at the hospital.

The babysitter spends a lot of time in town; she leaves as soon as Marguerite gets home, and she returns late at night. On a few occasions, she has returned early in the morning. She does not share details of her activities. She is twenty-three years old, and Marguerite does not feel entitled to ask her where she goes, who she meets. She returns and takes good care of the children. She remains cheerful and pleasant.

At the end of the third year in the United States, Pieter becomes eligible to take the internal medicine boards, and he decides to take the hematology boards at the same time. He passes both at the first try, he finds it easy. He is also interested in oncology—some of his patients have lymphoma or leukemia—and in infectious diseases. He is studying to pass those boards as well soon. It is very unusual for a physician to be certified in several specialties, but he finds correlations between the fields and his research straddles several areas.

Dan and Pieter discuss going on a tour of the United States in the summer, renting and sharing a large RV, heading west and north, then south, to visit several famous sites, the Grand Canyon, and return east on a monthlong vacation. The RV is reserved, but Dan decides to leave Boston and go to another state to specialize in a different field of pathology. Marguerite will miss her friends, but she is not in love with Dan. He provided comfort and tenderness. She thinks he is making the right choice for himself and his family, and Mariette is pregnant again.

Pieter, Marguerite, and their daughters embark on the planned vacation. The RV is huge; thirty-year-old Pieter does all the driving, they stop at camp sites, visit interesting sites along the way, Mount Rushmore in South Dakota. They drive for hours to reach the city of Pierre. The RV is slow, it is very hot, and the trip seems interminable. Pieter is irritable, he is very tired.

Marguerite is often afraid and lonely. The land is desolate. They could be attacked, they could have an accident and not find help. She is tense; she regrets having embarked on the trip. In Wyoming, they turn south and drive to Colorado, to the Grand Canyon. After Colorado, they make a turn east for the long trip home.

At a camp site, the hose to the toilet tank of the RV comes loose as Pieter tries to empty the tank, and he gets covered with the contents. Marguerite laughs when she sees him, and he is resentful for days.

The children are luminous, beautiful, healthy. They cuddle with their parents, play games, read books. For them, it is a wonderful trip; for Pieter it is very tiring, and he has a short temper. Marguerite is anxious, and the couple's relationship does not improve.

During the fourth year in Boston, in Marguerite's second year of fellowship, she starts working closely with a nephrologist, a kidney specialist. They collaborate on textbook chapters, they conduct research together and are coauthors on several scientific papers.

Marguerite invites the clinician, Bob, to come for dinner with his wife, Pamela, a nurse, and she and Pieter immediately bond. Marguerite does not like Pamela. She is critical, sarcastic, gives unwanted advice. Bob confides that his marriage is not going well.

"I got married because I was being drafted to go to Vietnam and we had been dating for a while, but I stopped loving Pamela long ago."

Pieter has joined the senior staff, he is an attending physician, with a commensurate salary. Years later, a woman who worked in Pieter's department and then came to work in Marguerite's hospital finds out that Marguerite had been married to Pieter. She rolls her eyes; "He was involved with several nurses there," she says, "a notorious Romeo."

Though they no longer are close to each other, the couple has independently decided to remain in the United States. Both their careers and training are going well, they both are very satisfied with their work. They decide to start looking for a house to buy.

In February of 1974, they buy a small Cape Cod–style house in a western suburb. It has four small bedrooms and two bathrooms, and a yard abutting a large park. The house is dirty and needs painting and updating, but it has potential and is in a desirable area.

The elementary school is around the corner, a few minutes' walk away. It is a safe neighborhood.

Maybe this will be a new start, hopes Marguerite. She is looking forward to owning her first house, to having a garden. Maybe our relationship can be mended, we could have a good life here.

CHAPTER 39

The family moves into their freshly cleaned and painted house in the first week of March.

Within a few days, Pieter is not feeling well, he complains of severe flank pain, and he develops a fever. Marguerite takes him to the emergency room; he is diagnosed with a large kidney stone blocking the ureter. He needs immediate surgery.

When he returns home a week later from the hospital, he is sullen, uncommunicative, short with everyone. The surgery went well, and Marguerite is at a loss. "Pieter," she asks, "what is going on? We are not doing well, we are unhappy. I would like to talk, to see if we could improve our relationship, have a new start."

Pieter is in his bathrobe, they are sitting in the living room. He looks at his wife, does not say a word, and goes upstairs to their bedroom. He closes the door. Marguerite overhears him talk on the phone. He moves around the room. Marguerite, hurt that he refused to talk with her, does not go to join him. Less than an hour later, the front doorbell rings. Pamela is on the front steps; she does not greet Marguerite who opened the door. Pieter comes downstairs, carrying a suitcase, and he leaves the house with Pamela. No words are exchanged.

Marguerite is stunned. She was hoping for the impossible: open communication with Pieter, and she was not prepared for the consequences.

Pieter has left a letter for Eve, whose ninth birthday is in a few days. Marguerite does not know what is in the letter, it is private, she does not ask to read it.

She goes upstairs. Pieter has taken his clothes and their savings book. They had sixty thousand dollars in the savings account and spent fifteen thousand dollars on the down payment for the house. Pieter has taken all the remaining money. Paralyzed, Marguerite sits at the top of the stairs. Eve has read her letter, and says: "We will be okay, Mom, we will be okay," as she puts her arms around her mother.

Pieter makes a lot more money than Marguerite, some of the savings were from his salary, most from gifts from Marguerite's parents. Marguerite's fellow's salary is only eleven thousand dollars a year. She has to pay the mortgage, the babysitter's salary, the house painter has not been paid—Marguerite has five hundred dollars to her name. It is still winter, the heating system breaks down two days later. It was old and needs to be replaced.

Bob was at a medical conference in Chicago. He calls Marguerite and says that Pamela told him he was not to return home. Could he stay at Marguerite's house until he can figure out what to do? "I will pay rent," he says, and they agree on an amount.

Marguerite talks to her parents, tells them that Pieter has left and that she has no money. "I will be there as soon as I can," says Maximilien, "I will bring money with me."

He arrives a few days later, with sufficient funds to cover the unpaid bills, replace the heater. Bob goes to a hotel while Maximilien visits.

"What will you do?" asks Maximilien. "You should come back home."

"I will manage, Dad, I need to finish the academic year, give myself time to think. I will come this summer with the children, it is only a few months away."

Marguerite has no news from Pieter for six months. He does not call or write, he does not check on his daughters. She does not receive any financial support for the care of the children. Pieter has vanished. She hears from his parents that he came to visit them with Pamela. "We do not like her, we are incredibly upset. How could he have left you and the children?" they say.

Pieter travels in Europe with Pamela for several months; he lives in her apartment when they return. At the beginning of the split, Bob, a big man, went back to his place to get some clothes, and he had a physical fight with Pieter, giving him a good beating. Pamela refuses to reunite with Bob who pays rent to Marguerite; he is generous, and it helps her manage for a few weeks. Then, Bob meets a woman, and moves in with her. He files for divorce from Pamela.

Marguerite has become eligible for, and passes, the pathology boards; she needs to find a senior staff position either in the US or in Belgium. She makes appointments with the chiefs of service at several hospitals in Brussels; but the Belgian system is one of seniority, not merit. Her training and expertise are not recognized; if she returns to Belgium, she will be reduced to doing autopsies in various hospitals, for low pay. She has no choice but to stay in the

United States and start applying in different cities, to find a position as a surgical pathologist with specialization in renal diseases.

The future feels frightening to her; she is very anxious. How will she find another position, how long will it take, what will she do in the meantime? How will she sell the house they just bought, move across the country alone with her small daughters?

She is back in Boston after her trip to Belgium, working for a few more weeks in her department, finishing her fellowship.

A few months ago, the chairman of pathology at Boston University and chief of service of her department retired. The two associate chiefs, one of them her mentor in renal pathology, vied for his position. Her mentor is the better scientist, more accomplished, but the other has more political support, and he was selected to be the new chief and chairman. Marguerite is not fond of him. He likes expediency and does not address problems. He is the man who laughed at her when she complained about the autopsy room assistant. He told her once: "If you wait, most problems go away; why waste energy confronting them?"

One day, as Marguerite is leaving at the end of the day, going to her car in the parking lot, she hears: "Marguerite, Marguerite, wait!" The new chairman, breathless, runs to her and says, "Your mentor is leaving to become the chairman at another medical school, we need a renal pathologist in the department. Will you join us on the staff?"

It is a monumental relief for Marguerite. "Thank you, I appreciate your offer, I accept," she says. She wishes the position had been offered more formally, sitting in an office. It is off-putting and disappointing to be offered the job by a breathless chief in a parking lot, but she overlooks the casual manner, the expediency.

She does not respect the chairman, but her immediate problems are solved.

She is an excellent renal pathologist, appreciated and trusted by the clinicians. She will not have to transplant her daughters to a faraway city, sell her house, re-create a reputation for herself. She will also soon be earning a salary sufficient to support herself and her daughters.

CHAPTER 40

Pieter left in early March, he vanished and did not get in touch. He rings the bell at the end of September; the children are surprised but happy to see him. "Where have you been?" they ask. "Where is your mother?" he says after hugging his daughters. "She is ironing in the basement," replies Eve.

Pieter approaches Marguerite: he does not look well, he smells of alcohol. She is guarded, does not say anything. "I am not feeling well," says Pieter, "I may have another kidney stone, and Pamela threw me out of her apartment. Would you let me come back, give me a second chance?"

"I need to think about it," says Marguerite, "but you should be checked at the hospital."

She brings Pieter to the emergency room. He has another kidney stone. The next day, Marguerite calls her husband and tells him that she does not want to get back together, that she intends to file for divorce.

Her life without him is peaceful; he gave her two wonderful daughters, but he does not provide the security, affection, and emotional support she needs. He only came back because Pamela threw him out. They have very different ways of dealing with money, he has been unfaithful and probably will be again. She and the children were abandoned for six months.

Pieter cannot be without a woman. When he met Marguerite, he was engaged to another young woman, and he abandoned her for Marguerite within days. He left Marguerite for Pamela; when Marguerite refuses to take him back, he convinces Pamela to get back together.

The divorce negotiations are very difficult, conducted back and forth by lawyers. Pieter is angry, and he is bent on revenge. He informs Marguerite through his lawyer that she will need to file their income tax returns. He will forward his documents. He always has taken care of official documents, of filing income tax returns. Marguerite has no idea how to go about it.

He initially refuses to pay any support for the children, and Marguerite is informed that her husband intends to ask for the custody of his daughters. Marguerite is frightened. "This will not happen," says Marguerite's lawyer, "no judge will agree to take children from a responsible mother and give them to a father who disappeared for six months; he is a well-paid physician, he has to financially support his children."

The negotiations are not progressing. Pieter offers to pay $250 a month, $125 for each child. It does not even cover a third of the babysitter' salary. Marguerite's lawyer scoffs, "It is totally ridiculous, insulting, we will demand much more, let the judge set the amount of support." "I am earning money as well," says Marguerite, "I can support my children, I want sole custody, the deed of the house in my name, and I want Pieter to pay for half of college tuition for each child." "You are making a huge mistake," says the lawyer. "I want to end this and put it behind me," replies Marguerite.

MARGUERITE DUVIVIER

In the end, it is what is agreed: $125 a month for each child, with visitation rights for Pieter. Marguerite does not want to deprive her daughters of seeing their father, who is intellectually brilliant and can enrich their lives. Pieter is granted visiting rights for one evening a week, every other weekend from Friday night to Sunday afternoon, alternating major holidays, and one month of summer vacation each year. Pieter and Pamela marry the day after the divorce becomes final.

The babysitter left last night and has not returned. She arrives early in the morning and she tells Marguerite that she is leaving; a car is waiting for her in the street. She quickly packs her clothes and kisses the children goodbye. What is she doing? wonders Marguerite. What will happen to her? What did she get herself into? And what will I do without a sitter? She takes the children to school; they are safe there for the day. She contacts an agency; "We can send someone well qualified right away," she is told.

A young woman is engaged to meet the children at the end of the school day and bring them back home. Marguerite takes them to school herself in the morning before heading to work. Anne likes the young woman, but Eve tells her mother that she does not. She does not explain why; "I do not want that woman in our house," she says. Marguerite listens to her daughter, a serious and bright young girl who has never been difficult nor demanding, and she lets the sitter go.

When she calls her parents, she tells them that she lost her babysitter. Maximilien knows a young nurse who is available and would be perfect for the job. For the next couple of weeks, Marguerite scrambles with childcare. It is nice to be by herself with Eve and Anne in the house in the evening, but the girls are too young at nine and six to be by themselves during the day; she needs a sitter to be with the children. She anxiously awaits the arrival of the young nurse, hoping that it will be a good fit.

CHAPTER 41

The mother and children have gone to the supermarket on Saturday. Marguerite forgot to lock the side door, and when they return, they find a diminutive young woman and suitcases in the living room. "I am Louisa, your new babysitter," says the woman. "The door was unlocked."

Louisa is godsent. The young Belgian nurse is chatty, hardworking; she is wonderful with the children who both like her. The little family has found a new equilibrium; Marguerite and Louisa are supportive of each other. Louisa, an orphan, had been raised by an older sister and her abusive alcoholic husband, taken advantage of, essentially raising her young nieces, her earnings confiscated by her sister and husband. She receives a salary from Marguerite, but she is more of a family member than an employee and she is grateful to have been able to leave an abusive situation. For Marguerite, it is the end of a long, precarious time of worry and loneliness. Marguerite is thirty-two years old, Louisa is twenty-two.

Marguerite was holding on by sheer willpower. Now that she has secured a staff position and has a responsible live-in babysitter, she can afford to become depressed. The depression hits her hard, she has never felt like this before. She cries, she wonders what happened to her, what happened to her marriage, what will happen to her children?

"You need to take a break, go away," suggests Louisa, "take a week's vacation, I will be fine here with the children. You should go and rest, you need it."

The young mother goes to Guadeloupe at Club Med for a week. She sleeps, she lies on the beach, she swims. Within days, two young men approach and befriend her. They find her attractive. I still am desirable, she thinks, I was just so tired and anxious. I will be okay, I am strong. It is healing to be in the sun, to banter; she regains strength and equilibrium. She returns home in better spirits, eager to be with her daughters, to work and to progress in her career.

She finds it is much easier to raise her children without Pieter. There is no tension in the house, no disagreement, no tiptoeing around a difficult man. They can be happy. The little house is comfortable; each child and the mother have a separate bedroom on the second floor, and the babysitter has a room and a bathroom on the first floor. There is privacy. The yard is wonderful. Marguerite starts planting a Japanese garden, she finds solace and great joy in nurturing her garden.

The weekday's visits of the children with their father last just a few weeks; "It is too complicated, I am too busy," says Pieter. The alternating weekend visits happen as long as Pieter is in town. He has taken and passed the oncology and infectious diseases medical boards in addition to the internal medicine and hematology boards. He often travels to do research, with Pamela acting as his assistant. They go away for long periods of time to foreign countries, Indonesia, China. When Pieter has the children on the weekend, Marguerite is forlorn. She is lost without her daughters, she misses them terribly.

Eve and Anne do not talk about the visits to their father, and Marguerite asks no questions. She is certain that they do not share information at their father's house either. They are naturally discreet and Marguerite marvels at her daughters. They are smarter, more intelligent than I am, more socially adept, she reflects. I sometimes talk too much, speak before I think, but not so my daughters. They have emotional elegance, innate wisdom.

She has not told them of the difficult divorce negotiations, how little financial support she gets from Pieter. She is careful not to criticize their father. It would hurt and confuse the children; she loves them too much to do so.

She finds out that Pieter and his wife bought a house in the South End; then Pieter sells that house and buys another beautiful one in Jamaica Plain. Marguerite is admitted to the huge designer kitchen when she comes to collect her daughters. A couple of years later Pieter moves to a third house, a mansion near where Marguerite lives. Her little house does not come close to those of her former husband. He must be spending all of his earnings, thinks Marguerite.

Pieter climbs the academic ladder, he becomes full professor, he publishes hundreds of scientific papers.

CHAPTER 42

Zilda visits for a couple of weeks at Christmas the year of the divorce. She brings many gifts, embraces her granddaughters; she enjoys cooking, shopping with her daughter. She appears relaxed and tells Marguerite that she and Maximilien spend the week at the main house in Aimeries, weekends at the farm; she often goes to the villa on the French Riviera and spends several weeks there by herself. She is happiest being alone at her French house.

Zilda is secretly writing her life story for her granddaughters to read after she dies. In her journal, after the visit to the United States, she writes: "Marguerite made me sleep on the floor, I almost caught my death, the house was cold."

Marguerite, who is struggling with money, had bought a comfortable, but low, folding bed for her mother, who did not sleep on the floor; she seemed happy during the visit, but she is critical of Marguerite in her secret journal.

"We have less money now," she tells her daughter during her visit: "the factories are receiving fewer orders." "Your father is still working but he is aging, he has fewer patients. He has retired from teaching at the nursing schools, and he gets two pensions, which really helps; the three houses are expensive to maintain. We are thinking of selling our main house, your father will retire, and we will rent an apartment. We still would have the villa in France and the farm."

She continues: "We rarely see Marie. The second adopted girl is causing a lot of problems."

"Maxine is having a love affair with an Egyptian man, though love has nothing to do with it," declares Zilda, "it's all about sex. Maxine is so difficult and demanding that we are avoiding her, but we are worried about our grandsons."

"Your sister has gained a lot of weight, you would be stunned, she has an enormous ass," says, with perverse satisfaction, the mother who was always concerned about the size of her own behind.

A few months later, Lucien, her fiancé in medical school, calls Marguerite.

"I found out that you are divorced," he says.

"How did you get my phone number?"

"It's on the list of our medical school students, I also have your address."

"How did you find out that I am divorced?"

"The grapevine," he responds, "you are collaborating with a urologist at your medical school who is doing a study with the chief of urology at my hospital here in Brussels. Your colleague sang your praises; he says you are a superb pathologist."

Marguerite has long suspected that Lucien was keeping an eye on her. "I want to see you," says Lucien. They get into a long conversation. Lucien got married just a few years ago to a much younger Jewish woman from Venezuela he met in Israel. He has two young daughters. "I went to Columbia University," he says, "and I got a PhD there. I am now a chief of service at the university hospital in Brussels. I do a lot of research and travel to the States frequently. May I come visit you?"

Marguerite is curious, she agrees to see him if he comes on a weekend when her daughters are with their father. He visits for a few hours, and they talk about their lives. They part on good terms, as friends.

A few weeks later, Lucien calls again from Belgium. "I am coming to New York for a seminar in a few weeks," he says. "Do you want to join me and spend a weekend together?" Marguerite is a free woman, it is a weekend when Pieter is taking his daughters, and she agrees to meet Lucien. They end up in bed; Lucien still has a big sexual appetite, Marguerite has not had sex or affection for a long time. "You are skinny," says Lucien, "my wife has more curves than you."

They part at the airport, they do not have plans to meet again. For Marguerite, this was a stroll down memory lane, an interlude. She is a little sad, but she knows that she made the right choice years ago when she broke up with Lucien. He is a very bright and successful man but he cheated on his wife with her, he is yet another unfaithful man, he is domineering. They live an ocean apart, they each have a family.

It is early morning about two weeks later when her phone rings. "It's me," says Lucien, "I call to warn you that my wife is trying to reach you. She knows that you work in a hospital in Boston, and she is systematically calling all the hospitals there to find you. She is threatening to take our children away and return to Venezuela if I meet with you again. I keep telling her the encounter meant nothing and we are in different countries separated by the Atlantic Ocean, but she is adamant that she wants to talk to you."

Marguerite is not pleased to hear that the encounter was meaningless, though she knows she would not want to meet again. What a jerk, she thinks, he must have told his young wife of our encounter in New York. He is hurting her, and he should just make things easier for her and give her my phone number.

It takes five days for the young wife to discover Marguerite's home phone. She calls and asks Marguerite to swear that she will never see her husband again. Marguerite feels sorry for her and admires her courage. "I have no intention of seeing Lucien again or corresponding with him," she says, "you have my word."

The medical school class has a reunion in Brussels every year. Marguerite always receives an invitation, and Lucien writes or calls every time to ask if she intends to attend. "I regret that I cannot," she responds each time.

Marguerite is applying for American citizenship for her herself and her children. On the day of examination, she is present with Eve and Anne; the official questioning her asks: "Have you or your children engaged in prostitution?" He looks directly at Eve and Anne, his eyebrows raised. Uncertain, they look at Marguerite. Marguerite is furious and shocked. They are granted citizenship and all three attend the swearing-in ceremony.

The mother and daughters and the babysitter Louisa settle into a peaceful life. The children go to school, they both excel. Anne's poems and stories are published in the elementary school newsletter; her teacher says she is unusually talented. Eve has already decided to go to medical school. She is very serious; Anne has a lighter disposition.

Marguerite leads a busy, organized life. She teaches pathology residents, medical school students at the university, she has a heavy workload of cases to diagnose, she conducts research, publishes papers.

At home, she spends time with her daughters, they talk at mealtimes. They go for long walks, to the swimming pool, the library. The children are avid readers. They never need help with schoolwork. Eve and Anne are organized, and homework is easy for them.

Marguerite does housework with the sitter, tends her Japanese garden. She is careful with money, systematically prepays her mortgage a little every month. She is afraid of being without money again. She has discovered the Goodwill store, and she buys clothing there for herself and her children. She and the sitter, Louisa, shop at Filene's Basement, where everything is cheap and automatically decreases in price every week. One can find designer clothes there at bargain prices. Marguerite is said to be the best dressed in her department.

She buys a few shares of stocks whenever she has some extra money. She keeps herself informed. Her small portfolio grows slowly. She craves security; she needs to save for her daughters' college education.

Pieter takes Eve and Anne for a month of summer vacation for the first time in 1975. The babysitter went to Belgium for the month. Marguerite is by herself, bereft, unmoored, lost without her daughters. Pieter and Pamela have rented a house on Cape Cod, and she decides to drive there, hoping to catch a glimpse of her children. When she gets to the beach, she sees Eve, Anne, Pamela, and Pieter nearby. The girls see her and run over to hug her. Pieter approaches, he is furious. He looms over her and threatens to sue for violation of the divorce agreement. His anger is palpable. Marguerite retreats, she is very afraid. He is nasty, she thinks, why is he so angry with me? It takes days before she can calm down.

The children are out of school for two months in the summer, Pieter has them for a month; Marguerite brings her daughters to Belgium to stay with her parents for the other part of the summer. There, they speak French—it is important that they remain bilingual; Marguerite returns to work first, and the girls fly home to the United States by themselves later. On each visit to Belgium, Marguerite visits Madame Leonce, her old landlady.

She learns from her daughters that Frank, her father-in-law, has died of a heart attack. "He was found in a ditch," says Eve, "he was walking on a dirt road in the countryside." Frank was only fifty-seven-year old. He was nice to her, she was fond of him. She wonders if Pieter will also die of a heart attack at a young age. He was a heavy smoker when younger.

CHAPTER 43

Marguerite identifies a couple of renal biopsies that do not conform to known diseases. She reviews the cases from the archives and finds three more that have been misdiagnosed. The previously unrecognized variant has critical implications for prognosis and treatment, and she decides to publish the cases.

Bob, Pamela's ex-husband and the nephrologist of record on one of the cases, immediately recognizes the importance of the findings. He tries to bully Marguerite into letting him be the first author on the scientific paper; "I am more senior, well known" he argues. "It is my discovery," she responds. Being the first author on such a publication is crucial for academic advancement, and in Marguerite's opinion, this will be a significant paper. Bob has some of Marguerite's documentation and photos of the cases, and he already has started a first draft of the paper. Afraid that he will use them without her permission, she retrieves the documents from his office.

The paper is published and is widely quoted, she is the first author. Bob grabs the opportunity to lecture and present the data at national meetings. It becomes his hallmark, but Marguerite does not mind. She does not want to present data at medical conferences. It is repetitive and time consuming, it requires travel that would take her away from her daughters. She is first author on the publication, her contribution is official. She becomes an assistant professor at the medical school.

She belongs to a group of renal pathologists who regularly meet to discuss cases and share information. She is respected. A colleague is editing a textbook of renal pathology, and Marguerite is asked to collaborate on a chapter in the book. It is peer reviewed and she receives accolades; "The best chapter in the book," says a reviewer. A personal letter comes for the United Kingdom praising her contributions. "By far the best chapter," says the letter, "thank you for your discovery and clear system of classification."

Marguerite has also become the recognized expert on prostatic and bladder pathology in her department. She does not want to be that person who has expertise on only one disease, one organ, and makes a career out of that expertise. There are several subjects that interest her.

She reads a scientific article from a well-known pathologist at the Mayo Clinic, describing two cases of what the author describes as a very rare finding in prostatic biopsies. Not so, she thinks, I have seen several cases here at my hospital. She corresponds with the Mayo Clinic specialist, sends him documentation of a couple of her cases, and tells him that she has many more. The specialist travels from Minnesota to Boston with a fellow, to review Marguerite's cases, and an important scientific publication ensues. This time, Marguerite is the senior author, but not after a long battle of will regarding authorship. Being the senior author on a publication indicates expertise and leadership.

At times, she feels that her professional life is a constant lonely battle. She recognizes important findings; others, always men, try to bully her and appropriate her discoveries.

She has two accomplished daughters, her career is progressing well, but love and companionship are missing from her life. She is thirty-five years old, she would like to have a relationship. She has gotten used to being alone every other weekend, and she tries to go out and meet people.

She signs up for a service that matches singles. It is expensive. She does not meet a single man she finds remotely attractive or interesting. She wasted money.

Invited to a party given by a younger resident, she walks into a crowded room with loud music and much drinking. She sees a gorgeous-looking man and goes to sit next to him. He smiles, introduces himself. "I'm Carl," he says. After a few minutes, he takes her hand, and they sit quietly. It feels good to hold someone's hand. "It is too loud in here," he says, "let's go out for a walk." The younger man is very handsome, he is slow talking. "I'm from the Midwest," he says, "a graduate of the Harvard School of Design. I am looking for a position in Boston."

Initially, Marguerite is interested in the man, who attaches himself to Marguerite. During the summer month when Eve and Anne are on vacation with their father, they travel together to Germany. Carl wants to visit public housing there, study the architecture. But there are things about him that bother Marguerite. He has no finesse in bed; sex is one sided with no regard for Marguerite's needs. He is slow talking and that irritates her. He is having a hard time finding and keeping a job. She has to loan him money when his car breaks down.

Carl and his sister visit at Marguerite's house, and the sister leaves marijuana on the dining room table for her brother. Marguerite is furious. She has never used drugs and she has kept her daughters safe from drug use. I am in another bad relationship, she reflects. What am I doing wrong? She makes an appointment with a psychologist to try to clarify her discontent, her uncertainties.

The first meeting with the therapist is not rewarding; she signs up for another session. This time she talks about how Carl irritates her, and she says: "The poor guy has a hard time keeping a job." "You are condescending and arrogant," exclaims the psychologist. Is a psychologist allowed to say something like that? Judge his patient? Marguerite does not return for additional sessions, though it helped bringing her doubts and feelings in the open. Yes, she realizes, I may be arrogant. I look down on Carl, he is not good enough for me, it is not a good relationship, I am feeling used, and she breaks up with him. She finds great relief when she makes the decision. Carl shows up at her house and calls several times, she tells him to stop.

Marguerite realizes that she may be looking for someone who does not exist. She needs an intelligent man, an interesting, healthy man, a man she can respect, decisive but not domineering. A man who is financially independent and secure. A man who can be tender and attentive, a man who will be faithful. She does not want a relationship with a man who has children; being a stepmother does not interest her.

I never will meet such a person, she realizes. Who would want to marry an independent, opinionated, set-in-her-ways, divorced woman with two children and such high standards?

Louisa wants to stay in the United States and find work as a nurse. She has met a young man and decides to move in with her boyfriend. Eve and Anne are twelve and nine years old. Marguerite initially hires babysitters, but they do not work out well.

Eve is more mature at twelve than the two eighteen-year-old girls who come babysit. "I can take care of my sister when we get back from school," she argues. "I do not like the babysitters." Marguerite is distressed to find the house in disarray, dirty dishes in the kitchen when she comes back home. The sitters are not tidy.

The school is five hundred yards away on the next street in a safe suburban neighborhood. The children are responsible, and Marguerite agrees to let them come home by themselves. For a few years, the mother calls home precisely at three o'clock, to check on the children. She is tense from the time school gets out until she gets back home, but there are no incidents. The two girls do their homework and keep the door locked until their mother returns.

CHAPTER 44

"We have news," says Marguerite's mother at the next phone call to Belgium; "We are selling the main house. It needs a lot of repairs, the park is difficult to maintain. We no longer have the cash to take care of it properly." Zilda and Maximilien rent an apartment in another town, in the same building where Maxine is also renting while building her house.

Maxine's love affair with the Egyptian man has ended. She now lives with a Yugoslav, the stocky, muscular, physical education teacher at the high school where she teaches art history. Zilda and Maximilien abhor the man, a boor, they find him loud and obnoxious; he is not treating Maxine's two boys well, he bosses them around, and the grandparents are worried. They hope to mitigate the situation by living in the same building. Maybe the boys can find refuge with their grandparents.

Instead, the relationship with Maxine worsens. She stands by her lover, and the children are caught between their mother and their grandparents. The older boy sides with his mother and is rude to Zilda and Maximilien. The younger, a smart and sweet young boy bullied by his mother's lover, is emotionally withdrawn. He keeps to himself, avoids confrontations.

"Maxine is crazy about sex," says Zilda; "Your sister is just like my younger sister."

Maxine is slowly building a small house on the lot she bought a couple of years ago. She builds the house in stages, and she adds to it when she has sufficient money.

At the farm, Zilda and Maximilien discover that Maxine has installed a padlock on the door of the bedroom she usually occupies, with a sign saying: "Private Property". They are aghast, speechless. The farm and the bedroom belong to them, not to Maxine.

Maxine is convinced that the farm will eventually be hers. Her older son loves the property, he likes to work on old cars and is mechanically gifted. He uses the barn to work on his projects. He comes to the farm to work in the barn and leaves without greeting his grandparents, which upsets them greatly. Maxine dreams of leaving the farm to her son.

"Marie never visits at the farm," she tells her parents, "and Marguerite lives in the US, so, of course the farm will be mine when you die." She is callous, takes no note of her parents' feelings. "It is obvious, logical," she goes on, "Hurlebise is my patrimony."

Once, while Zilda and Maximilien are staying at the farm, Maxine, her lover, and the two boys come to spend the weekend. They come frequently, unannounced, eat all the food, do not clean after themselves. Maxine views the place as hers and she is not tidy. The Yugoslav enters the den, a fire is lit in the fireplace. The room is lovely, warm and cozy, it smells of burning wood. Maxine's lover sits in Maximilien's favorite armchair, reclines, spreads out his legs, and says: "Ah, it feels so good to be in my own house." The parents are again stunned, outraged.

It is not a good weekend for Maximilien. Zilda has severely trimmed his beloved cotoneaster at the corner of the farm building; "It was getting much too big," says Zilda. "You had no right to demolish it," replies Maximilien; "It was my plant, it was so beautiful." He is angry, sad. He does not speak to Zilda for a week.

They resolve to sell the property in the near future. They do not want to leave it to Maxine. For now, they are still using it, and they do not want open warfare that might hurt their grandsons, but their mind is set.

Zilda is determined to cut all contact with Maxine, the child she favored when young. Maximilien has become afraid of his daughter, a young female embodiment of himself. Her hands on her hips, a virago in an aggressive stance, she makes demands and orders him to pay for improvements of the property; she asks for money to complete the building of her own house. Maximilien is getting old and does not have the funds, energy, or desire to oblige her. He gets very upset when Maxine comes to him with her demands, and at times, Zilda is afraid that he is having a heart attack.

Marie is largely absent from her parents' and sisters' lives. Ashamed, she is hiding the fact that Jacques is now regularly beating her when he is drunk. She has had to make a couple of visits to the emergency room. The nurses there recognize her and say, "It's you again, poor Madame Marie." Her own life has many echoes of her mother's.

Jacques tried to rape her after a late evening of particularly hard drinking. Marie ran to the garage and locked herself in her car to escape the assault. She is deeply Catholic, divorce is not an option, and she does her best to hide the abuse from her children and family.

The balance of power has shifted in Zilda's marriage. Maximilien no longer is the powerful, muscular man she married. He no longer teaches, he has stopped practicing medicine. He is no longer planting trees. Neither he nor Zilda has cultivated friendships, and they are largely dependent on each other. Zilda is a wonderful cook, she takes care of the farm and the French villa, the rented apartment. Younger by seven years, she still has the energy to clean, do laundry, but she complains to Marguerite that she is getting old and tired.

"Your father gets on my nerves," she says. "He sits in his armchair and waits for lunch and dinner. He drinks a lot of whisky every night. He has a couple of teeth that need to be removed but he is a coward, and he is afraid to go to the dentist. He has bad breath. He is not paying attention to me, he thinks that I am his maid."

"Your mother is demanding sex," says Maximilien in another phone call. "She is acting crazy, I am impotent, there is nothing I can do. Last week, she accused me of being a pedophile." His voice is trembling.

Marguerite is silent for a few heartbeats—she would prefer not knowing those details of her parents' lives. She now is the one they are turning to with their problems. They each need to talk to someone, confide. They both are unhappy, and Marguerite is the only one they can talk to. "You are not a pedophile," she tells her father, "try to ignore Mother if you can." "I will come visit in a few weeks," she tells them. "We can talk then."

Just before her trip, Marguerite receives a phone call from Belgium. A man introduces himself and says that he was Madame Leonce's lawyer. "She has died," he says, "and she left you money.

I will not know exactly how much money you will receive until we settle her estate. She left gifts to several people."

A day later, she gets another call. This time a man introduces himself as a jeweler in Brussels. "Madame Leonce had commissioned and designed a ring for you," he says. "I have the sapphire and diamond ring waiting for you; could you pick it up on your next visit to Brussels? It has a 4.3-carat cabochon sapphire surrounded by twelve perfect diamonds. Madame Leonce loved you. It was a surprise for your next visit."

Marguerite would never have dreamed that her old landlady had named her in her will. For years, she visited her old friend every time she returned to Belgium, she faithfully called and wrote to the lonely old woman out of affection and a sense of duty. She is stunned.

In the capital, she finds Madame Leonce's jeweler. The ring is huge, gorgeous, the diamonds are flawless, the sapphire has a deep rich blue color. Marguerite is touched, emotional.

Driving from Brussels, she arrives at her parents' apartment. She has never seen it before. It is a big place with a large entryway. The oak, custom-made bookshelves installed over forty years ago in Maximilien's office in their big house in Aimeries have been dismantled and reinstalled in the apartment's entryway. "I didn't know you kept the bookshelves," says Marguerite. "They were too beautiful to leave at the old house," states Zilda.

The apartment is very nice; Zilda always had good taste in decorating. "We kept what we liked the best," says the mother, "we sold all the big paintings, the heavy furniture." The antique bijar rug that Zilda gave as a housewarming gift to her mother thirty-five years ago is also there, in the living room.

Marguerite listens to her parents talk. One at a time they complain bitterly about each other, but there is very little that she can do. The parents complain but do not accept suggestions.

Marguerite sees Maxine and her nephews. She is Maxine's oldest son's godmother, and she gives him a very generous gift of money. The next day, she is sitting at the dining room table with her parents; they just finished dinner. Maxine enters the apartment, she is very agitated, and without saying good evening, or asking how her parents are, she starts a tirade: "I just came back from the farm," she says, looking directly at her father, her hands on her hips. "The fence along the long driveway to the farm is sagging, you have to replace it immediately, you are not taking good care of the farm. I do not want to inherit a property with problems."

Maximilien swears profusely, he is red and sputtering. Zilda tells him to calm down, making him angrier. Marguerite intervenes: "Maxine," she says, "don't you see that you upset Father?" Maxine storms out after a few choice words about the sister who lives in the US and never takes care of her parents. How does she dare to say anything?

"This is what we face all the time," sighs Zilda, "we are at a loss about your sister. What happened to her? She was a such a sweet, fun-loving little girl."

Marguerite has some theories about what happened, but she keeps them to herself. It would upset her parents to be told that Maxine was overprotected and coddled growing up. Out of the fear that her long-ago proteinuria could have adverse effects, she was indulged in all her whims. And she has Maximilien's personality.

Ten minutes after Maxine storms out, Marguerite's godson walks in. He has the money that Marguerite gave him in his hand, and he throws it on the table without a word, turns around and leaves the apartment.

Her parents are difficult, Maxine is impossible. Marguerite feels powerless to help her family. She does the best she can for the next few days, but she is happy to return home. She does not see Marie nor her children. Marie is hiding, too busy to meet.

CHAPTER 45

Marguerite divides her time between two hospitals; her expertise in urology pathology is recognized. She is needed in both places.

A new cytology technique intrigues her: instead of doing biopsies of suspicious lesions, a thin needle is used to aspirate cells from the abnormal areas. It is called the fine needle aspiration technique. The patient is spared surgery or open biopsy, and the diagnosis can be made immediately by looking at cells spread on glass slides. A clinician can quickly perform the procedure in the clinic, or a radiologist is enlisted to obtain the cells under X-ray guidance. Therapeutic decisions are made faster.

As all anatomic pathologists, Marguerite has had some training in cytology, but she is not proficient.

Cytology is the microscopical review of cells spread out on a glass slide. The best known example is the Pap smear, the examination of cells from the uterine cervix, which has saved countless lives.

Marguerite attends an intensive, two-week-long, course in cytology in Baltimore; Louisa comes to stay with the two girls, fifteen and twelve. The course is spectacular. She is learning by leaps and bounds. Back at home, she studies textbooks and offers to take responsibility for signing out the cytology specimens at one of the hospitals where she works and can consult with an old, experienced pathologist. She sits for the cytopathology boards examination and easily qualifies. She has become the only board-certified cytopathologist at both hospitals where she works, and at the medical school.

One morning, Anne, a sixth grader, has already left for school. Eve, who usually takes the school bus to the high school, is in the shower. Marguerite is about to leave and lock the door when she hears a frightening scream. She runs to the first floor bathroom. Eve is on the floor of the small shower stall, her leg appears broken. Marguerite turns off the water, covers her daughter with a towel, and rushes to call 911. She is frantic, her daughter has not stopped screaming. When the medics arrive a few minutes later, they immediately give a morphine injection and Eve finally stops her cries.

The bathroom is tiny; the shower stall is narrow and its glass door is facing away from the bathroom door. The medics are not able to maneuver the stretcher, and they eventually stick it out the window. Sedated, strapped on the stretcher, Eve is unaware of the difficulties. The ambulance takes her to the nearby hospital, Marguerite follows in her car. "The knee is dislocated," she is told, "we will reset it, then take X-rays; there does not appear to be a fracture." Marguerite returns home with a sleepy daughter, whose leg is in a cast; she will have to stay home for a few days, be driven to school, picked up. It is not an easy time for the little family. Marguerite shudders: what would have happened if she had already left the house? It is yet one of the most stressful and disturbing events of her life and she thinks of it frequently. Her daughters are sacred, precious, she fears for them.

In high school Eve, who is fluent in French, opts to study Spanish. The school has a student exchange program and Eve travels to a family in Venezuela, to be immersed in the language. Back home, she wins the state's best student in Spanish award. She is still intent on studying medicine; she wants to be an internist like her father. She already knows which college she wants to apply to, her path is decided, and Marguerite has no input.

Eve has gained weight, she seems depressed at times, she dresses in black, wears a black hat. When Marguerite tries to probe and asks her daughter if she wants to talk, see a psychologist, Eve refuses. She stays by herself in her bedroom. She works at the local supermarket as a bagger. "I like to work there," she says. Her grades do not suffer, and there is little that Marguerite can do except to worry and say that she loves her daughter. The mother, a doer, is powerless to help; it is a difficult, anxious period.

Anne is very social, she likes to play in the yard with friends, she too remains an excellent student, and as soon as she reaches the age when she can work, she looks for a part-time job; first she works at the Gap at the mall, then as a salesgirl at a local pottery store. My daughters are motivated thinks Marguerite, I don't have any input in their schooling or extracurricular activities. And she is glad, her professional life is so busy, there are diagnoses to make, papers to write, students to teach, a house to take care of.

At a hospital she just joined half-time, she is ordered by her chief of service to review and diagnose cases from another hospital; he tells her that she will be paid for the extra work. She welcomes the additional income. From half-time, she is offered a full-time position a few months later. It would simplify her life, travel between institutions is time consuming; the salary, benefits and security of a full-time position at that hospital, and the range of cases, are very attractive. She agrees and resigns from her other half-time position.

As a fulltime pathologist, Marguerite will no longer be allowed to do side work for additional pay. It is against the by-laws of the hospital. Her chief there says to ignore the rules. "I cannot," says Marguerite, "when I become full time, I can no longer handle your cases from the other small hospital." "Then, I will not make you full-time says the chief."

There is no security for-part time employees, fewer benefits and vacation time. Marguerite hires a labor lawyer to negotiate with the chief, but he is adamant that she will not be made full time unless she continues to do side work for him.

She is anxious, stressed, alone. She wants, needs, the position that was offered, and she does not want to break the rules. She is resentful that she was made false promises. She is again facing difficulties and unfair pressure, another battle to fight, and this one is important for financial and security reasons. The hospital has a Human Resources officer who can give advice. She goes to him and explains the situation. He listens and says that he will get back to her.

Shortly after, she is called to a meeting of several administrators and chiefs of services. She tells them she was promised a full-time position but that in order to get it, she would have to do unsanctioned side work, and she refused. She is asked by one member of the committee if her chief has ever made any sexual advances or inappropriate comments. "No, he has not," she replies. She does not say that the chief made her keep his dog when he went on vacation. It sounds too petty, though she was very annoyed at the time.

The chief of pathology is investigated for his illegal side activities. It is also discovered that he is conducting HIV research in his laboratory without official approval, oversight, and adequate safety measures, and he is fired.

Marguerite is expecting to be given the full-time position, but nothing is said. She goes to the Chief of Staff to ask when she will be notified. "We are not bound by offers and promises made by a former employee," she is told. Her lawyer intervenes and threatens to sue.

Marguerite is made full-time soon after. But she is not well regarded by the administration. She threatened to sue the hospital. Whistleblowers are not treated kindly. Marguerite is heartsick, it has been several hard and stressful weeks. She receives a large bill from the lawyer who represented her.

CHAPTER 46

Marguerite, finally a full-time employee and the chief of the cytology department, wants to introduce the fine needle aspiration technique. The clinicians are interested, a radiologist is enlisted, he is very enthusiastic. The little laboratory is a happy place; there is great energy and enthusiasm, and the clinicians are doing more and more fine needle aspirations. Marguerite is extremely busy; she still has a heavy load of renal biopsies, prostatic and other specimens to review, papers to write. She has been put in charge of the residency program and asked to write a manual for the pathology department in preparation for accreditation. No one else is willing to do it.

The hospital has hired a new chief of pathology, and he wants to build a large regional cytology laboratory, one that would process the specimens from multiple hospitals in New England. He is looking for a chief for the expanded laboratory. Marguerite, head of the current, smaller cytology section, is interested in the position—she is one of several applicants.

At the interview, the new chairman, a large imposing man, bluntly says to the small woman: "Your colleagues do not like you."

"I know," responds Marguerite, and, in one of those instances when she speaks before thinking, she adds: "They are jealous." The chief looks at her, eyebrows raised. "They are resent my successes. I am the only one who is board certified in cytopathology in the department; I have introduced a technique that decreased the number of biopsies my colleagues see, there is competition."

All her pathology colleagues are men; she privately considers them to be lazy, with blown egos.

She continues: "I have written several papers on cytopathology and fine needle aspirations. I am the department's expert in kidney, prostate, and bladder biopsies. I carry administrative duties. I have a great rapport with the clinicians," she adds. "You could ask the clinicians what they think of my services."

The chairman grills her with many difficult questions and after the long, draining interview, she gets to her car and starts crying, she feels defeated, desperately alone.

Two weeks later, she is offered the position and given great leeway in building the new cytology department. Her new chief is very supportive, and they get along well, after that first difficult interview. She creates the regional system he envisioned. Her laboratory is staffed by diligent, capable technicians. It is a wonderful place to be. She still has a general pathology workload and teaching to do, but asks to be relieved of handling renal biopsies. "I am too busy to handle them, and I have not kept up with new developments in the field," she says.

Marguerite is promoted to associate professor at the medical school, and her thirty-eighth birthday is near.

She decides to celebrate and give herself a big birthday party. She invites the people she likes to her house, medical colleagues and their wives, a few residents whom she finds intelligent and personable, a couple of friends from the neighborhood. The little house is filled with people; Eve and Anne mingle and are having fun.

The party runs late, it is one o'clock in the morning and only one person remains. His name is Lev, a resident in pathology. "I am staying to help you clean up," he says, and he works side by side with Marguerite to straighten out the house and do the dishes.

CHAPTER 47

Lev is Jewish, almost thirty years old, born and raised in New Hampshire. He is of medium height, slim, with reddish hair, not the type of man she usually notices. But she has been impressed by his work ethic. He is punctual, thorough, a perfectionist. His work is always well done, he works hard. He was just named resident of the year.

After medical school, Lev started a residency in surgery but was disappointed by the routine. He assisted in gallbladder surgeries a few times and asked the chief resident, "Is this all there is to it?" "Yes," said the chief resident, "it is pretty much the same every time." Lev transitioned to research for a year, then became a first year resident in pathology.

He does not have Marguerite's gift for diagnosing diseases at the microscope, but he is doggedly persistent. When shown abnormalities in a specimen and told this is representative of such-and-such disease, he wants criteria. "Why is this a specific tumor?" he asks. "Well, it looks like it," tells Marguerite, "it is like differentiating a Picasso from a Monet, you can tell the difference right away." Lev is not satisfied, he wants clear-cut criteria that he can check off.

Marguerite respects and admires his work ethic, his persistence. They have different abilities; he is analytical, she is visual.

It is easy for me, she thinks, it must be hard for him. She forces herself to describe findings in a way he can relate to and reproduce later. He is making great progress.

If only he did not have that big moustache and those sideburns, the longish hippie hair, thinks Marguerite, he could be attractive, I like his personality, his energy and drive. They become friends at work. Lev is reliable, pleasant, and he has a great sense of humor. He is impatient with sloppiness, demands perfection from himself and others.

A few months after the party, he asks Marguerite: "What are you doing this weekend?" "Not much," responds Marguerite, "some gardening and cleaning, my daughters are spending the weekend with their father." "I don't have plans either," says Lev, "would you like to go to the movies?" It becomes a routine, they do something together every other weekend. Lev says that he broke up with his nurse girlfriend; "She wanted to get more serious than I was ready for," he tells Marguerite.

One day, he takes Marguerite's hand to cross a busy street to the movie theater and he keeps holding it for a few minutes. He is good company, he finds interesting things to do, he behaves like a gentleman. Marguerite is enjoying the friendship, but Lev is more than eight years younger than she is; she is not sure where this is going and whether it should continue. They work in the same department, she is part of the senior staff, he is a first year resident, it is not wise to let the relationship progress. They are careful at work; she cannot show preferences.

Lev tells Marguerite that he will be away the coming weekend. "I am taking my ex-girlfriend to New Hampshire to look at the fall foliage," he says, "I promised her that I would take her there." "But you broke up," exclaims Marguerite; "Yes, but I promised months ago," responds Lev, "I do not break my promises." Well, this is interesting, reflects Marguerite, he keeps his promises.

Back from the weekend drive with the girl, Lev asks Marguerite if she would like to date. "I will not share," says Marguerite; "You will not have to," responds Lev. They take it easy, go on dates when Marguerite is free. "Why do you have the big mustache and sideburns?" Marguerite is curious. "My ex-girlfriend thought I looked good with them" is the reply. "I wonder how you would look without them," muses Marguerite.

The next time she sees Lev, he has shaved his mustache, shortened the sideburns, and is smiling broadly. Marguerite laughs, he is attractive, and he tries to please her.

They have been friends for months, done outings and gone to movies and shows. They work well together. Lev takes her hand regularly now, and has asked if he could kiss her. One day, he tells her, "I am falling in love with you, we could stay together." "I am not sure about this," Marguerite replies. "I am divorced with two teen daughters, I am not Jewish, and I have no intention of practicing any religion. What if you decide later that you want children?" "I do not want to have children, I never intended to father any."

After months of slowly getting to know each other, they finally find themselves in Marguerite's bedroom. Lev's pants come off so fast that Marguerite laughs. In bed, he is gentle and patient, attentive. There is a lot of tenderness, he smells good, his skin is warm. She feels at peace and cherished. Maybe this will last, it could work.

The money from Madame Leonce arrives. She has left Marguerite seventy-five thousand dollars, a huge sum. She can make needed repairs to the house.

The front bow window is sagging; "Termites," says the contractor. Marguerite installs a big picture window, siding on the house and a new roof. A deck is built at the back. She has repainted all the rooms one by one by herself. The ceilings are the hardest, but she can paint a room in a single Sunday if there are no distractions. The little house looks good, she will update the kitchen when she can afford it.

The next spring, Pieter calls: "I would like to take Eve and Anne on a six-week trip to China and Indonesia this summer," he says. "Pamela and I will conduct research there, I would cover all the costs, take care of the necessary vaccinations and visas." Pieter has contracted malaria on one of his research trips, and some exotic skin worm infection, but he promises to be extremely careful with his daughters. Eve and Anne, both in high school, are enthusiastic, and it is agreed.

CHAPTER 48

"Why don't we take a vacation together?" suggests Lev. "I have friends who are doing their annual canoe trip on the Allagash in the North Woods of Maine, we could join them for the two-week-long trip."

Marguerite has never canoed, but with experienced outdoorsmen along, she thinks that they will be safe, and she agrees to go.

It is an adventure, physically demanding, and she loves it. They camp at night in remote areas, sometimes they encounter pouring rain, and they get soaked a time or two. The men catch frogs and they eat roasted frog legs which are delicious.

At midmorning one day, they beach the canoes and Lev tells her they have to empty the boats of all luggage; "We are at the Churchill Dam," he says, "there is a portage. A truck will bring our belongings further down, on the other side." They get back in the canoe on the other side of the dam; "What is this roaring noise?" she asks. "Keep paddling," he yells. He does not tell her that they are about to enter the Chase Rapids. Lev has canoed before, he does a great job getting them through the Devil's Elbow, a difficult section of whitewater. "You could have warned me," says Marguerite. "I did not want to scare you," replies Lev.

One morning, they get up at dawn and pack the canoe to cross the Umsaskis Lake. "There is too much wind in the afternoon," they are told, "you have to get across by noon." The water is choppy, her arms and back are sore and tired, but it is exhilarating; she can do this. They are alone on the lake, the banks are barely visible. Lev and Marguerite are a good team, they work well together. "I want to travel," says Lev, "I want to go everywhere, on each continent. I like adventures." He has pushed Marguerite out of her comfort zone, and she enjoyed it thoroughly.

Eve and Anne return from their trip to Asia. Marguerite goes to the airport to meet them. They walk toward her, wave, they look happy, they are beautiful, tanned, thinner, they are wearing new clothes. "We had the clothes made to measure, overnight, in Hong Kong," they say; "Daddy bought each of us two outfits," explains Anne. "They were made from fabrics and patterns we chose." The two girls tell many stories. "Bali was the best, it is dreamily beautiful there. The beaches are stunning. The Forbidden City in Beijing is incredible, you should try to go visit. We walked on the Great Wall."

"In China, we were accompanied everywhere by officials, minders and translators, we were not allowed to deviate from a set itinerary. We took many long train trips, the trains were very uncomfortable, it was very hot. We traveled to the countryside. The people there had never seen white people before—we were treated like royalty, sat at interminable meals with inedible food. We survived on rice."

"Daddy and Pamela conducted research, they took blood samples from people, collected data. It was interesting but tiring, and we are happy to be back home."

Anne, who is enrolled in a photography class in high school, brings back gorgeous pictures from the trip, photos of small children, floating mosquito nets, luminous pictures of her sister walking on the beach in Bali. She is talented.

Eve is seventeen, Anne is fourteen years old. Marguerite finally introduces them to Lev. "I am dating him," she says, "we are serious about each other."

Eve is not pleased, she is reserved toward Lev; he is interfering with her family life, an intruder in their rhythm. Anne is receptive, she likes him, and she and Lev go together to lunch, to McDonald's; they interact well. They have the same sense of humor, they love jokes.

Lev has an older sister, married with two daughters younger than Eve and Anne. The sister and her husband are very wealthy, religious. They observe the Sabbath, all the religious Jewish traditions, they go to the synagogue. "I will not attend the synagogue if we stay together," says Marguerite to Lev. He reassures her, "I am not religious, I am not interested in any of the Jewish traditions."

Marguerite discovers that Lev has a temper; he does not tolerate incompetence, he is impatient, he gets mad at himself if he is not happy with his own work, and he can be upset for days. Marguerite does not like that aspect of his personality, and they argue sometimes. She talks to a friend, who advises: "He is not angry at you, he is angry at himself, let him cool off."

Nothing makes Lev angrier than talking to his parents. He does not get along well with them. He was a surprise, born when his mother was in her late forties, his father in his fifties. The mother is chronically depressed. Whatever love and attention the parents had to give were spent on their firstborn, the daughter. The father is often overwhelmed by his wife's depression and complaints; she has a litany of ancient resentments and imagined ills; both parents infuriate Lev.

He brings Marguerite to his parents' house in New Hampshire for the first time. "I warn you," says Lev as they are driving there, "my mother is not a good cook, she serves canned vegetables, we will be offered canned pineapple and store-bought angel cake, kosher wine."

When they arrive at the house, the parents are guarded, polite. Lev's mother, in her late seventies, is strikingly made up with heavy turquoise eye shadow and bright red lipstick and nail polish, she has an elaborate hairdo, she is agitated. Marguerite, who never wears makeup, is oddly fascinated. She walks into the living room with pale blue carpeting, a pale blue silk-covered sofa. She sits on the sofa, Lev seems nervous. "I was not allowed in the living room," he says, "we should move to the den."

The mother has prepared lunch. The chicken is overcooked, they are served canned peas, they are offered kosher wine. The wine is not good, Lev and Marguerite barely touch theirs and there is wine left in each glass. Lev's mother collects all the glasses and carefully transfers the contents back into the bottle. She serves angel cake and canned pineapple for dessert.

Lev shows his childhood bedroom to Marguerite; it is utilitarian, but there is a lovely small antique rug, which is damaged. "It came from my grandparents," says Lev, "if you like it, we could take it with us, get it repaired."

Seeing his parents always angers Lev; he drives too fast on the way back to Boston. "Slow down," says Marguerite, "you're scaring me." "I can't," says Lev, "I cannot stand my parents, their demands; seeing them brings back the memories of my childhood, my teen years, how they neglected me. They always favored my sister, she was the princess, I felt unwanted. My mother screamed at me when my cousin clogged the toilet. She is a crazy woman." He goes on: "She has never written a check in her life, my father has never taught her. I blame my father too. My parents left me alone for two months when I was thirteen," he adds. "My father needed complicated aortic surgery and they went for it to Texas."

Favoritism raises its ugly head again, reflects Marguerite silently. She is gaining an understanding of Lev's personality, why he always tries to please, to excel. Lev cannot stop talking. Marguerite lets him rant. What kind of woman waits for others to teach her things, she wonders to herself.

Marguerite is deep in thought; she too experienced favoritism, her mother did not seem to like her as much as her sisters, but she was her father's favorite; maybe there was a balance there? She let it go a long time ago. She turns to Lev in the car: "You are thirty-one years old," she says, "a physician, you have proven yourself. You should let go of your parents, forgive them, they probably did the best they could. Detach yourself. We are together now."

"I cannot forgive them," replies Lev.

"Then, you are wasting emotional energy," sighs Marguerite.

CHAPTER 49

Eve has applied to several colleges, all top schools. She decided on her own where to apply; the school counselor and her father gave her some advice. Marguerite had no input, she does not know how the American system works. The University of Chicago accepts her application. "It is a top school," says Lev, "congratulations. It really is a hard school to get into, it is on a par with the Ivy League schools of the East Coast, you should be proud."

She learns how to drive, Marguerite tries to teach her, but they end up arguing. Lev takes over the lessons, spends time with her practicing in the neighborhood.

Eve has not dated in high school. "I love Mel Gibson," she says, "I love his blue eyes." She has a picture of the actor in her bedroom. She is a late bloomer, thinks Marguerite, she will date in college.

Lev and Marguerite have decided to marry. They have dated for two years. He has finished his residency; he passed the anatomic pathology boards, has decided to become a dermatopathologist, a specialist in the diagnosis of skin diseases, and he is now working as a fellow at another hospital. With the age difference between them, it would have been awkward to be married and work in the same department. They have waited to announce their wedding until Lev moves to the other institution. Marguerite is accused of cradle robbing, of being a cougar; the unsolicited comments are uncomfortable.

She is older, she no longer knows what love is; they are compatible, life is fuller with him, more secure; he is supportive and affectionate, protective. It did not work out the first time in spite of the strong attraction. She and Pieter were too young, they were not suited. But she has no regrets. She has her two daughters. She hopes that this time, it is the right decision.

Lev has a fever; one side of his neck is painful, red, and swollen. The ENT specialist diagnoses a blocked duct of the parotid, the large salivary gland below the ear, and the gland has to be removed. It is a delicate, complicated surgery; he could end up with damage of the facial nerve coursing through the gland and paralysis of one side of the face. He has surgery at the hospital where he is training as a fellow. Marguerite visits every day. His parents, his sister, his colleagues at the same hospital do not visit. He is crushed by the lack of support, Marguerite is the only one who cares. Lev asks about moving in with her, they are getting married soon.

Eve is not happy about the decision. "You are almost eighteen years old, you are leaving for college in a few months," says Marguerite, "you will have your own life, your own career and relationships. I do not want to spend the rest of my life without companionship. I have been divorced for over eight years." Eve accepted her father's immediate remarriage after the divorce, why can't she

MARGUERITE DUVIVIER

accept her mother's? Anne is happy for her mother. She likes Lev, he is like a father to her, she has let him into her life.

When Lev tells his parents that he is marrying Marguerite, they are very upset. "She is not Jewish," they say, "she is divorced, much older, she has two teenage daughters, what are you thinking!" Lev's father offers him one hundred thousand dollars to break up with Marguerite; he refuses and does not tell Marguerite of the offer from his father. "You can gain a daughter or lose a son," he tells his father.

Zilda tells Marguerite that she will be coming to Boston to help find a wedding dress. She forgets that I do not like wedding dresses, thinks Marguerite, I did not want one the first time. But she is happy to see her mother and goes shopping with her. Marguerite settles on a red silk outfit, the only one she sees that she likes.

A very small wedding is planned for a Saturday in February. Lev's parents are upset again; Jews cannot marry on the Sabbath. The date is changed to the next day. Marguerite just turned forty years old, Lev is almost thirty-two; they are married on Valentine's Day. The new couple is honeymooning in Peru, they want to visit Lima, Cuzco, Machu Picchu.

Before they leave for the honeymoon, Eve takes Lev aside and says: "You have to take good care of my mother, watch over her, I am holding you responsible." "I will take good care of her," promises Lev.

Traveling with Lev is easy, he takes care of all the details, he prides himself on giving Marguerite a wonderful experience. When she gets altitude sickness in Cuzco, he leaves the hotel late at night to try to find a pharmacy. He comes back shaken; "It is very dark everywhere," he says, "I was followed in the streets, it was scary."

Back home after their honeymoon, Lev and Marguerite work hard. They have a plan—work and save all their vacation days, and go on a big trip every year.

Eve has decided that she will travel on her own this summer, backpacking in Europe before leaving for college. "I forbid you to go," says Marguerite, "it is too dangerous. If you go," the frightened mother threatens, "I will not pay your college tuition." It is not the right approach, Eve is her mother's daughter. "I will take a loan," she says, "Dad is paying for half anyway." She is undeterred.

She calls collect from Amsterdam one evening, it is around two in the morning there, she is very afraid. "I'm scared," she says, "I'm lost, and I do not have a place to stay. I am calling from a phone booth. What should I do?" What can Marguerite say? Her heart stops when her daughter calls; "Try to find a policeman, a police station," she urges, "stay where there are people around, do not go in deserted streets. Please call me back as soon as you can in the morning." Marguerite is both anxious and furious, powerless. How can Eve have put herself in such a position, and call her mother when there is nothing she can do? But Eve trusted her mother enough to call home and admit she needed help. Maybe, talking to her mother gave her a little bit of courage, reassurance. She calls again the next day, "I am safe, she says, I was so scared last night."

CHAPTER 50

Eve leaves for college. For Marguerite, it is a hard thing to see her daughter go, she is very sad. But there was tension between Lev and Eve; maybe the distance will smooth out the relationship. Eve does not call home until Thanksgiving. She has built a wall around herself, she does not confide. She suffered the most from the divorce; she has a hard time accepting her mother's remarriage. She has been solemn and serious, uncommunicative.

Anne continues to take photographs. She has a great teacher at the high school, and she spends extra time there, in the photography laboratory. She is taking close-up photographs of old rusting objects, old trucks, enlarges the color photographs. It is a strange subject, but the series of images is arresting, unusual. She finds the angle and the lighting that make ordinary objects appear mysterious.

Lucien has been calling Marguerite every few years. He usually calls to ask if she plans to come to Belgium for the annual medical school reunion. "I am not," she always says. "We had another child," says Lucien, "a little boy this time. My wife got pregnant after we met in New York." "I got remarried," shares Marguerite, "his name is Lev." There is a silence, then Lucien asks: "So, you finally married a Jew?" "I did," confirms Marguerite.

"I still have all the love letters you wrote to me when we were together," offers Lucien. "They are full of burning love." Marguerite laughs: "A different life, a long time ago, you should throw them away, your wife might find them." "I am keeping them," replies Lucien.

A couple of years ago, Marguerite introduced her daughters to horseback riding. They both had several lessons, and neither was interested in that sport. Marguerite tells Lev how much she loved riding horses when she was young; "There are stables around, would you like to try horseback riding?" Lev is interested. He takes lessons, and he is soon comfortable enough to go on long rides. Marguerite loves to gallop, she is relaxed with her horse; Lev is more cautious, tense, and the horse senses it. "Why do I always get the more difficult horse?" he asks. "It is not the horse, you are not relaxed, your horse senses it."

Anne spends a summer month in Belgium, at the farm with her grandparents, while Lev and Marguerite take their first horseback-riding vacation in Ireland. They land in Shannon, rent a car, travel through the country. They spend a week riding, going from inn to inn to castle along the Connemara Trail. The Irish-bred horses, the Connemara ponies, are swift and sure footed, they love to gallop. The guide is reckless, he takes the riders galloping over dunes riddled with rabbit holes. The horses jump over the tip of the dunes, gallop down on the other side, gallop to climb the next hill, they race each other. Marguerite is a little scared. On the beach, the horses gallop with abandon and she cannot slow down her mount. It is exhilarating. They swim in the sea with their horses. The riders strip to bathing suits, the saddles are taken off. With just the reins to guide their mounts, the riders advance in the surf until the horses lose their footing and swim. The water is cold, the horse is warm. The ponies love to swim, and they go far into the sea, until reined back in toward the beach.

In Dublin, Marguerite calls her parents. "Anne had a scooter accident," she is told; "she broke several bones in her hand, had an operation, and she has metallic rods that will have to be removed in a few weeks, in the States." Maximilien is upset with Anne. "She was flirting with the son of our maid," he says, "I do not want her to be friendly with that young man. Can you believe," he adds, "the son of our maid!" When the family gets back together in Boston, Anne explains: "The son of the maid is very bright, he wants to go to medical school." Marguerite says nothing—the boy is in Belgium, Anne is in the United States, it is normal for her to start flirting.

Eve is nearing the end of her first year in college, she is getting top grades as usual. Anne too, is doing extremely well in high school. The girls joke that they are smarter than their mother, they have their father's brain. "But I have more experience than you," counters the mother.

In the spring, Eve calls to say that she wants to come home to spend the weekend; can her mother pay for the airplane ticket? "Of course," says Marguerite, "we cannot wait to see you."

Eve arrives, and they settle on the back deck. "A group of people at the University of Chicago has made a list of gay people and are sending letters to the gay students' parents, outing them. I did not want you to get that letter," says Eve. "I came to tell you myself that I am gay, I am in a relationship with an African American woman."

Marguerite is stunned. She had never thought of that possibility, that her daughter could be gay. After a few seconds, tearing up, she tells Eve, "I will always love you no matter what." Lev echoes, "It does not matter to us." "Dad knows," tells Eve, "he has gay cousins, it seems to run in his family." That is news to Marguerite, and it hurts to know that Eve confided in her father first. The mother's immediate emotion is fear, fear for her daughter. It is 1984. Life is not easy for gay people, they are discriminated against, she will have to hide her relationships, how will she have children? Her life is going to be so difficult, she fears for her. Eve has always said that she wants to have children. She embraces her daughter. "I love you," she repeats, "I will always be there for you." "I will be fine, Mother," says Eve, "this is who I am." Lev hugs his wife, tells her that Eve is strong, she will build her own life.

The next week, at the mall, Lev takes Marguerite by the hand and makes her walk into Tiffany, the jewelry store. "I did not buy you an engagement ring," he says, "I want to buy you one now." Marguerite knows that he wants to console her, she lets herself be loved and Lev buys her a beautiful diamond solitaire. He is a sweet and generous man, she is lucky to have found him.

Anne turns seventeen in early summer. She is joining a bicycle-riding group spending several weeks touring in Nova Scotia; it is organized by the high school, supervised. The young people will camp every night. "It was very hard bicycling up the hills," she reports when she returns, "we all had to carry our packs and tent on the bicycles, I never exercised so hard."

She gets a bad report from the staff, for flirting and kissing a young participant. "We almost sent them back home," they say, "we separated them, we made them stop."

The young man lives in the next town, and Anne sees him on the weekend. Marguerite finds birth control pills on the bedside table in Anne's room. She wants me to know she is sexually active, realizes Marguerite, at least she is careful. Years later, her daughter confides: "My first boyfriend was very inventive, he bought a small tent, and he set it up in an out-of-the-way area. That's where we met. He's a ballet dancer now."

Anne is very attractive, men turn to look at her, she always is the prettiest girl in the room. Marguerite hopes that she will be careful and safe. She gives the usual advice; "I know all that, Mother," says Anne.

CHAPTER 51

There is news from Belgium. Maxine's house is finished, she is leaving the rented apartment and moving into her house.

Marie and Jacques have bought a large piece of land and are building a house too. It is located in farmland. "They are crazy," says Maximilien, "it faces a potato field, there is a dilapidated stable behind it and it is reached by an unpaved road. It is isolated, far from the town, but Marie wants to have a large garden. The second adopted Indian girl has run away from home."

Zilda and Maximilien still divide their time mostly between the French Riviera and the farm; they are thinking of leaving the apartment. Their health is okay, aches and pains from arthritis, Maximilien's teeth are in bad shape.

Lev has been a dermatopathologist for three years. "It's boring," he says, "I cannot envision diagnosing the same diseases day after day for the rest of my working life. I am thinking of going to business school." He is restless. He often says to Marguerite: "We are living in your house, it is not a house that I chose. Why don't you sell it, and we can buy another one, in another city, another state?" Marguerite temporizes; "Maybe later," she says. "The mortgage is paid off, the house is comfortable, in a great location, Anne is still in high school."

Marguerite loves her house, her beautiful Japanese garden, she put a lot of time and care into making her home pretty and comfortable. The kitchen has been redone. She needs security, control of her own money; the house is a valuable investment. In truth, she does not want to share ownership of a house with a man ever again. She would feel too vulnerable. She keeps her finances separate from Lev's. Lev is generous, they share the living expenses, but they have not joined their assets.

A few months earlier, Lev wanted to move to California for a new job. Marguerite said no, that is an uncertain scheme, and my career is here. She always tells Lev that he may go if he wants, that he is free to choose his own path, but that she makes decisions for herself. Now, Lev wants to apply to business schools in other states. "There are several good ones in Boston," says Marguerite. "If you want to go study elsewhere, I will wait for you here, you can commute, but I am not moving."

As Marguerite refuses moving to another house, another state, she knows that it may not be fair to Lev, but she protects her independence and her own livelihood. Lev knew her position when he married her. At forty years old, she had carved her own life, they were not two young people starting life together with nothing in their names. There is no guarantee that she could restart a career somewhere else, she has invested in her current position, built seniority; she does not want to depend on a man; she will have tuitions to pay. She cares for and supports Lev in every other way, she is his emotional anchor and she hopes that it is enough to sustain the relationship. He tends to get bored, wants to move and try new things. Who knows where it would end, how many moves they would make over the next few years?

Lev starts business school in Boston. He is using his savings for tuition and living expenses, never asks Marguerite for any financial support. He is very happy in business school, the happiest Marguerite has ever seen him. He loves to learn, closets himself in his upstairs office, spends hours solving difficult problems, never quitting until they are resolved. Curses are heard, some things hit the floor. He graduates with the highest honors.

As a physician with a master's in business administration, he immediately finds a position in a biotechnology start-up as the assistant to the CEO, gets promoted to chief medical officer within the year. He makes much more money than Marguerite ever made, but they keep their financial agreement in place. The house belongs to Marguerite, they share living expenses, they each cover their own cost of travel. Marguerite pays her daughters' college tuitions and expenses.

Lev likes to give financial advice to his wife, he wants to help. "I have an MBA," he says, "the success to investing is asset allocation. You only buy stocks, you should have bonds, gold, cash." "I am doing well," says Marguerite, "do what you want with your money, and let me do what I want with mine." Lev gets frustrated, Marguerite does not budge. She buys and holds her equity positions, rides the ups and downs of the stock market, she has saved quite a bit.

CHAPTER 52

The cytopathology laboratory Marguerite created is very successful. The chief who hired her to start the regional laboratory has retired and Marguerite misses him dearly. He had vision, he was fair, appreciated Marguerite's efforts and accomplishments.

His replacement is a difficult man, a poor administrator and a careless pathologist, though he leaves Marguerite largely alone to run her department. She has built a computer-based quality control system. The system is thorough and easy to use. A few keystrokes on the computer bring up a list of cases by diagnosis, or the list of all samples for a given patient.

A case of invasive cervical cancer is diagnosed by Pap smear cytology. The diagnosis is confirmed by biopsy, and a hysterectomy is performed. According to the protocol she has set up for the laboratory, Marguerite reviews all of the patient's previous cytology specimens to see if prior abnormalities have been missed. She is dismayed. The laboratory has reported progressively more severe Pap smear abnormalities over the last several years, all curable stages of disease, and the patient has never been biopsied. She could have been cured and spared the hysterectomy if the clinician had intervened earlier. A second similar case is seen six months later.

Another patient has a hysterectomy for invasive cancer that could have been entirely avoided. The same clinician was following the two patients.

Alarmed, Marguerite pulls out and reviews all the cases of abnormal Pap smears for the past ten years. It is a huge task. There are eight other women following the same course of progressively worse changes in their cervical specimens. They are all patients of the same clinician.

Marguerite talks with her new chief of service." It is not our problem," he says," it is a clinical issue, we should not be involved."

She tries to talk with the gynecologist responsible for the care of the patients; he throws her out of his office.

The gynecologist reports to the chief of surgery. Marguerite makes an appointment with the head surgeon; the tall man barely listens, paces in his office, he appears annoyed. Marguerite presses him for some reassurance that he will intervene but gets no answer. She is told to leave.

Her last resort is to speak to the chief of staff, a woman, who oversees the entire medical staff at the hospital; she will understand that this is an avoidable tragedy, thinks Marguerite. The chief of staff impatiently listens to Marguerite, who stresses that it is crucial to recall the women who have precancerous lesions, to reevaluate them.

The woman says, "It's water under the bridge, we are not recalling patients." Marguerite presses on, she is in disbelief; "You are a woman," she says bluntly, "and it is malpractice." "Water under the bridge," repeats the chief of staff who is getting angry at the challenge, "We will damage the hospital's reputation if this comes to light, if we recall the patients."

Marguerite feels physically and emotionally ill, she too is angry.

Her team, who also worked hard in the lengthy review of the cases, is incensed as well. "You have to go public, go to the *Boston Globe*, the city newspaper," they tell Marguerite. "It should be investigated and disclosed." "I will think about it for a week or two, get advice," she tells the cytotechnologists.

She has been a whistleblower before, instrumental in the firing of her chief a few years ago. She bitterly recalls the consequences, the emotional toll it had on her, the need for and the cost of hiring a lawyer. It was a painful time.

She learns three weeks later that the responsible clinician is retiring; a young female gynecologist has been hired to replace him. Marguerite was not given the courtesy of a follow-up conversation with either the chief of surgery or the chief of staff. As soon as the new gynecologist comes on board, she meets with her; the young doctor shares her concerns, she promises to recall the patients.

The entire episode has shaken Marguerite. Once again, her professional life has been difficult, disheartening, she is bitter and has lost trust in her superiors. It was particularly upsetting to witness the callousness of the chief of staff, a woman. Is it always going to be like that? she wonders.

CHAPTER 53

Anne is applying to colleges, and she is going to Costa Rica for a month of immersion in the Spanish language, as her sister did in Venezuela. Like Eve, she applies to top schools. She has an interview with a Princeton alumnus. She takes her portfolio of photographs with her. "The interview went really well," she reports, "the man liked my photos, we had a wonderful conversation." She is abroad when the acceptance letters arrive. She has been accepted at Princeton and Duke Universities.

Marguerite replies to Princeton that Anne will be attending. When she gets back home, Anne is very upset; "You should have waited for me to come back and decide," she says, "I was interested in Duke as well." "Princeton is prestigious," says Marguerite. "You are a lucky girl."

Princeton offers a week of camping and bicycling to freshmen, as a way to get acclimated before starting classes. "I would love to go," says Anne. It is quite expensive, and Marguerite asks Pieter if he would share the cost. He agrees; Marguerite pays the entire fee and waits for Pieter to reimburse her for half. She does not hear from him and finally sends him a note. "I changed my mind," writes Pieter, "this type of expense was not in our divorce agreement."

Lev and Marguerite bring Anne to Princeton, they hug her hard; the second child has left home, Lev and Marguerite are now alone together.

Eve is in her final year of college, she has applied to several medical schools. She graduates again with high honors. Lev and Marguerite travel to Chicago for the graduation. Never again, decides Marguerite. They are sitting far away, packed elbow to elbow on hard wood benches for several hours, they do not see Eve walk on the platform and receive her diploma. But they have a chance to visit Chicago with Eve, spend a few days together.

Eve starts medical school at Columbia University. "Medical school is easy compared to college," she says, "it takes a lot of reading, studying, memorizing, but it is not that hard. I could earn a master's of public health at the same time," and she enrolls in the second program. Pieter is willing to share the cost; Marguerite was anxious since postgraduate school cost was not part of the divorce agreement, but there is no dispute.

Lev and Marguerite plan a vacation in India and Nepal. They are going to hike in the Himalayas after spending several days in India. Marguerite does not feel safe in India. It is mayhem at the airport, bodies are packed together, the custom lines are interminable, chaotic. They stay in New Delhi for a couple of days, then head to the Taj Mahal. The unpaved road to Agra is crowded by buses, camels, donkeys. It is all very foreign, very dirty. Dirt and chaos upset Marguerite.

When they arrive at the Taj Mahal, they are told by their guide to run from the bus to the entrance of the Taj, to hold their belongings against their chest, look ahead of them, to not make eye contact with people. "There are aggressive beggars, do not stop for anyone."

The Taj Mahal is stunning, its history touching, they are very moved. On the ground near the Taj, two children approach Lev, they beg. It is impossible to ignore them, they look desperate. Lev empties his pockets of change. One child received a little more than the other and she attaches herself to Lev, who tries to move away. The child is crying, kicking and screaming. "I told you to ignore the beggars," says the guide. "They are trained to do this, some beggars are even maimed on purpose, to attract pity. It is the reality here." It is an alien world for the American tourists, troubling, sobering.

Lev has been reading books on Nepal, Kathmandu, and its surroundings. He likes to be prepared, and he is thorough. He has booked seats on the left side of the airplane; "Sit at the window," he tells his wife. Later, Marguerite points, "Look at the strange clouds!" "They are not clouds, they are the Himalayas," says Lev, who is beaming, "You can only see them from the left side of the plane." And as the plane pivots and swoops down to the valley to land at the airport, they fly over yellow mustard fields. It is gorgeous.

Lev often asks Marguerite why she does not get prepared for trips. "Don't you want to read about it?" he asks, "The places to visit, the culture?" "You always know everything there is to know. I follow you, you are my guide." Lev rolls his eyes; "You are lazy," he says. Lev has more time to reads books on countries they visit, she has no guilt benefiting from his knowledge.

And Lev is well prepared. He knows the topography of Kathmandu, all the places to visit, restaurants to go to. They walk in the street, in awe of the people, the culture, the smell of spices, the sights. It is much cleaner than India, less frenetic, more spiritual. In the street, they are discreetly approached by people who softly say, "Hashish?" They say, "No, not interested." They visit Bhaktapur, the highlight of their trip. They visit temples, artisan shops, they buy handmade rugs to take home as gifts for Eve and Anne.

It is easy to walk in Kathmandu, they feel safe. They are transplanted into a different world, the people are beautiful. Marguerite takes photos of children. There is no or very little begging, in contrast to India, although the children ask for money if one wants to take their photo.

They meet the guide who will be taking them trekking in the Gorkha region, an American woman who has lived in Nepal for many years. She inspects everyone's hiking boots. "We will be walking for ten days on rough terrain," she explains, "there are eight hikers in the group, and we will have porters, a cook, trekking along with us. People do not have to stay in a close group, walk and climb at your own pace, one of the porters will stay with you until we all meet for lunch and at the end of the day."

The group travels several hours by jeep on unpaved roads to the starting point of the mountain trek. They stop by a river with a long, narrow, suspended bridge. There are several Nepalese men waiting there and the guide walks by them. "You, you," she says, pointing to men, choosing porters. She goes to a young woman carrying a baby, talks to her briefly; "You come too," she says. The porters take the tourists' luggage, the hikers have a personal backpack with items needed for the day. The young woman also takes a bag, her infant is strapped to her chest.

The next day, when Lev and Marguerite come close to the young mother, they notice that the child's entire scalp is badly infected, it is oozing pus. "The child was burned," says the guide. "The mother hired herself to go to the other side of the mountain, where there is a medical clinic." "We are both physicians," says Lev, "we carry some medical supplies, we could start treating the burns; this child could die soon, he is badly infected." "I forbid it," says the guide, "we would have sick native people following us on every trek, to get free treatment."

Lev and Marguerite ignore the order; they approach the mother, mimic looking at the child with gestures. The mother understands and extends her arms, the baby in her hands, she lets Lev and Marguerite examine the child who is underweight, listless. Marguerite cleans the wounds and applies antibiotic ointment. The guide is furious, she has a loud fight with Lev, but they continue treating the baby. The other hikers are subdued, the fight affects the entire group.

At night, in the mountains, the stars are amazing, wondrous, and it is very cold. The young mother sleeps on the ground with her baby and Marguerite gives her warmest sweater for the child, but she notices that the sweater has disappeared the next day. She guesses that it has been sold or traded. The scalp is healing well, the baby is more alert. The trek is physically demanding, full of incredible sights and lessons in humanity.

From there, Lev and Marguerite leave to raft on the Trishuli River, down to a national park where they will get the chance to ride elephants and maybe see a tiger in the wild.

The rafting is easy, in big inflatable boats, with Nepalese men paddling; the guide and the cook are still with them. Along the river, gigantic vultures perch on trees, the biggest birds they have ever seen. A man approaches the riverbank, gestures, he holds a scrawny live chicken. A quick transaction is made, the chicken is now in the raft, the cook breaks its neck. "Dinner," he says, with a big smile.

As they approach a small sandy beach in the distance, the guide announces: "If anyone wants to get in the water, now is the time. Let yourself float down to the beach." Lev slides out of the boat. He floats for a long time, and when they get to the beach, he has to be pulled out of the water, hypothermic and almost unconscious. The guide, still angry, does not intervene. "We need to bury him in the warm sand," says Marguerite; she is very worried and also furious. Trust Lev to try crazy things.

They arrive at Chitwan National Park and enter a lodge, a huge structure on posts, elevated for protection from elephants and other wildlife. It is a luxury staying at the lodge, after the mountain and riverbank camping, and there is a lot to do and see. They take a canoe trip and see gharials and crocodiles, they go on elephant back in the tall grasses and find rhinoceroses. The mahouts bring the elephants around the rhinoceroses, and the rhinos charge the elephants. The mahouts laugh; the elephants easily outrun the other beasts. They communicate well with their respective animals by touch; at one point, the mahout sees a puddle on the ground; he is very excited, slides down from the elephant's back, and gets down to collect the fluid. "Rhino's urine," he says, grinning, "very valuable."

It is nighttime, a Nepali comes in the dining room of the lodge and says: "Time to see wild tiger, remove shoes, walk slowly, no make noise, get behind blind." They are brought to an area of the forest where a live goat had been tied to a stake in a clearing. A huge tiger is there, it just killed the prey. It is extremely upsetting to see; tigers need to eat, but the goat did not have a chance. Marguerite and Lev are subdued.

CHAPTER 54

Back from the trip, Marguerite calls her daughters; they are doing well. "College is fun," says Anne. She chose courses she likes, art, literature; she is heading for a liberal arts degree. "You should take some science and math courses too," pleads Marguerite. "No, I do not want to, no more mathematics for me," replies Anne.

Marguerite does not ask personal questions, she knows that her daughters are very discreet and will not disclose love affairs. They will talk when they are ready, ask when they need help or money. Both daughters are given a stipend from Marguerite—she assumes, hopes, that their father is also helping out.

Anne and Eve are coming home for Thanksgiving. "May I bring someone home?" asks Eve. She brings Carrie to visit. Carrie is a lovely young woman, an LGBT activist. She is animated, interesting. Marguerite and Lev like her at first sight; Eve, who is slow to love and loves deeply, is happy.

Soon after, Marguerite calls her parents. "Your mother has a problem," says Maximilien, "I will let her tell you about it."

"We went to dinner at some friends," relates Zilda, "you may recall the old radiologist in Aimeries? I told him that I feel some heaviness in the right side of my belly. 'I still have my old X-ray machine,' he said, 'we will take a radiograph after dinner.' Well, it turns out that I have a mass in the abdomen, I will have surgery in a few days in Brussels."

"I will come visit as soon as I can," replies Marguerite.

Zilda has surgery. "A large mass has infiltrated several organs, the surgeon believes it originated in the ovary, he could not remove the entire tumor; we are waiting for the pathology results, it does not look good," relates Maximilien. "Your mother has a lot of pain, but she is very brave."

The pathologist in Brussels diagnoses ovarian carcinoma. Marguerite asks her father to immediately send her the pathology slides for review. She looks at the slides made from her mother's tumor, one of the hardest things she has ever done. The cancer has infiltrated several organs, the surgeon had to cut through skeletal muscle, and it is full of tumor cells, but it does not appear to Marguerite that it is an ovarian carcinoma. She suspects that her mother has a large cell lymphoma, a more treatable type of tumor. She has access to several specialists; they concur with the diagnosis of lymphoma.

Zilda's tumor has been misdiagnosed in Belgium. Marguerite immediately notifies her father and gets in touch with a Belgian pathologist specializing in lymphomas.

"The diagnosis of lymphoma has been confirmed here, in Brussels, and your mother is starting chemotherapy in a few days," says Maximilien. "We have been given a good chance of survival, the oncologist trained in the United States, he is very competent and reassuring."

Marguerite travels to Belgium. Her mother has already lost most of her hair, she is wearing a pink turban, she looks small, resigned, sitting in her hospital armchair. Maximilien is sitting nearby, sullen. They both look lost. "I will be able to go home soon," says Zilda. "Your father will bring me to Brussels for the chemotherapy sessions. I am so glad to see you."

Back home, Marguerite calls every few days, asks Maximilien to call her if there is any change. A couple of weeks later, she gets an alarming call. "Your mother is back at the hospital, she is very ill, she may not survive, her white blood cells are alarmingly low. You should come see her now," says Maximilien.

Marguerite books a flight for the next day. When she gets to the hospital in Brussels, she finds that her mother is weak but conscious. The oncologist suspects that she has tumor cells in the spinal fluid, that the tumor has reached the brain. "I need to give the chemotherapy agents by spinal injection," he says. Marguerite has had a spinal tap herself, when she was ill with sarcoidosis. It was fairly easy to do, with minimal pain. She tells her mother that she has had the test done herself; "It is not difficult," she says.

Zilda agrees to the procedure but asks for Marguerite to be present. "I will not do it without my daughter," she says in a weak voice. Marguerite gowns up, she holds her mother's hand. "Do not leave me," Zilda pleads, "I am afraid, stay with me, hold my hand." She is agitated. The doctor tries to insert the needle in the spinal space, but Zilda moves, she screams. There is another attempt, Zilda screams continuously, and she eventually passes out. The physician is finally able to inject the fluid into the spinal canal. Zilda does not recover consciousness for a long time.

When Maximilien asks how the procedure went, Marguerite simply says, "It was difficult." She heard her mother scream, witnessed her revert to a helpless, frightened childlike state. She has to return to the States to work, but she is in daily contact with her parents. In the next couple of weeks, Zilda's white blood cell count is normalizing. "We have turned a corner," says the oncologist to his patient, "we can space out the chemotherapy, you need to regain strength, go home and we will do regular checkups."

CHAPTER 55

Lev has become the chief executive officer of a biotechnology start-up. It has taken many months of negotiations and planning to start the small company. He has raised money from venture capitalists, rented laboratory and administrative spaces, hired scientists; as one of the founders, he owns stock options; he is happy, engaged, extremely busy. He is gone for long hours, works all the time. Within a year, there is talk of a buyout by a large biotech company.

Marguerite too, is busy, her laboratory is receiving increasing numbers of specimens, she has to hire more cytotechnologists. "You should open your own laboratory," suggests Lev, "I am certain that we could raise the necessary funds, you would be successful, you would earn a lot more money."

Marguerite has no intention of going out on her own. "It is not for me," she says, "one entrepreneur in the family is sufficient, what if I fail?"

They have planned a long trip to New Zealand and Australia, they have saved every minute of vacation time, they have almost four weeks of travel and a lot of horseback riding planned. Both daughters are in school, Zilda is in remission. Lev is in telephone contact with lawyers negotiating the acquisition of his start-up company.

Their trip starts in the southern part of New Zealand, in Christchurch. They travel to Queenstown, visit the Milford Sounds. It is amazingly beautiful, I wish I lived here, thinks Marguerite, it is breathtaking.

Lev wants to go whitewater rafting and try bungee jumping. They talk a long time about the bungee jumping; Marguerite is hesitant. "I don't want to jump from a bridge, go up and down like a yoyo, hanging by my feet," she says. "It is safe," argues Lev, "we could go together, attached to each other, it would be a lot of fun." They book the bungee jumping at the Kawarau Bridge for the afternoon and the whitewater rafting on the Shotover River for the morning.

They arrive at the Shotover River at the appointed time. Each raft holds four tourists and a guide. The rafts leave the starting point at wide intervals. The river guide with Lev and Marguerite looks fit but young, he cannot be much older than twenty, thinks Marguerite. He sits at the back, to direct the raft. The two additional passengers are slight-built young Japanese women. Everyone dons a wetsuit, gloves, a helmet. The guide tells Lev and Marguerite to sit in front, they are stronger than the Japanese women. The descent down the river is exciting, a little scary at times. There are many rapids, it is very fast, everyone paddles hard. The rapids have names: Double Trouble, Death Spiral.

At one point, the guide stops the raft on the left side of the river just before it divides into two parts. He points to a small tunnel on the right side and says, "That is the Oxenbridge Tunnel where we are going, we all have to paddle as hard as we can to cross over and go into the tunnel which is 560 feet long and has very low clearance. You have to bend down, be careful not to bang your head, keep your hands and your body in the raft."

He signals: "Ready, paddle hard" and starts the raft into the rapids. The two Japanese women are slow to start, the raft misses the entrance, bounces up the left side of the tunnel and Marguerite is ejected into the current. She is in front and under the raft, which rights itself and engages into the tunnel. Lev, quick-witted, abandons his paddle and tries to reach for Marguerite in front of the boat. The current is very strong in the narrow space. He feels Marguerite's helmet and manages to lift and hold her head above the water, but he is not able to drag her back into the raft. She is pinned under, and banged around until they emerge into wider and calmer waters. Lev and the guide are both livid. Marguerite is dragged onto the riverbank, she is dazed, barely conscious, she can hardly breathe. Lev has saved her life. She is helped out of the wetsuit, she already has bruises, her entire body is battered and painful. Lev is blaming the young guide, he is absolutely furious. "You will hear from me if my wife has serious injuries," he says.

The bungee jumping is that same afternoon. Subdued, sore, Marguerite has lost any intention of participating, but Lev gets strapped for the 134-meter high jump over the river. "Do you want to go into the water or stop over it?" ask the people measuring and weighting him to adjust the length of the bungee cord. "I do not want to get wet," says Lev. Marguerite watches from the side as he flies over the river, graceful with arms extended, going down, bouncing back up several times until he comes to rest, head down just over the surface of the water. I would have chickened out at the last minute anyway, reflects Marguerite. Lev is a little crazy.

They land in Sidney, in Australia. The city is as pretty as its pictures. Their first weeklong horseback trip is in the Snowy Mountains, where their guide gets lost and they wake up one morning in a flooded area, with leeches on their legs.

They then travel to Queensland to ride in remote wilderness with an Arabian horse breeder and endurance rider. The guide will take three riders on a 250-kilometer, weeklong journey through inhabited land and forests. The horseman teaches them to gallop downhill, one leans over the horse's neck. Lev learns to gallop without holding reins. Marguerite refuses to try. They go on a midnight gallop in the forest; it is pitch black, there is no moonlight. "Trust your horse," says the man, "it can see in the dark."

The horseman sometimes jumps off his mount at a gallop and runs alongside. "It's what endurance riders do," he says, "it spares the horse for a while."

One day, the guide stops. "Hold your horse perpendicular to the trail," he says, "I will leave first, each of you wait for five minutes, then leave, one at a time. You will gallop alone, and where the trail branches off in three prongs, stay in the middle, you will be in a kind of green tunnel of vegetation. At the end, follow the trail and we will get back together."

Marguerite is the last to leave. Her Arabian mare, Victory, is fast and smooth, they gallop as one as fast as they can, and it is magical. The green tunnel is long and narrow, the horse silently gallops on moss and grass. Marguerite feels ecstatic, she is flying, weightless;

time slows, peace and happiness nestle in her soul, where precious memories go.

At the end of the tunnel, she takes the wrong trail, she is far behind the others, she should have met them already. She urges the mare, but the horse hesitates. Marguerite slows down, stops, guides the horse perpendicularly to the trail, and let the mare find her way. She turns back and regains speed, takes another path. Lev is coming toward her, he is pale, anxious. "We were afraid you got hurt," he says. "I just took the wrong turn, I am safe, I am happy, my horse knew what to do."

Today's ride, the communion with her horse, is etched in her soul forever, a memory she turns to in difficult times, one of the happiest moments in her life.

The Australia trip ends with a visit to the Great Barrier Reef. They take a catamaran to Heron Island, a paradise surrounded by turquoise waters, sitting in the ocean on the reef. Their bungalow is feet from the ocean, they swim among small sharks and huge manta rays. They can walk at low tide from the bungalow onto the reef. They discover that they are visiting at the time when giant green turtles come back from the ocean to lay their eggs on the beach. At midnight, small bobbing heads emerge from the sea; the huge turtles drag themselves on the sand, dig a hole, drop their eggs, cover them back with sand, return to sea. It is eerie, surreal; it fills them with wonder, awe. They look at each other and grin; we are so lucky, feels Marguerite.

Travel, horseback riding are the adventures that bind Lev and Marguerite together. Over the years, they spend weeks on horseback in Colorado, Wyoming, Northern California, Costa Rica, Hungary, Chile. They ride the five-gaited horses in Iceland.

They attend to an unconscious man thrown from his horse in Wyoming. Lev sutures the forehead of a fellow traveler in a remote place, and a deep gash in the leg of a horse while the guide twists the animal's nose. Twisting the nose releases endorphins and calms the animal, they learn. In Costa Rica, Lev is given a stallion to ride. "Stay way back," he is told, "one of the mares is in heat." The rope halter of Lev's stallion breaks. Lev throws himself off the horse as it starts to surge forward.

In Chile, at a remote location near the ocean, Lev eats abalone and gets food poisoning. He is very ill for a couple of days, and while he recuperates in bed, Marguerite and a young guide go galloping on a beach, then in hills where they race through streams, screaming and whooping. Lev would never have let Marguerite take those risks; he fears for her, but on a horse, she is a different, reckless person. She cherishes the moments of abandon, of freedom, of pure joy. She needs to be her own person.

CHAPTER 56

Zilda is in remission, she has regained some weight. On her birthday, Maximilien says he wants to make a confession. Confession implies the hope for forgiveness.

"I had a mistress for over forty years," he tells Zilda. "I think that you should know."

He goes on. "It started when Marguerite was born. I thought that with her black hair and green eyes she could not possibly be my daughter; you have to understand, I was very upset. I thought that you had slept with another man."

Zilda, vulnerable, diminished by her illness, the chemotherapy, is frozen, silent, aghast; today is my birthday, she keeps thinking, today is my birthday. I have been so sick. He tells me now! Forty years?

Maximilien goes on, heedless of the shock on Zilda's face. "I was crazy about her," he reminisces; "in the beginning we made love every day, she excited me, she loved sex, she was uninhibited, inventive." Maximilien has forgotten that Zilda is sitting nearby; his mistress was all that Zilda never was. He sighs. "She died at fifty-nine," he says, "I still miss her."

Forty years! "Who was she?" asks Zilda in a trembling voice. Maximilien tells the name. His whore worked in my house, realizes Zilda, she and my husband made me a fool.

She descends into a brew of fury, anger, and depression. Her resentment and humiliation have no bounds; she recalls all she has done over the years for Maximilien and how little she received in return.

He is a monster, I washed his dirty underwear, I cleaned around the toilet when he missed the bowl, I picked fleas from the waistband of his pants, I cooked for him, kept house for him; all we have comes from my family. I gave him three daughters, I raised them for him. She now thinks of her three daughters as the monster's daughters, she hates them.

He would not let me touch him, he was not making love to me. I thought that he was cold, but mine, but he belonged to that woman.

Zilda tries to commit suicide by slashing her wrists; she is hospitalized, returns home to the apartment. She tries to kill herself a second time, she swallows sleeping pills. She is taken to the emergency room, has her stomach pumped.

Back at the apartment, she physically attacks Maximilien. Marie and her husband Jacques, who brought her back from the hospital, have to drag them apart. Zilda is screaming, waving the old German gun from the war. Jacques grabs the gun from her and throws it in a canal on his way home.

She is committed to a psychiatric hospital in Brussels. Maximilien argues that she is crazy, dangerous. The psychiatrist is sympathetic to Zilda, supportive; "You have been wronged," he says, "but you are severely depressed, we can make you better here."

She finds herself locked up with mentally ill people. Her nightmare is getting worse. I am not crazy, she pleads; she calls Maximilien, "Please, please get me out of here." He refuses; "You should stay," he says, "you are safe there, under good care." He is afraid to be alone with Zilda.

The psychiatrist relaxes the lock-up rules for Zilda, she is allowed some visits, and her fourteen-year-younger sister comes to be with her. She too has been wronged by her husband, she understands, she commiserates, she hugs and rocks her older sister, lets her cry.

Zilda is allowed to leave the hospital for a couple of hours a day. She buys sweets for the other patients. Some of them are beyond recovery, they cannot be made better; some are aggressive and dangerous. I do not belong here, I am not crazy, thinks Zilda, I have been horribly hurt, humiliated, wronged, taken advantage of by a monster. She does not want to see her daughters—Marguerite is in the US, untold and unaware for a couple of weeks that Zilda has been institutionalized; Marie and Maxine do not visit.

When she is released from the hospital, Zilda goes to live by herself at Hurlebise, the farm, separate from Maximilien. They end the lease for the apartment, Maximilien moves into a tiny apartment in an assisted living facility. He has acted stupidly, selfishly, with cruelty. He wanted to unburden himself of his secret, be forgiven; he has no excuse. But he is lonely, and he was supportive of Marguerite in her own times of need, a devoted father in his own fashion. Though mad at him, Marguerite stays in touch with her father.

Oddly, she reflects that Maximilien was faithful to a woman for forty years, his mistress. He remained married to Zilda, a woman he did not love, for the sake of his children, and for the money she brought into the marriage. He never professed love for his wife. He followed in his father's footsteps, a man who also had two women in his life and had a child with his mistress.

Marguerite pities and aches for her mother, a fragile woman too young to marry, the victim of an ill-fated, arranged union between incompatible people. Marguerite knows about needs and infidelity, and in a way, she understands her father, though she is upset that he so deeply wounded her mother who does not have much self-worth or emotional resources. She is upset about his timing: Zilda just survived cancer, she is physically diminished. How could he have been so stupid, so callous? Did he really hope that she might forgive him?

She understands Zilda's rage and pain, she aches for her mother, and she reaches out to her. At first, Zilda refuses to communicate, she is defiant, defensive, she has isolated herself, but she eventually accepts Marguerite's offer to come and help her get settled at the farm. Marguerite thinks that her mother is making a huge mistake, living there by herself, isolated, far from any town and support.

When Marguerite arrives at the farm, she finds a tragic, guarded mother surrounded by packing boxes; the house is cold, dirty. Marguerite cleans and organizes; the old oak bookcases from the family home are there. Marguerite arranges them, empties the packing boxes, unrolls the old antique bijar rug from Lydie's castle; she drives three-quarters of an hour to town to get supplies.

"You are making a mistake, Mother," she says, "you will not be able to get help if you need it. The winter here alone is going to be unbearable. If there is snow, you may be stranded for days." She goes on. "How will you get food, wood for the fires?"

"Then I will freeze and die," says Zilda, "your father will be happy."

After a week spent helping her mother, Marguerite tells she will go visit her father the next day. "He is my father," she says, "I cannot return home to the States without seeing him."

Zilda starts crying, then she screams. "Traitor, I forbid you to visit the monster," she yells. She starts climbing the stairs to the second floor, halfway, she turns around to face Marguerite.

"Mother, I will be back soon, let me hug you, it is only for a few hours." She tries to calm her mother, but Zilda is now in a frenzy, she holds on to the stairs' banister and kicks at Marguerite every time she tries to approach. She screams: "You are a traitor, I hate you, traitor, daughter of a monster."

Marguerite is shaken, powerless; she leaves the farm.

The visit with Maximilien is sad. He cries when he sees his daughter. He has aged a great deal. He is unkempt. His apartment is small, dreary. He has never cooked for himself, he eats sardines, salami, cookies and chocolate, drinks large amounts of whisky and beer.

He has brought a few antiques and paintings from the farm and the apartment, says that Maxine brings him soup, some food, but she demands to be given the old valuable objects one at a time in return. "She sells them," says Maximilien, "I am afraid of her, but I now depend on her goodwill. Marie rarely visits." Her father is a broken man. The physically powerful, dynamic man is now a ruin, shaken, all alone, of his own doing. "I thought of getting divorced before we had children," he confesses "but I stayed."

When Marguerite returns to the farm at night, she finds it dark and locked. The front door is barricaded from the inside; all the heavy wooden window shutters on the first floor have been barricaded too. She knocks on the door for a long time, her mother does not respond. Now afraid for Zilda, she drives from the farm and looks for a farm with lights on. She finds one a mile away, knocks on the door, and asks if she can use the phone.

Maxine is the only person who could help. She has a key to the farm. Maxine tells her, "If the front door is barricaded from inside, we will not be able to enter, but I am coming with my son, he might be able to get in the barn and use a ladder to reach the second floor." Maxine and her son arrive, it is close to midnight. The teenager gets a ladder, manages to pry open a second-floor window, and he opens the front door.

Zilda is asleep in her bed, she has posted a big sign on her bedroom door; "I hate you," it says, "go away, leave me alone." She cannot be roused but is breathing regularly. She has protected herself with incontinence pads. "That is what she does," says Maxine. "She took sleeping pills, she will not wake for many hours."

Marguerite is sad, drained, she traveled from the United States to help her mother, did the best she could to deal with two impossibly difficult people, her parents. She packs her suitcase. She returns to Maxine's home in the middle of the night, sleeps a few hours on a sofa and leaves for the airport at dawn.

Deeply hurt, she does not communicate with her mother for a long time. Zilda sends letters that are full of anger, venom, insults. "My daughters would not give me a glass of water if I were dying of thirst," she writes. After opening and reading a couple of those letters, crying and depressed each time, Marguerite stops reading them. They go in the trash, unopened.

Marie calls, incensed, angry. "Mother came to the cemetery here," she says, "she desecrated the tomb of Father's mistress. I do not dare show up in the community, it is a big scandal here." "What did she do?" asks Marguerite. "She broke the vases, stomped on the flowers, and she wrote 'whore' on the tombstone," says Marie. "How do we deal with her? I do not want to see her ever again, I am so embarrassed."

Marguerite keeps in touch with her father. "Your mother is now in France, on the Riviera," he says. "She had rented her villa for a year; she took an apartment in the next town, waiting for the renters to leave the villa. She has moved her belongings from the farm. We communicate through lawyers, we are selling the farm."

After several months, Zilda calls Marguerite. She sounds hesitant; "I am calmer now," she says. Marguerite is guarded. "I am glad that you are better," she tells her mother. "Would you come visit at some point?" asks Zilda, "I'm moving back into my villa, the renters are gone." "I will think about it," replies Marguerite.

The farm has been sold, Maximilien calls Marguerite and tells her that he immediately needs twenty thousand dollars to pay taxes, could she loan it to him? Marguerite is surprised, they just sold a big property. "What have you done with your money?" she asks. "It is none of your business," he replies, "I will repay you, but I need that money now." Her father supported her when she was in need—she wires the twenty thousand dollars.

On the phone, Marie says: "Father claims that he lost the check from his half of the proceeds of the sale of the farm. I cannot deal with either of them, I have my own problems, and by the way, both daughters of our father's mistress are flaunting brand-new cars. He has not lost the check, he gave the money away to the daughters of that woman."

"Do we have half-sisters?" asks Marguerite. "I do not know," replies Marie.

CHAPTER 57

Anne graduates from college, with a Bachelor of Arts degree. She has a show of photographs at Princeton, and Lev and Marguerite drive from Boston to see the show. There, they meet a young man in a black leather jacket who speaks with a strong brogue. "This is my boyfriend, Patrick," says Anne.

Anne is wearing new shoes. "Nice shoes," points Marguerite. "I got them at the shoe store where Patrick works," replies Anne. Marguerite had assumed that Patrick is a college student; she finds out that the young man is on a visitor's visa, works in a shoe store, is to return home soon to Dublin when his visa expires.

Anne hopes to get a master's degree in fine arts and museum administration; her heart is set on pursuing a career in fine arts. "Apply to schools near us," says Marguerite, "I will talk to your father and see if he is willing to share the cost of the tuition."

"I am done paying for education" is Pieter's answer. Marguerite will shoulder the cost alone. She does not want her daughters to take loans. Anne has been accepted at Tufts University in Boston. She comes home with a new blue dress; "Do you like it?" she asks Marguerite. "It is very nice," replies the mother. "I am getting married to Patrick, this is the dress I will wear," says Anne.

A small wedding is arranged; Pieter and his wife, Lev, Marguerite, and Eve and a sister of Patrick are there for the small civil ceremony outside of a local inn. Eve is sad, Carrie has broken up with her. Anne and Patrick have rented a small apartment, Patrick is enrolling at the Massachusetts College of Arts.

Lev is interested in investing in the real estate market, which has collapsed. "We could go look at apartments," he says, "invest together, and Anne and Patrick could live rent free while they are in school." He is still very critical of the way Marguerite invests her money. "When you buy a stock," he asks, "do you read the annual report? How much research do you do? The key to success is to diversify, you put all your money in the stock market," reiterates Lev.

Marguerite has heard it all before, Lev is probably right; she does not read annual reports, she would not understand them, but she is doing well. He tries to control Marguerite and she pushes back. He is moody for a while after each confrontation. He invests his own money in start-up biotechnology companies.

They buy a small condominium in Boston and Anne lives there rent free. Marguerite pays Anne's tuition. The young couple takes loans to cover expenses and Patrick's tuition. Patrick is a good singer, and he plays the guitar. He has gigs at bars, makes some money.

Marguerite is still working full-time, life is more complicated now. Her father is in Belgium, her mother is on the French Riviera. It is impossible to visit both parents on the same trip, work, see her daughters, and carve vacation time with Lev. Travel is curtailed.

Eve finishes medical school; she has earned two degrees: a doctorate in medicine and a master's of public health. She will be a medical resident in Boston. Both of Marguerite's daughters are now close by, for the first time in eleven years.

MIDDLE SISTERS

The sisters are the very best of friends, they love to spend time together and sometime Marguerite feels excluded, but she rejoices at the love her two daughters have for each other. She always treated and praised them equally. She feels lucky in her accomplished, well-balanced children; I have raised them well; she congratulates herself.

She had hoped to see her daughters frequently. Eve is working long hours, she often is on call or too tired to come visit. Anne too is working hard at the fine arts school. She finishes the two-year program and earns her master's degree in fine arts and museum administration. It is difficult to find a good salaried position in her field, and she is working as a poorly paid copywriter, unsatisfied with her work.

Marguerite tells her, "Get in a good business school program, I will cover the tuition." Anne now regrets that she shunned mathematics in college. But she is determined, takes mathematic courses, and she applies to business schools. She is admitted at MIT. My daughters are smart and hardworking, thinks again Marguerite, though it took a while for Anne to land on her feet.

Lev's father has been sick, he broke his femur, is bedridden, and a nurse has been hired to take care of him at home. Lev and Marguerite go visit; the father's doctor has just recommended that he be moved to a nursing home. Lev's father says to him, "I am not going to a nursing home," and he dies that same night. After the funeral, Lev's mother is moved to a nursing home. The house will be emptied and put up for sale. Lev offers to share the work of emptying the house, but his sister says, "You are working, and I am not, I will take care of it."

A few weeks later, Lev's sister calls: "I have taken some things out of our parents' house, you should go and see if there is anything you would like to keep before the house goes on the market." When Lev and Marguerite arrive, they are stunned. The mother's antique pale blue convertible car, the rugs, furniture, anything of any value is gone. They find a few pieces of old furniture, broken dishes, old clothes in the basement. Lev is speechless at first, he walks around the empty house. Then: "I have nothing from my parents," he says to Marguerite, "nothing from my childhood. My parents never visited our house, they refused all our invitations. You are the only one I love, the only one I trust, the only important person in my life." Lev feels betrayed. Marguerite hugs her husband, keeps her thoughts to herself.

Lev, his start-up company acquired, becomes an associate at a venture fund, the firm's expert in biotechnology. He goes on frequent business trips to the West Coast, Tokyo, Moscow. He has started to drink more, he works very long hours, he is stressed. I need the drinks to relax, he says, and Marguerite does not like it. They have occasional fights.

He has booked a flying lesson without telling Marguerite. When he returns home from the lesson, he announces that he is learning how to fly a Cessna plane. "I took my first lesson," he says, "I loved it." He flies as much as he can with a private instructor. He dreams about buying a plane. He anxiously checks the weather forecast for the weekend. The sky ceiling is too low, the wind is too strong, it is too cold in the unheated Cessna in the winter.

Lev is frustrated but he persists, and he comes home one spring day with the entire back of his T-shirt cut off. "What happened?"

asks Marguerite. Lev shows the cut-off panel of his shirt, dated and signed by his instructor; "First solo flight," he beams. "We will frame the T-shirt" says Marguerite." "You have to take a pinch-hitter course," continues Lev. "We will fly across the country when I buy a plane, and you have to be ready to take over if I become incapacitated during a flight."

Lev is stretching Marguerite's willingness for adventures, but she agrees to take a flying lesson. She studies a list of rules and instructions. The big day arrives, she is in the pilot seat of the small Cessna, the instructor is sitting next to her, Lev is in the back, confusing and annoying her with comments and instructions. Taking off is easy, flying in a loop and keeping the plane horizontal is not too taxing. Landing is another matter—the instructor has to take over. Once on the ground, Marguerite cannot reach the floor pedals to guide the plane on the tarmac, her legs are too short. The instructor communicated with the tower during the flight. Marguerite is certain that she would not be able to keep track of all there is to do to fly an airplane; no wonder Lev comes home exhausted after flying. Marguerite tells him: "I was willing to try, but it is too stressful, I am not taking any more lessons."

Lev flies for a couple of years; he learns to do acrobatics, flies upside down, and then he mercifully loses interest, to Marguerite's great relief. She was anxious every time he set out to fly solo, to do crazy things in the air.

He finds an Israeli instructor to teach him self-defense Krav Maga; loud shouts and grunts are heard from the basement. "I need to be able to defend you in case of danger when traveling," says Lev.

Next, he hires a masseuse to come to the house. A young woman comes with a portable massage table, rolls up the rug in the first-floor bedroom, and closes the door. The woman wanders around the house after she finishes the massage. "I love your house," she tells Marguerite and Lev. "I want this woman out of here," declares Marguerite. "Go get massages elsewhere." Lev is restless, he is stretching Marguerite's tolerance.

CHAPTER 58

Pieter has a massive heart attack and gets a quadruple coronary bypass. He is told that his heart is in bad shape, with a guarded prognosis.

Lev and Marguerite have just left for a safari in Tanzania, and Eve and Anne do not tell their mother of Pieter's medical emergency. They spend several days at their father's bedside.

In Tanzania, the couple visits Tarangire National Park, marvel at the herds of elephants, the giraffes, the massive water buffaloes, the brazen baboons and the velvet monkeys. Then they travel to the Serengeti. Lions are easy to find; the cheetahs are elusive, but the guide is experienced; he can find a cheetah in the distance, perched in a tree. "I look for the tail," he says, "it hangs below the branch." At the immense Ngorongoro Crater, they see a pride of lions surrounding a young hippopotamus lying in a small pool of mud, patiently waiting for the animal to move. "When we have grandchildren, we will bring them here," says Lev.

They fly to Uganda, over Lake Victoria, and land in Entebbe. They travel to the Bwindi National Park, camp in tents guarded by armed men. Gorillas move each day in search of food, and they are not easy to find. The hike is extremely arduous; they walk for hours in the heat behind guides slashing vegetation with machetes.

Toward the end of the day, they encounter the huge primates. "Do not make eye contact," they are told, "crouch on the ground, do not make any noise." An enormous silverback paces back and forth a few feet in front of the group, watching them intently. Baby gorillas and mothers are behind, the babies balance from branches, curious, looking at the intruders. Marguerite and Lev are awed by the experience. It was a dangerous adventure, the end of their African trip.

The next year, the camp where they had stayed is attacked by rebels, and eight tourists, American and Britons, are massacred. Bhaktapur, in Nepal, was destroyed by an earthquake the year after they visited. It is sobering to think that they have twice skirted tragedy.

Pieter recovers and retires. He is only fifty-five years old, he was at the apex of his career, a full professor at Harvard University; he sells his big house and buys a sailing boat. He and Pamela plan to sail the Atlantic Ocean south in the winter, and north in the summer. After being attacked by pirates off the coast of Venezuela, having lost all their instruments and valuables, abandoned in a drifting boat with only their clothes on their backs, they are rescued by another sailboat and they move to Costa Rica to an artist colony. Pieter rarely calls his daughters, he does not show much interest in their lives.

CHAPTER 59

Zilda, living alone on the French Riviera, makes another suicide attempt. She takes sleeping pills and calls Marie. "I am calling to say goodbye, I will be dead in the morning." Marie is in Belgium; she finds the phone number of the police in the small resort where Zilda lives, asks if they can go check on her mother. They bang on the front and terrace doors for a long time, and Zilda finally appears. She is obviously sluggish, drugged. Taken for observation to the hospital, she sleeps for many hours, then she is released.

After that episode, her mother asks Marguerite to come and visit her in France. She has been in touch with Eve and Anne; Eve visited her a couple of months ago. "I have a dog," says Zilda in her call to Marguerite, "she is good company."

As difficult as she can be with her own daughters, Zilda is loving with her grandchildren, and they love her in return. Unbeknown to anyone, she is still writing her memoirs, and she dedicates them to Eve and Anne, her beloved granddaughters.

"I do not have pretensions of being a good writer," she writes, "and I know that I don't have a perfect grasp of spelling, but I write to entertain you, I write so that you can know me better. I am giving free rein to my memories. Everything I write has happened, and you will learn of long-ago times and customs."

The first journals are factual, memories of events. As years pass, she documents happenings, writes about her daughters, the disappointments in her marriage, her relationships with her own mother and siblings, the shock of Maximilien's revelations, the immense pain and humiliation she suffered. The journals become repositories of anger, cries for help. But she tells no one that she is writing.

Zilda has severed all relationship with Maxine. "I hate her," she writes in her journal. Maxine embodies all the resentment and fury she has for Maximilien. Her relationship with Marie is guarded. Marie keeps a distance from both parents; she has little time for their dramas and antics.

It is now to Marguerite that Zilda turns for support. When asked to come visit, Marguerite is hesitant; she remembers the last time she saw her mother, at the farm, and how she was kicked, insulted. Marguerite was deeply hurt, it would be emotionally wrenching to see her mother again. She has received many angry, insulting letters since the last time she saw her.

She finally resolves to visit her mother, a long and expensive trip, with an airplane change in Paris, a long taxi or train ride from Nice to where her mother is living. The night before her departure, Zilda calls: "I no longer want you to visit." "Mother," says Marguerite after a long pause, "if you do not want me to come tomorrow, you will never see me again." There is another long silence, then Zilda says, in a small voice, "You may come, I would like to see you."

When she arrives, both women are guarded, they eye each other, then embrace after a few moments. "Where is your dog?" asks

Marguerite. "I drove to a beach and let her loose, then I drove away; I did not want her anymore," replies the mother. Oh, Mother, thinks Marguerite, her heart sinking, how could you? There is no point talking about the dog, Zilda is obviously still fragile, she does not apologize for what happened at the farm, does not feel remorse for abandoning the animal. Zilda is hard to love.

She seems happy to see Marguerite. They avoid controversial subjects. Marguerite helps her mother around the villa, she pulls weeds in the garden. Zilda has difficulties keeping track of her bills, Marguerite sorts it out. They go for walks and visit antique stores, one of Zilda's pleasures. The antique bijar rug that belonged to Lydie and followed Zilda around from house to house is there in the living room. "I am glad you brought the rug," says Marguerite, "it is such a gorgeous one."

They spend a few peaceful days together. It worries Marguerite that her mother is living alone, has no social or emotional support, but it is what Zilda wants to do. She has bought comfortable leather furniture for the living room, she listens to opera, she has regained some peace of mind. When her daughter leaves, Zilda cries; they promise to talk on the phone every week.

CHAPTER 60

Anne graduates from business school. She finds a position at a consulting firm.

Eve completes her residency in internal medicine. She is staying in Boston to specialize in infectious diseases. She has not mentioned a relationship since she broke up with Carrie in college. "I do not have time to date," she says, "but I hope to have children one day."

Marguerite receives a notice from US Customs. There is an import fee on a package sent from France. "I did not order anything," says Marguerite when she calls Customs. "It is an old rug," she is told, "it was appraised, and you need to come pay the fee, retrieve the package."

Zilda has sent the old bijar rug to Marguerite. How did she manage to send it, she wonders, it is a very large, heavy rug. Marguerite is touched, she loves the beautiful antique rug, it is a precious gift, a tie to her mother and her grandmother Lydie.

A couple of months later, Marguerite travels to Belgium to visit her father, who sounds despondent on the phone. Maximilien, ninety-one years old, has moved to a nursing home. When Marguerite arrives, he is sitting in an armchair in a small room, looking shrunken and very old; he bursts into tears. He holds Marguerite's hand in his own deformed ones for a long time, he says that he is sorry. "I have many regrets," he says, "I should not have told your mother that I had a mistress, we could have grown old together, I caused her such pain, and now I am all alone." He pauses. "I have a lot of chest pain," he complains.

There is nothing that Marguerite can say or do. Her father has an enlarged heart, hypertension, he is on medication. He has regrets. She visits Maximilien again the next day. Again, he cries; they both know that it is the last time they will see each other. "I will call often," says Marguerite when she leaves. On July 31, 1999, two days after her return to the United States, Maxine calls to say that their father has died.

When informed of Maximilien's death, Zilda rejoices; "I told him that I would bury him," she laughs. When asked if she wants to be involved in the details of the funeral, she says: "Put his body in the trunk of the car, he is going to be cremated anyway, he does not deserve a casket; I am free of the monster at last!"

Marie relates that she met with Maximilien's lawyer; "Father hardly left us any money, she says." What did he do with his money, they wonder. He and Zilda sold the big family house with the park in Aimeries, and more recently the farm, a large property. He earned a lot of money during his career. The sisters guess that he gave his money to other people, his mistress, and her daughters.

Several months after Maximilien's death, Maxine calls on Marguerite's birthday. The call is unusual, Maxine does not call for birthdays. "Jacques has died," says Maxine, "he drank himself to death."

Marie is fifty-nine years old; she starts calling Marguerite regularly. She needs a friend to talk to. All the details of her difficult life come pouring out. How Jacques raped her, the visits to the emergency room. How he drank anything he could put his hands on. "At the end, he drank rubbing alcohol." Marguerite has never been close to her sister, barely knows her. Now they are making up for lost time.

"I did not like either of our parents," says Marie, "I do not have any good memories of my childhood except for the years that I spent with our grandparents. You are lucky you live in the US, you did not have to deal with them."

Lev's mother passes away.

"You are the only person in the world who matters to me," Lev tells Marguerite again. Marguerite is pensive; to be the only person to count in someone's life is sobering, daunting.

Shortly after, Anne and Patrick come to visit. Anne, smiling, pretty in a pale blue coat, hands a small package to Marguerite. "A small gift for you," she says. She brought baby booties, she and Patrick are beaming. "We need to look for a house," they say, "we don't want to raise a baby where we live now."

They find a property they can afford west of Boston, half of an old Victorian home, with a tiny yard, and it needs repairs. Marguerite gifts the down payment, and Lev pays to have the roof re-shingled and the windows replaced, air conditioning installed. It is not a house the parents would have chosen, but Anne and Patrick are twenty-nine and thirty-two years old, they like the house, and they cannot afford a better one. Mine was also in need of repairs when

I bought it, thinks Marguerite, they will make it work, remodel later on.

Eve has moved to Washington, DC. She is an infectious disease specialist at a big teaching hospital. She calls her mother frequently, discusses her cases. Lev and Marguerite visit her occasionally, and she comes to Boston for short visits to see Anne's baby boy. At one visit, Eve announces that she has met a woman, and that she is happy. "We are thinking of moving in together," she says, "Rachel is a librarian, seven years older than I, and we want to raise children together." Marguerite is happy for her daughter, that Eve might have children soon. It is wonderful news.

Lev and Marguerite travel again, they visit China, Japan, Southeast Asia, Scandinavia. One trip every year. Marguerite regularly visits Zilda, who is aging, isolated, and the villa needs major repairs and upkeep. There are termites in the roof supports, and mice run under the eaves. Marguerite is worried about her mother. "Would you consider moving back to Belgium?" she asks. "Marie would help, I have discussed it with her. You could have your own apartment in Brussels, it would be easier for you than living alone in a big house, easier for me to visit in Brussels than come to the Riviera." "Or do you want to come to the States, live near us?"

"No," says the mother, "I am staying here. I have contacted a pest service, they are coming to treat the framework, kill the mice."

She is sometimes confused about paying her bills, but she is careful with her money, she has sufficient assets to live well.

A few weeks after Marguerite's last visit, Zilda calls, upset and angry. "I received a huge bill for real estate taxes on my villa. The state claims that I owe taxes on my own home after your father's passing." Zilda argues with officials at the revenue service. "They claim the villa was owned by both your father and me," she reports, "and that I owe money to the state for his half ownership. I tried to tell them the villa is mine, I paid for it with my own money, but I was reminded that your father co-signed the purchase agreement when I bought the land so many years ago. I will never pay those taxes, Maximilien did not own the villa." She is consumed with anger, Maximilien is again ruining her life. The tax dispute unsettles the hard-won balance that she had finally achieved.

Maxine calls Marguerite: "Mother is crazy," she says, "I believe that she is no longer capable of handling her money, she is giving large sums to some of her grandchildren. I consulted with a lawyer, and if her three daughters agree, she can be declared incompetent and we will take control of her assets. I will manage her accounts. I talked to Marie, she is waiting to hear from you."

"Mother has been disturbed recently," agrees Marguerite, "but she is calming down now, and I would not dream of having her declared legally incompetent, it would kill her for sure." "I need your approval," insists Maxine, "if you give it, Marie will come along; all three daughters have to sign the papers. She is spending money that should come to us." "It is her money to do with as she pleases," replies Marguerite, "I am not signing any papers, I am not giving my approval." Maxine swears and slams the phone down.

Marie tells Zilda about Maxine's scheme to declare her incompetent. Marguerite is upset when she hears about it, it unnecessarily agitates and infuriates their mother. Her peace is fragile, and Marguerite makes another visit to the French Riviera to reassure and check on Zilda. "I want to give you my money," says Zilda; "invest it in the United States, and send me money when I need it. I trust you to distribute the assets according to my instructions after I die."

"Mother, I cannot do that, it would leave me open to endless lawsuits from Maxine after you pass away. She would accuse me of having stolen your assets. It would have tax implications for both of us. It is not simple, quick, nor easy to transfer money from country to country. We should go talk to your banker, a lawyer, ask for advice about protecting and investing your money." Zilda is upset, disappointed, she lets the subject drop.

She pours all her feelings into her journals. She writes every day, a strange mix of factual events and feelings of anger, sorrow. She has conversations with her long dead father, and Victor, her teenage fiancé. She writes: "I spoke with Marguerite today, she refused to help me, to help protect my assets. Maxine is trying to steal my money, how I hate her, she truly is the monster's daughter. Help me, Father, I miss you so much. Victor, come lie with me, hold me in your arms. I am so alone."

Then she follows with the events of the day: "I went to the supermarket, the traffic was terrible." She mixes in global events and comments on them. "The world has become crazy, dangerous, Saddam Hussein is a monster." she writes. She is partway in the real world, partway in an imaginary one. "The day was long," she tells Victor, "I could not wait to be with you. Put your head on my breast, my love, let me hold you. I am so sad."

CHAPTER 61

Eve and Rachel have moved in together in a small house in Bethesda, Maryland. Lev and Marguerite visit and meet Rachel. "We have decided to have children," says Eve, "we are researching semen donors' profiles, I am on hormonal therapy." "I so much hope that it works out for you," wishes Marguerite.

Months pass and Eve is not getting pregnant; she is very sad. She talks on the phone to Zilda, shares her feelings and her disappointments with her grandmother. Zilda is supportive; she rallies and finds the right words when she talks to Eve whom she adores. Later, Zilda tells Marguerite: "Eve has so much love to give, I pray for her every day; she would make a wonderful mother."

"We are stopping with the hormonal treatments for a while," announces Eve.

A few months later, she calls. "I am pregnant! I want to be close to you and Anne, I am applying to hospitals in Boston. I want to raise my child near my family. Rachel agrees to the move, you are the only family we have." Eve is thirty-seven years old.

Anne visits with her husband and her little boy. He is just over two years old, and he already talks like a magpie. He is mischievous and delightful. Lev and Marguerite are in love with him, they are besotted. Lev has taken to the role of grandfather with relish. "When are you retiring, Mom?" asks Anne. Marguerite looks at her daughter: "Are you pregnant again?" "Yes," beams Anne, "and we would love to have you help raise the children."

When Marguerite talks again with Eve, she learns that her daughter is carrying twins; "Two boys," says Eve, "we are so happy!"

Rachel and Eve are moving near Boston; they buy a small house and Marguerite gives money for the down payment as she had done for Anne and Patrick.

Marguerite is turning sixty years old soon, and she will be eligible for a pension. She has a solid portfolio of securities, she calculates that she can safely retire. The desire to spend time with grandchildren is strong. She was working long hours when her own children were growing up. Her career has been bittersweet with professional successes and administrative crises. She is proud of what she has accomplished, but it is time to move on while she can still help her daughters. The decision is to retire is easy and she never regrets it. She is about to embark on a different journey, a different life as a grandmother.

Anne has a second baby boy, Marguerite is retiring in two weeks.

The day after delivering her baby by cesarian section, still at the hospital, Anne receives a telephone call from her employer saying that she has been terminated. The firm is laying off personnel. She will not be getting severance or maternity leave pay. She is the family's breadwinner, Patrick stays home with the children. The callousness and the timing of the notice are abhorrent. Lev visits Anne at the hospital and hands her a very big check; "This should cover your expenses for a while," he says, and "I am talking to a lawyer I know well. He will be in touch with your firm."

The benefits are reinstated, but Anne is unemployed. She starts a job search, often coming to Lev and Marguerite's house to be able to work without distractions. She brings her newborn, strapped to her chest as she works on the computer, or Marguerite takes care of the baby.

CHAPTER 62

Zilda calls and complains of great fatigue. "I have itchy blisters on my legs, they break and turn into small ulcers," she reports, "and I also have some on my arms." "Did you see a physician?" asks Marguerite. "I saw one and he gave me some pills." "What type of pills?" "I do not know," replies Zilda.

Alarmed, Marguerite departs for a couple of weeks to take care of her mother. She brings with her steroid and antibiotic ointments. When she arrives, she examines Zilda's legs and arms. They are indeed covered with oozing lesions, small bleeding ulcers, and some are surrounded by short stiff hair. It is very strange, Marguerite does not know what to think, she has limited knowledge of dermatology.

"Show me what the doctor prescribed," she asks. Zilda brings out a container of pills marked with her name, but there is no medication name. "Who is this doctor?" asks Marguerite. "He is a homeopath, I like him, and he is the only one who will see me. It is isolated here, the doctors are far away, it takes over an hour to drive to Nice, it takes weeks to get an appointment."

Zilda is agitated, obviously tired and listless; she also complains of severe neck pain. Marguerite is not familiar with the area or the medical system on the Riviera, but she urges her mother to find a good physician and see a dermatologist as soon as possible. She cleans her mother's legs and arms, applies steroid cream on all the lesions, and they start clearing up very rapidly. She buys a neck collar for her mother, it seems to help with the pain. Zilda has arthritis, a nerve in the neck may be affected. She needs a thorough medical checkup. Within a week, the skin lesions are practically healed. "Mother, you can no longer stay here by yourself, without proper medical care," she says. "I will kill myself if you make me leave," replies Zilda, who is again combative, belligerent. "Let's find a doctor," insists Marguerite. Zilda says that she found one who makes house calls, who will be coming next week. "I can start there, see what the doctor says."

"Let's go grocery shopping together, show me how you drive," suggests Marguerite.

Zilda is tense, she drives slowly but they make it to the supermarket. She is able to select the food and supplies she needs. It was not an easy experience, but her mother still managed, reflects Marguerite. She is in a quandary—let her mother be, or force a move back to Brussels or to an assisted-care facility? Zilda has shown herself capable of attempting suicide. "I am better," declares the mother, "my legs and arms are almost healed, I promise that I will take better care of myself. I promise to see a doctor."

When it is time for Marguerite to return home, Zilda seems much improved. She tells Marguerite that she wants to give her some artwork. "Look around the villa," she says, "tell me what you like." Marguerite points to two small landscape paintings; "I like these, they are lovely and small enough to fit in my carry-on bag," she says, "give me one or the other." "I want you to have both," insists Zilda, forcing them into Marguerite's hands.

Before Marguerite leaves, Zilda urges her daughter to honor her wishes when she dies. "I want to be buried with Victor," she says; "Marie knows where he is buried, near Brussels. I made her promise the same thing." They embrace, Zilda is sad to see her daughter leave. Marguerite wonders if she has done enough for her mother, if she made the right decisions. Her most pressing concern is to let her mother live the life she wants, to enjoy her freedom, make her own choices.

The mother and daughter talk regularly on the phone. "Have you found a doctor?" "Not yet, I am fine, I am fine, just tired, I feel like sleeping in the afternoon." "It is okay to take naps," reassures Marguerite. "How is your neck?" "I am wearing the collar," says Zilda, "it helps a little bit."

CHAPTER 63

Zilda is not better, she is hiding the truth from Marguerite. She is still awake at three o'clock in the morning, takes pills and sleeps until the afternoon. She is slipping into despair and finds refuge in her journal, in talking to her father, to Victor.

She has a photo of her nineteen-year-old fiancé on her bedside table. She puts fresh flowers next to the picture every day. She speaks to the young man: "I brought you roses from my garden this morning, and look at those lilies, they are for you also, don't they smell heavenly?" Next to Victor's photo is a medallion picture of her father. "The flowers are for you too, father."

To Zilda, Victor was perfect, the love she has lost, the man who would have made her happy had he lived.

Her journal writings have become a jumble of daily events and delusions, and she writes long poems, laments to lost love. "I had a pretty good day today, she writes. I went to a plant nursery this afternoon, I bought two large clay containers, they will be delivered in a couple of days, with soil and laurels; I could not wait to tell you, Victor, I missed you all day, I am so lonely, I have such relentless pain, what happened to me? Why have I been so unlucky?

Misery and bad luck cling to me like a second skin. Come with me to bed, my love, lie next to me, hold me, kiss me, how I miss you!"

The next evening, she writes: "I could not sleep last night. I found an old bottle of liquor and drank it, I was very sick during the night, I slept most of the day." She rallies and writes: "Then I went into the garden, the roses are blooming, they smell wonderful. The containers were delivered, they look fabulous with the laurels. How I love my house, I am never leaving from here. But I long to be with you and Father, I miss you so much. Come and lie with me, Victor, kiss me, put your head on my breast. I need you so much, why are you not coming for me?" "And you, Father, have you abandoned me? You were my hero, my protector, why have you abandoned me?"

Zilda tells no one that the skin lesions have reappeared; she has made no attempts to book a doctor's appointment. She is not eating properly, she is not hungry and sleeps erratically, takes sedatives, various pills hoarded through the years. She is falling into despair. "I can no longer wait," she writes in her journal; "Father, Victor, I beg you to come and get me, I am so miserable, so angry, nobody loves me, I have been humiliated, ignored, abandoned. I suffer so much, I want to be with you, my life has been so hard, why have I been so punished? What have I done to deserve this?"

She writes every day, laments her fate, is asking to die. There are glimpses of clear thinking. "I paid my bills today," she writes, "the prices have gone up. I am tired now, I will take a pill and go lie down. Come sleep with me, Victor."

After a couple of weeks, she no longer answers her phone when Marguerite calls. "Have you heard from Mother?" Marguerite asks Marie. "No, but my son is vacationing nearby with his wife and children, I will ask him to go check on her, we should hear back in a day or two."

The grandson stops at Zilda's house. She opens the door for him; he is shocked when he sees his grandmother. She is again covered with small skin ulcers and looks thinner, unkempt, very tired. "I am fine," she says, "I just need a nap, I had a bad night." Marie's son had not planned on visiting the aging Zilda, the generous grandmother who made lavish gifts of money, who hosted him and his family many times at her villa. He is annoyed that he had to make a detour. "Pack your suitcase," he says, "I am taking you with us to Belgium, you have an hour to get ready."

Zilda spends the next ten hours in a corner of the car, silent, largely ignored by her grandson and his family. Later she tells Marguerite: "The wife and children avoided me as if I had leprosy, no one talked to me in the car." In Belgium, she is unceremoniously dropped at the emergency room of the hospital nearest to where his mother, Marie, lives; he calls his mother and tells her Zilda is at the hospital near her. "I made the decision to bring grandmother back to Belgium," he says, "she is now your problem." He never visits nor checks on his grandmother again.

CHAPTER 64

Zilda calls Marguerite from her hospital room. "I am in Belgium," she says, "I was brought here against my wishes, and I know that I will never see my villa again. It is the end for me, I can feel it and I am happy that I will join Victor and my parents. You promised me that I would be buried next to Victor."

Marguerite asks to talk to her mother's physician; "Your mother has bullous pemphigoid, a rare treatable autoimmune condition in old people," she says. "We have put her on steroids, but some of the lesions are infected. She is also receiving antibiotics, she is malnourished, somewhat confused; it seems that she is addicted to all kinds of sedatives. Is she an alcoholic?" "No," replies Marguerite, "not to my knowledge, I have never seen her drink. It has been difficult to take care of Mother," adds Marguerite, who feels defensive and guilty, "she chose to isolate herself far from the family, she can be intractable." "Your mother's liver and renal function tests are abnormal, we do not know what is going on," says the doctor.

Marguerite calls every day. She is told the skin lesions have totally healed, but that her mother is becoming incoherent; she rants on the phone with Marguerite. "I am going to see Victor soon," she says. The doctor explains to Marguerite that Zilda now has multisystem failure; "Everything is awry," she tells her, "we are out of ideas for how to help her; you should come see your mother before it is too late."

Marguerite books an overnight flight the same day. She arrives early in the morning in Brussels, Marie and Maxine meet her at the airport. Two hours later, they arrive at the hospital. Zilda is unconscious. "I came to be with you, Mother," says a teary Marguerite, holding her mother's hand, caressing her hair.

After staying for an hour at the hospital, Marie and Marguerite drive to Marie's house. Marguerite did not sleep on the overnight flight, she needs to rest for a few hours. When they return to the hospital, they find their mother lying on the bed in a flowered dress, her hands are joined, she looks peaceful; "She passed away an hour ago," they are told.

Marie and Marguerite return to Marie's house. They are silent, dispirited. They brought Zilda's suitcase from the hospital. At the house, they place the small old suitcase on the kitchen table, and they open it. Their mother had packed a couple of cheap dresses, underwear, a nightgown, worn shoes, a hairbrush, Lancôme face cream. They find Zilda's passport, her medical insurance card, Victor's photo, and Clement's medallion from Zilda's bedside table. They have tears in their eyes; it is so ordinary, so sad, so little. "That's it," says Marie.

Zilda was eighty-nine years old. An incongruous thought comes to Marguerite's mind. Our parents fought bitterly about who would die first, who would live longer, she reflects; each hoped to outlive and bury the other one, they taunted each other in ugly battles. Father died first, at ninety-one, he lived longer; mother survived him for five years and is now gone at eighty-nine. One lived longer, one buried the other.

The three sisters visit a funeral home to discuss details of the wake, the burial. Immediately, there is tension. Maxine wants the most expensive, most ornate casket; Marguerite, who heard many times her mother state her wishes, wants a simple casket. Marie sides with Marguerite. "You are so cheap," accuses Maxine. "We are doing what Mother wanted," counters Marguerite. Zilda will be cremated. In spite of her ardent pleas, there is no hope of burying her ashes in Victor's grave. How would they find the grave, obtain permission, locate distant relatives of the long-dead Victor?

Maximilien's ashes were placed in his parents' modest tomb; Zilda's will be placed in her parents' pretentious marble mausoleum.

Before the cremation, the sisters view their mother's body for the last time. Zilda, dressed in a summer dress, still has two rings on her fingers, simple rings that she wore all her life. Marguerite asks that the rings be removed. If her sisters have no objections, she would like to give them to her own daughters.

Maxine starts a fight, next to her mother's body. "You are so cheap," she says again, "and everything is always for you," she raises her voice. "You would swim the Atlantic Ocean to pick up a penny on the beach on the other side." She goes on and on with insults; "You stole Mother's money," she accuses, "I have proof that you stole works of art from her villa."

Marguerite and Marie recoil. "Mother is here," says Marie, "lower your voice." Marguerite, outraged, feels ill and stays silent. Without thinking, she flips her middle finger to Maxine, which sends the younger sister into a paroxysm of rage. Mother must have told someone that she gave me the two small paintings, reflects Marguerite.

Before the cremation, the funeral director asks if anyone would like to say a few words, give a eulogy to Zilda. None of the daughters rise. Marguerite is choked with emotion, she is still reeling from Maxine's outburst. Some of Zilda's grandchildren are here too, none rise to say a word. It is the saddest funeral in the entire world, thinks Marguerite.

While the body is cremated, everyone is silent. Marguerite takes Maxine's youngest son aside. She always has liked the gentle, intelligent young man, and she does not want him to think badly of her. She came from the States for his wedding, made a generous gift to the young couple. His brother, Marguerite's godson, turns his back. "I want you to know that contrary to what your mother claims, I have not stolen a penny of your grandmother's money," she tells her nephew. The young man does not respond, he looks at his aunt and moves away.

At the cemetery, the gravediggers cannot find the opening to the huge grave of Zilda's parents, though Marie remembers that it can be opened from the side. It is very hot on that day in July 2003. The few family members present walk around, subdued, sit on nearby graves. Marguerite and Marie avoid their sister Maxine. There is time to reflect.

Mother was a tragic figure, hard to love, thinks Marguerite, at times she was a victim, sorry for herself, at times she could be imperious, throwing her name and connections around, "I am the daughter of…, the wife of doctor…"

The tomb is finally opened. It is filled with black dirty water almost to the top. The urn with Zilda's ashes is placed on a small lip of cement near the top and the tomb is resealed. The gravedigger is not sure the ashes will remain where they were placed.

Marguerite thinks: the ashes of Mother, the woman who could smell cemeteries, will soon float in that brew. She has finally rejoined her mother and father.

She cannot wait to leave, breathe a different air, return to the States, her own family, regain balance, distance herself from the strange thoughts.

CHAPTER 65

The sisters have an appointment with Zilda's lawyer in Belgium. She had a lawyer in France as well, they will meet with the French lawyer later, on the Riviera. The Belgian lawyer has tended to the family for a long time. "Your mother has left written instructions," he says. "It is not an official will, but her instructions are clear; her estate is to be divided in four parts, a quarter goes to each daughter, the fourth part is to be divided equally among her seven grandchildren. The adoptive daughters of Marie are not included."

Maxine explodes. "It is illegal," she says, "the grandchildren are not entitled to money, I will sue you and contest the will."

"Madame," responds the lawyer, "I assure you that it is perfectly legal. According to Belgian laws, children cannot be disinherited, but the estate can be divided in as many parts as there are children, plus one. One can gift the extra part to whoever he or she wishes. Your mother could have bequeathed a fourth of her assets to a single person or entity; she chose her grandchildren in equal parts."

"My sisters' children received more money than mine during her lifetime," argues Maxine. "They have to repay that money.

Marie's youngest son got money to redo his kitchen, I know that Mother gave money to Eve and Anne." The lawyer loses patience; "The gifts made during life cannot be reclaimed," he says, "and they were not made to your sisters." "I will see you in court," replies Maxine, "I will contest this, it is not a formal will," and she storms out of the office.

When she is gone, the lawyer sighs; "Your mother warned me, she wanted to disinherit Maxine, but I told her that she could not. The law is clear." "Could Maxine really cause problems?" ask Marie and Marguerite. "She could try, but the written instructions, though not notarized and witnessed, are very clear. I would testify to her wishes, I had made notes of them on several visits. Unless you find another, different document, this will go forward exactly according to your mother's wishes."

"I have no idea how much money Mother gave to my children," says Marguerite. "They never told me, and I did not ask." "It is the same with me," says Marie.

The three sisters have to go to the French Riviera, look through their mother's papers, banking records, empty the villa and put it up for sale. Maxine is seething, furious, on the attack, bent on revenge. She has been cheated and she is demanding that they go to France and arrive at the villa on the same day, at the same time, enter the villa together. "I do not trust either of you," she sneers at her sisters.

"I am willing to go there when it is convenient for you," Marguerite offers. "I am returning to Boston. Decide on the date and time and I will meet you at the front door of the villa."

"And I forbid both of you to come with a companion," orders Maxine, "it should be just the three of us."

A week later, three days ahead of the mutually agreed meeting time, Marguerite receives a phone call from Marie. "We are at the villa," announces Marie. "But I thought that we were to arrive there at the same time!" exclaims Marguerite. "Maxine was threatening to come early, by herself, and my boyfriend offered to drive us," replies Marie. "She is furious that my boyfriend is here, though she was happy enough to travel in his comfortable car. She sat on the backseat, and constantly ate candy during the ten hours' drive, like father used to do. She has invited a friend to come join her, since my boyfriend is here. 'Tit for tat,' she said. She also says that she plans to drive to Nice with her friend and will pick you up at the airport; tell me the name of your airline and time of arrival."

"Our sister is unhinged," adds Marie; "she is tearing through Mother's papers and records. She discovered another will, with the same terms described by the Belgian lawyer; I saw the handwritten, signed, and dated document, too late for Maxine to destroy it. She also found out that Mother bought a large certificate of deposit at an insurance company where she invested all her money. All the money you had allegedly stolen," says Marie.

Marguerite is dismayed but not surprised, Maxine is behaving as usual. At the Nice airport, she waits for her sister to pick her up at the place and time she had confirmed, and Maxine never comes. After over one hour of waiting, she takes a cab to the train station, then, after the hourlong train ride, another taxi to the villa. She is exhausted, it is a long trip, she changed planes in Paris.

"Where is Maxine?" asks Marie. "I waited for her for over an hour, then decided that she was not coming, I took cabs and the train," replies Marguerite. "She left hours ago with her friend to pick you up," states Marie. The entryway of the villa is full of packed and taped moving boxes. "Maxine went through the house and Mother's closets and took all she wanted," says Marie. The boxes are marked "Maxine's property, hands off." "She is unmanageable, I let her do what she wants," sighs Marie.

Maxine arrives an hour later, she is in a fury. "I went to get you," she rages. "I waited for an hour," replies Marguerite, "I am sorry that we missed each other." Maxine is sobbing, she is hysterical. She grabs a bottle of fruit syrup and throws it at the wall; the wall and floor are sticky with the syrup. There is broken glass everywhere. Her woman friend tries to calm her, they go outside on the terrace, Maxine's sobs can be heard inside. "No one loves me," she wails, "everyone takes advantage of me." Marie's boyfriend disappears in the garden, Maxine's friend announces that she will be leaving tonight. Maxine refuses to clean up the mess she has made.

From there on, Maxine is on the warpath. She disappears for several hours the next day and returns to announce she has contacted several antique store owners and will be having an open house to liquidate furniture the next day. Zilda had nice furniture, some valuable antique pieces. Maxine has marked a couple of them and declared that she will be taking them for herself. "I am taking Mother's car too," she declares, "and the leather sofa and armchair are for my son," defying anyone to disagree.

The next day, several dealers arrive at the villa with vans and trucks. Marie's boyfriend offers to buy a small desk that he likes, at whatever price Maxine deems it is worth. She ignores him. "I said that we could not bring companions," she says, "get out of my way." She sells all the valuables in a few hours, she negotiates the prices, collects the money. She is in a frenzy. In the evening, she divides the proceeds of the sale and gives a third to Marie; she throws Marguerite's share in front of her and says, mocking: "Here is to the millionaire."

There are small items to divide among the sisters. They take turns picking objects each wants to keep, Marie picks a small painting, Marguerite takes a vase that had been at the family home since she was a child and some silverware as souvenirs of her mother. She cannot carry much on the plane. Eve had asked for a set of linen sheets that she slept in on a visit, but it has disappeared, most likely into one of Maxine's "hands off" boxes. There was a lovely antique oil painting, an oval portrait of a young woman, over Zilda's bed. It too has disappeared. Marguerite keeps silent.

When they contact the firm holding Zilda's certificate of deposit, they learn that the three daughters and seven grandchildren are beneficiaries, as in her will. Maxine tries to overturn the terms again, but she fails. "Your mother's instructions were clear and legal," she is told. I can no longer be accused of having stolen Mother's money, thinks Marguerite.

The three daughters meet with the French lawyer. The villa will be sold, the lawyer will handle the formalities, pay overdue utility bills and taxes. At the meeting with the lawyer, Maxine is aggressive, insulting. Privately, the lawyer asks Marie and Marguerite: "Can you control your sister?" "We cannot, no one can, we are sorry."

Maxine offers to return to the Riviera to sign documents when a sale is finalized. "I need to come back with a truck to transport the furniture I am taking," she says. Marguerite and Marie give her power of attorney, Marguerite flies back home to Boston.

On the plane, Marguerite reflects on her parents, her sisters. I will never again speak with Maxine, she decides, never deal with her. The lawyer will handle the estate. Marie and I can be friends. Father and Mother are now dead. They both were deeply flawed, difficult, ill-suited to each other; they made many mistakes. But they did the best they could as parents, Father was supportive of me, Mother became close when she was older, and she loved my daughters. My own strange upbringing in a dysfunctional family made me strong, independent. I have a good marriage, two strong, intelligent daughters. I have been lucky.

Over the next several weeks, Marguerite receives correspondence from Belgium and from France. "I am duty bound to inform you that your sister Maxine has made allegations that you stole valuable paintings from your mother in the months before her death," writes the Belgian lawyer. "Your sister demands that the paintings be appraised and sold, to be part of the estate. I would appreciate if you would address these allegations."

"I was given two small paintings by my mother a few weeks before she passed away," replies Marguerite. "They have sentimental value and I have no intention of selling them."

"I am satisfied with your explanation," replies the lawyer, "I consider the matter closed."

Maxine writes to Marguerite: "I demand that Mother's two paintings be appraised at both Christie's and Sotheby, sold, and the proceeds added to the estate." She adds: "I filed a complaint with both our lawyers." Marguerite throws the letter away, does not reply. A letter also comes from the office of the French lawyer. "Out of courtesy, I wish to inform you that your sister has made allegations of theft against you," states the letter. "I do not intend to pursue the matter," writes the lawyer.

The French lawyer calls Marguerite: "Your sister is harassing me," she says. "I am asking again, can you do something to control her?" "I am sorry to hear that," replies Marguerite, "she is harassing me too, I ignore her, that is all I can advise."

The villa has buyers. Maxine returns to the Riviera to complete the sale; she accompanies the lawyer and the buyers on a last visit to the house before signing the sale's agreement. "I will join you at the office and bring the keys," she says, "I will lock the house." There is a laundry room at the back of the garage. Maxine opens the faucets in the laundry room before leaving. The lawyer calls Marguerite hours later, distressed, angry; "The buyers went back to the villa after the sale was finalized," she tells her, "the lower level of the house is flooded, you should consider indemnifying the buyers. I have never encountered such malice in my life."

"I am sorry," replies Marguerite, "you have been very patient, but no, I am done paying for my sister's actions."

CHAPTER 66

Eve, seven months pregnant, calls from the hospital. "I went for a routine checkup," she tells Marguerite, "and found out that my cervix is fully dilated. I am lying with my feet up and my head down and I am receiving steroids to help the babies' lungs. We are hoping to delay the delivery as much as possible."

She delivers a few days later, needing a C-section for the second boy who was in distress. The two boys are tiny, each could fit in the palm of the hand, they are in incubators, with lines and oxygen masks. Marguerite chokes up and fears for them when she sees them. The babies go home after four weeks of intensive care. "We are going to need you, Mom," says Eve.

Eve and Anne rarely see their father; he did not meet Anne's second son for the first time until the boy was eighteen months old. Pieter visits with Pamela after the twins' birth, and they return to Costa Rica.

Eve and Anne are unaware that Pamela has advanced breast cancer, they are not told of the disease until Pieter calls to say his wife has died. Now, in poor health, lonely, he gets in touch with his daughters more regularly. He is scheduled to have elective surgery in Boston, and, in 2014, he dies of a heart attack, alone, in Costa Rica, the day he was to depart for the States. Pieter was seventy one.

After his passing, Anne tells Marguerite that both Pieter and Pamela were heavy drinkers, that Pamela was intensely critical of Marguerite, mocking, sarcastic and mean when she was drunk. "But she adored and idolized father," says Anne, "even though he was unfaithful. She turned a blind eye and stayed at his side."

"I was hoping to finally get to know my father, it was impossible while Pamela was alive," says Anne, "and now, I never will." She has a heavy heart.

Time has passed. Every week, each of Anne's sons, and later, Eve's sons, come to spend a day alone with their grandmother. Marguerite awaits eagerly for those visits, she feels as though she has dates.

One evening, as Marguerite is driving the oldest grandson back to his home, she turns on the radio in the car. The news is grim, someone has been killed, the police is investigating. Not something that young children should hear, decides Marguerite, and she turns off the radio. A small indignant voice at the back of the car pipes in: "I am *frusterated*, I was listening to that story, turn the radio back on." The boy just turned three years old, he talks incessantly, he likes big words, "awesome" is the current favorite.

"What did you hear?" asks Marguerite. The boy repeats the entire story exactly as he heard it on the radio. Oh, that is interesting, realizes Marguerite. We have a lot to look forward to. When she relates the story to Lev, at dinnertime, he raises his hand: "I object, your honor; our grandson is going to be a lawyer," he predicts.

Time passes, and Marguerite spends countless hours with her four grandsons. Each one is unique, each one is smart, each one is her favorite. They have different talents. They are raised differently by loving parents, two with a father present, the twins have two mothers.

Anne's boys have farting contests with their father; they streak through the house, undressed, yelling: "Naked boys, naked boys!" One day, the father and the two boys return from the barber; all three are beaming, they all sport a mohawk. The twins are the sweetest, all hugs and wet kisses. One is a wizard with construction sets; "An architect or engineer in the making," declares Lev; the other loves stories; "A writer," predicts the grandfather.

Anne's second son is artistic, creative, he gets stuck on laughing, cannot stop. Other children are drawn to him as to a magnet. He beats his grandmother at all the board games they play together. He is incredibly smart, she tells Lev.

It is mayhem in the grandparents' house when all four boys visit together. Lev puts on music and the boys have dancing shows in the living room. Marguerite has to use all her willpower to not fall on the floor laughing; these are wonderful times.

Lev is still working, he has become a consultant, rarely travels. He is less stressed and has curtailed his drinking. He too wants to be part of the children's lives. "We could take the grandkids on the weekend," he proposes, "that would give free time to the parents, I could spend time with them." Eve is delighted. "My boys need a man in their lives," she says.

Lev has taken on archery; he learns to fish. "I will teach archery to the boys, I could take them fishing," he says. We will travel with the grandkids."

Anne is pregnant for a third time. She delivers a baby girl who she names Maggie.

A girl, I am so glad, thinks Marguerite. The line of women is alive.

The years have passed. Lev and Marguerite take their entire family to Tanzania, on the same safari they went on twenty years earlier. A year later, Anne and her family join them to Ecuador and the Galapagos.

Maggie, Anne's daughter, is determined from an early age. She grows into an assured little girl, falls in love with horses, and is an expert equestrian at fifteen; she and her horse fearlessly jump over obstacles, and she raises her fist in the air.

ACKNOWLEDGEMENTS

A large part of the book could not have been written without the information contained in my mother's journals.
Thank you, Mother.

My eighty-four-year old sister has a wonderful recall of people and events. We did not get to know each other well until we were in our late fifties and started sharing confidences and memories.
Thank you, big sister.

Susan Okula, friend, journalist and fellow writer, offered advice, and shared resources.
Thank you, Susan, for your graceful help.

Katherine Pickett skillfully edited a first book by a non-native English speaker. Any remaining mistake is my own.
Thank you Katherine, your help was invaluable.

I thank my talented team at Palmetto Publishing; my Publishing Consultant Cassie Arendec, Project Manager Julia McKenna, Cover Designer Danna Mathias Steele, and Interior Designer Jessica Horton for their dedication and skilled work.

My two daughters are always there for me when I need them.
Thank you, my strong and wise daughters.

My husband provides love, encouragement and support.
Thank you my best friend, you make my life richer.

ABOUT THE AUTHOR

Marguerite Duvivier, a pseudonym, was an academic in the field of anatomic pathology who spent her formative years in Belgium where she also attended medical school. Her career led her to Boston, Massachusetts, where she pursued further training. Although she made significant contributions to her field, the author seeks to address a wider audience through her book, Middle Sisters. Her work delves into various themes that resonate with a broad spectrum of readers, including women's challenges in personal and professional life, world history, poverty, affluence and religion, all imbued with a dash of humor.